# Kitchen Guide to Hotel Management

# Kitchen Guide to Hotel Management

**Pradeep Paul**

**Kitchen Guide to Hotel Management**

ISBN 978-93-5111-337-9


Published in 2014 in India by

**RANDOM PUBLICATIONS**

4376-A/4B, Gali Murari Lal, Ansari Road
New Delhi-110 002
Phone : +91-11-43580356, +91-11-23289044
e-mail: randomexports@gmail.com, sales@randompublications.com,
info@randompublications.com

*Type Setting by* : Keystoneprintads, Delhi-110051
*Printed at* : Thomson Press (India) Ltd

# Preface

Kitchen managers supervise the operations of kitchens in places like restaurants, hospitals, and hotels. Restaurant and canteen kitchens found in hotels, hospitals, educational and work place facilities, army barracks, and similar establishments are generally (in developed countries) subject to public health laws. They are inspected periodically by public-health officials, and forced to close if they do not meet hygienic requirements mandated by law.

The purpose of kitchen hoods is to remove the heat, smoke, effluent, and other contaminants. The thermal plume from appliances absorbs the contaminants that are released during the cooking process. Room air replaces the void created by the plume.

If convective heat is not removed directly above the cooking equipment, impurities will spread throughout the kitchen, leaving discoloured ceiling tiles and greasy countertops and floors. Therefore, contaminants from stationary local sources within the space should be controlled by collection and removal as close to the source as is practical.

In the beginning of the hotel kitchen design process, the designer defines the type and process type as an input. The space dimensioning includes hotel room estimates for all functional areas, such as receiving, storage, preparation, cooking and dishwashing, that is required to produce the menu items. The space required for each functional area of the facility is dependent upon many factors.

Many manufacturers of hotel kitchen ventilation equipment offer design methods for determining exhaust based on cooking appliances. Any method used is better than no quantification at all.

The method of determining exhaust levels based on the heat generated by the cooking process is referred to as heat load based design and is the premise for this manual. It is the foundation of accurate and correct design fundamentals in a hotel kitchen environment.

The book will be found immensely informative and useful for all and for students and scholars.

I thank all members of my team who have helped in the preparation of the book. My special thanks go to "Random Publications" who have published the book.

*—Pradeep Paul*

# Contents

# 1

# Introduction to Kitchen

A kitchen is a room or part of a room used for cooking and food preparation. In the West, a modern residential kitchen is typically equipped with a stove, a sink with hot and cold running water, a refrigerator and kitchen cabinets arranged according to a modular design. Many households have a microwave oven, a dishwasher and other electric appliances. The main function of a kitchen is cooking or preparing food but it may also be used for dining, food storage, entertaining, dishwashing and laundry.

## HISTORY

The evolution of the kitchen is linked to the invention of the cooking range or stove and the development of water infrastructure capable of supplying water to private homes. Until the 18th century, food was cooked over an open fire. Technical advances in heating food in the 18th and 19th centuries, changed the architecture of the kitchen. Before the advent of modern pipes, water was brought from an outdoor source such as wells, pumps or springs.

### Antiquity

The houses in Ancient Greece were commonly of the atrium-type: the rooms were arranged around a central courtyard for women. In many such homes, a covered but otherwise open patio served as the kitchen. Homes of the wealthy had the kitchen as a separate room, usually next to a bathroom (so that both rooms could be heated by the kitchen fire), both rooms being accessible from the court. In such houses, there was often a separate small storage room in the back of the kitchen used for storing food and kitchen utensils.

In the Roman Empire, common folk in cities often had no kitchen of their own; they did their cooking in large public kitchens. Some had small mobile bronze stoves, on which a fire could be lit for cooking. WealthyRomans had relatively well-equipped kitchens. In a Roman villa, the kitchen was typically integrated into the main building as a separate room, set apart for practical reasons of smoke and sociological reasons of the kitchen being operated by slaves. The fireplace was typically on the floor, placed at a wall—sometimes raised a little bit—such that one had to kneel to cook. There were no chimneys.

**Middle Ages**

Early medieval European longhouses had an open fire under the highest point of the building. The "kitchen area" was between the entrance and the fireplace. In wealthy homes there was typically more than one kitchen. In some homes there were upwards of three kitchens. The kitchens were divided based on the types of food prepared in them. In place of a chimney, these early buildings had a hole in the roof through which some of the smoke could escape. Besides cooking, the fire also served as a source of heat and light to the single-room building. A similar design can be found in the Iroquois longhouses of North America.

In the larger homesteads of European nobles, the kitchen was sometimes in a separate sunken floor building to keep the main building, which served social and official purposes, free from indoor smoke.

The first known stoves in Japan date from about the same time. The earliest findings are from the Kofun period (3rd to 6th century). These stoves, called *kamado,* were typically made of clay and mortar; they were fired with wood or charcoal through a hole in the front and had a hole in the top, into which a pot could be hanged by its rim. This type of stove remained in use for centuries to come, with only minor modifications. Like in Europe, the wealthier homes had a separate building which served for cooking. A kind of open fire pit fired with charcoal, called *irori,* remained in use as the secondary stove in most homes until the Edo period (17th to 19th century). A *kamado* was used to cook the staple food, for instance rice, while *irori* served both to cook side dishes and as a heat source.

The kitchen remained largely unaffected by architectural advances throughout the Middle Ages; open fire remained the only method of heating food. European medieval kitchens were dark, smoky, and sooty places, whence their name *"smoke kitchen"*. In European medieval cities around the 10th to 12th centuries, the kitchen still used an open fire hearth in the middle of the room. In wealthy homes, the ground floor was often used as a stable while the kitchen was located on the floor above, like the bedroom and the hall. In castles and monasteries, the living and working areas were separated; the kitchen was sometimes moved to a separate building, and thus could not serve anymore to heat the living rooms. In some castles the kitchen was retained in the same structure, but servants were strictly separated from nobles, by constructing separate spiral stone staircases for use of servants to bring food to upper levels. An extant example of such a medieval kitchen with servants' staircaseis at Muchalls Castle in Scotland. In Japanese homes, the kitchen started to become a separate room within the main building at that time.

With the advent of the chimney, the hearth moved from the center of the room to one wall, and the first brick-and-mortar hearths were built. The fire was lit on top of the construction; a vault underneath served to store wood. Pots made of iron, bronze, or copper started to replace the pottery used earlier. The temperature was controlled by hanging the pot higher or lower over the fire, or placing it on a trivet or directly on the hot ashes. Using open fire for cooking (and heating) was risky; fires devastating whole cities occurred frequently.

Leonardo da Vinci invented an automated system for a rotating spit for spit-roasting: a propeller in the chimney made the spit turn all by itself. This kind of system was widely used in wealthier homes. Beginning in the late Middle Ages, kitchens in Europe lost their home-heating function even more and were increasingly moved from the living area into a separate room. The living room was now heated by tiled stoves, operated from the kitchen, which offered the huge advantage of not filling the room with smoke.

Freed from smoke and dirt, the living room thus began to serve as an area for social functions and increasingly became a showcase for the owner's wealth. In the upper classes, cooking and the kitchen were the domain of the servants, and the kitchen was set apart from the living rooms, sometimes even far from the dining room. Poorer homes often did not have a separate kitchen yet; they kept the one-room arrangement where all activities took place, or at the most had the kitchen in the entrance hall.

The medieval smoke kitchen (or Farmhouse kitchen) remained common, especially in rural farmhouses and generally in poorer homes, until much later. In a few European farmhouses, the smoke kitchen was in regular use until the middle of the 20th century. These houses often had no chimney, but only a smoke hood above the fireplace, made of wood and covered with clay, used to smoke meat. The smoke rose more or less freely, warming the upstairs rooms and protecting the woodwork from vermin.

**Colonial America**

In the Colony of Connecticut, as in other states of New England during Colonial America, kitchens were often built as separate rooms and were located behind the parlor and keeping room or dining room. One early record of a kitchen is found in the 1648 inventory of the estate of a John Porter of Windsor, Connecticut. The inventory lists goods in the house *over the kittchin* and *in the kittchin*. The items listed in the kitchen were; silver spoons, pewter, brass, iron, arms, ammunition, hemp, flax and *other implements about the room.*

In the southern states, where the climate and sociological conditions differed from the north, the kitchen was often relegated to an outbuilding, separate from the big house, the mansion, for much of the same reasons as in the feudal kitchen in medieval Europe: the kitchen was operated by slaves, and their working place had to be separated from the living area of the masters by the social standards of the time. Separate summer kitchens were also common on large farms in the north. These were used to prepare meals for harvest workers and tasks such as canning during the warm summer months.

## Technological Advances

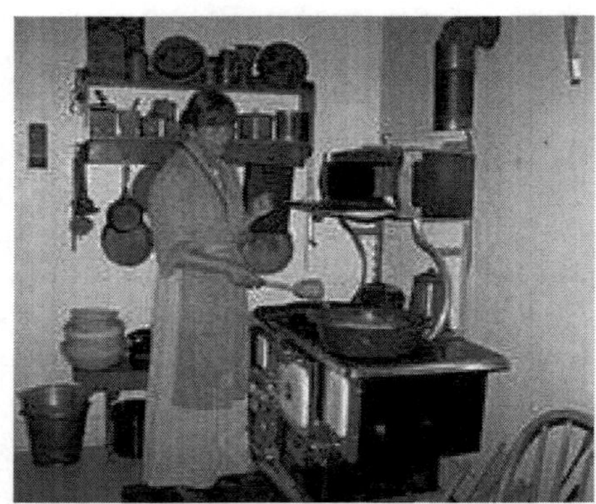

**Fig.** A typical rural American kitchen of 1918 at The Sauer-Beckmann Farmstead, Texas

Technological advances during industrialization brought major changes to the kitchen. Iron stoves, which enclosed the fire completely and were more efficient, appeared. Early models included the Franklin stovearound 1740, which was a furnace stove intended for heating, not for cooking. Benjamin Thompson in England designed his "Rumford stove" around 1800. This stove was much more energy efficient than earlier stoves; it used one fire to heat several pots, which were hung into holes on top of the stove and were thus heated from all sides instead of just from the bottom. However, his stove was designed for large kitchens; it was too big for domestic use.

**Fig.** A typical Hoosier cabinet of the 1920s.

The "Oberlin stove" was a refinement of the technique that resulted in a size reduction; it was patented in the U.S. in 1834 and became a commercial success with some 90,000 units sold over the next 30 years. These stoves were still fired with wood or coal. Although the first gas street lampswere installed in Paris, London, and Berlin at the beginning of the 1820s and the first U.S. patent on a gas stove was granted in 1825, it was not until the late 19th century that using gas for lighting and cooking became commonplace in urban areas.

Before and after the beginning of the 20th century, kitchens were frequently not equipped with built-in cabinetry, and the lack of storage space in the kitchen became a real problem. The Hoosier Manufacturing Co. of Indiana adapted an existing furniture piece, the baker's cabinet, which had a similar structure of a table top with some cabinets above it (and frequently flour bins beneath) to solve the storage problem.

By rearranging the parts and taking advantage of (then) modern metal working, they were able to produce a well-organized, compact cabinet which answered the home cook's needs for storage and working space. A distinctive feature of the Hoosier cabinet is its accessories.

As originally supplied, they were equipped with various racks and other hardware to hold and organize spices and various staples. One useful feature was the combination flour-bin/sifter, a tin hopper that could be used without having to remove it from the cabinet. A similar sugar bin was also common.

The urbanization in the second half of the 19th century induced other significant changes that would ultimately change the kitchen. Out of sheer necessity, cities began planning and building water distribution pipes into homes, and built sewers to deal with the waste water. Gas pipes were laid; gas was used first for lighting purposes, but once the network had grown sufficiently, it also became available for heating and cooking on gas stoves. At the turn of the 20th century, electricity had been mastered well enough to become a commercially viable alternative to gas and slowly started replacing the latter. But like the gas stove, the electric stove had a slow start. The first electrical stove had been presented in 1893 at the World's Columbian Exposition in Chicago, but it was not until the 1930s that the technology was stable enough and began to take off.

## Industrialization

Industrialization also caused social changes. The new factory working class in the cities was housed under generally poor conditions. Whole families lived in small one or two-room apartments in tenement buildings up to six stories high, badly aired and with insufficient lighting. Sometimes, they shared apartments with "night sleepers", unmarried men who paid for a bed at night. The kitchen in such an apartment was often used as a living and sleeping room, and even as a bathroom. Water had to be fetched from wells and heated on the stove. Water pipes were laid only towards the end of the 19th century, and then often only with one tap per building or per story. Brick-

and-mortar stoves fired with coal remained the norm until well into the second half of the century. Pots and kitchenware were typically stored on open shelves, and parts of the room could be separated from the rest using simple curtains.

In contrast, there were no dramatic changes for the upper classes. The kitchen, located in the basement or the ground floor, continued to be operated by servants. In some houses, water pumps were installed, and some even had kitchen sinks and drains (but no water on tap yet, except for some feudal kitchens in castles).

The kitchen became a much cleaner space with the advent of "cooking machines", closed stoves made of iron plates and fired by wood and increasingly charcoal or coal, and that had flue pipes connected to the chimney. For the servants the kitchen continued to also serve as a sleeping room; they slept either on the floor, or later in narrow spaces above a lowered ceiling, for the new stoves with their smoke outlet no longer required a high ceiling in the kitchen.

The kitchen floors were tiled; kitchenware was neatly stored in cupboards to protect them from dust and steam. A large table served as a workbench; there were at least as many chairs as there were servants, for the table in the kitchen also doubled as the eating place for the servants.

## World War II Cooking and Dining Trends

The urban middle class imitated the luxurious dining styles of the upper class as best as they could. Living in smaller apartments, the kitchen was the main room—here, the family lived.

The study or living room was saved for special occasions such as an occasional dinner invitation. Because of this, these middle-class kitchens were often more homely than those of the upper class, where the kitchen was a work-only room occupied only by the servants.

Besides a cupboard to store the kitchenware, there were a table and chairs, where the family would dine, and sometimes—if space allowed—even afauteuil or a couch.

Gas pipes were first laid in the late 19th century, and gas stoves started to replace the older coal-fired stoves. Gas was more expensive than coal, though, and thus the new technology was first installed in the wealthier homes. Where workers' apartments were equipped with a gas stove, gas distribution would go through a coin meter.

In rural areas, the older technology using coal or wood stoves or even brick-and-mortar open fireplaces remained common throughout. Gas and water pipes were first installed in the big cities; small villages were connected only much later.

## Rationalization

The trend to increasing gasification and electrification continued at the turn of the 20th century. In industry, it was the phase of work process optimization.

Taylorism was born, and time-motion studies were used to optimize processes. These ideas also spilled over into domestic kitchen architecture because of a growing trend that called for a professionalization of household work, started in the mid-19th century by Catharine Beecher and amplified by Christine Frederick's publications in the 1910s.

**Fig.** The Frankfurt kitchen using Tayloristprinciples

A stepstone was the kitchen designed in Frankfurt by Margarethe Schütte-Lihotzky. Working class women frequently worked in factories to ensure the family's survival, as the men's wages often did not suffice. Social housing projects led to the next milestone: the Frankfurt Kitchen. Developed in 1926, this kitchen measured 1.9 m by 3.4 m (approximately 6 ft 2 inby 11 ft 2 in, with a standard layout. It was built for two purposes: to optimize kitchen work to reduce cooking time and lower the cost of building decently equipped kitchens. The design, created by Margarete Schütte-Lihotzky, was the result of detailed time-motion studies and interviews with future tenants to identify what they needed from their kitchens. Schütte-Lihotzky's fitted kitchen was built in some 10,000 apartments in the housing projects erected in Frankfurt in the 1930s.

The initial reception was critical: it was so small that only one person could work in it; some storage spaces intended for raw loose food ingredients such as flour were reachable by children. But the Frankfurt kitchen embodied a standard for the rest of the 20th century in rental apartments: the "work kitchen". It was criticized as "exiling the women in the kitchen", but post-

World War II economic reasons prevailed. The kitchen once more was seen as a work place that needed to be separated from the living areas. Practical reasons also played a role in this development: just as in the bourgeois homes of the past, one reason for separating the kitchen was to keep the steam and smells of cooking out of the living room.

**Unit/fitted**

**Fig.** A kitchen produced by the German company Poggenpohl in 1892

The idea of standardized was first introduced locally with the Frankfurt kitchen, but later defined new in the "Swedish kitchen" (Svensk köksstandard, Swedish kitchen standard).

The equipment used remained a standard for years to come: hot and cold water on tap and a kitchen sink and an electrical or gas stove and oven. Not much later, the refrigerator was added as a standard item. The concept was refined in the "Swedish kitchen" using unit furniture with wooden fronts for the kitchen cabinets.

Soon, the concept was amended by the use of smooth synthetic door and drawer fronts, first in white, recalling a sense of cleanliness and alluding to sterile lab or hospital settings, but soon after in more lively colors, too. Some years after the Frankfurt Kitchen Poggenpohl presented the "reform kitchen" in 1928 with interconnecting cabinets and functional interiors. The reform kitchen was a forerunner to the later unit kitchen and fitted kitchen. Poggenpohl presented the form 1000, declared as "the world's first unit kitchen", at the imm Colognefurniture fair in 1950.

Unit construction since its introduction has defined the development of the modern kitchen. Pre-manufactured modules using mass manufacturing techniques developed during World War II greatly brought down the cost of a kitchen. Units which are kept on the floor are called "floor units", "floor cabinets", or "base cabinets" on which a kitchen worktop, originally often formica and often now made of granite, marble, tile or wood is placed. The units which are held on the wall for storage purposes are termed as "wall units" or "wall cabinets". In small areas of kitchen in an apartment, even a "tall storage unit" is available for effective storage. In cheaper brands, all cabinets are kept a uniform color, normally white, with interchangeable doors and accessories chosen by the customer to give a varied look. In more expensive brands, the cabinets are produced matching the doors' colors and finishes, for an older more bespoke look.

**Technicalization**

A trend began in the 1940s in the United States to equip the kitchen with electrified small and large kitchen appliances such as blenders, toasters, and later also microwave ovens. Following the end of World War II, massive demand in Europe for low-price, high-tech consumer goods led to Western European kitchens being designed to accommodate new appliances such as refrigerators and electric/gas cookers.

**Fig.** Stainless steel home appliancespopular in modern western kitchens

Parallel to this development in tenement buildings was the evolution of the kitchen in homeowner's houses. There, the kitchens usually were somewhat larger, suitable for everyday use as a dining room, but otherwise the ongoing technicalization was the same, and the use of unit furniture also became a standard in this market sector.

General technocentric enthusiasm even led some designers to take the "work kitchen" approach even further, culminating in futuristic designs like Luigi Colani's "kitchen satellite" (1969, commissioned by the Germanhigh-end kitchen manufacturer Poggenpohl for an exhibit), in which the room was reduced to a ball with a chair in the middle and all appliances at arm's length, an optimal arrangement maybe for "applying heat to food", but not necessarily for actual cooking. Such extravaganzas remained outside the norm, though.

In the former Eastern bloc countries, the official doctrine viewed cooking as a mere necessity, and women should work "for the society" in factories, not at home.

Also, housing had to be built at low costs and quickly, which led directly to the standardized apartment block using prefabricated slabs. The kitchen was reduced to its minimums and the "work kitchen" paradigm taken to its extremes: in East Germany for instance, the standard tenement block of the model "P2" had tiny 4 $m^2$ kitchens in the inside of the building (no windows), connected to the dining and living room of the 55 $m^2$ apartment and separated from the latter by a pass-through or a window.

**Open kitchens**

Starting in the 1980s, the perfection of the extractor hood allowed an open kitchen again, integrated more or less with the living room without causing the whole apartment or house to smell. Before that, only a few earlier experiments, typically in newly built upper-middle-class family homes, had open kitchens. Examples are Frank Lloyd Wright's *House Willey* (1934) and *House Jacobs* (1936). Both had open kitchens, with high ceilings (up to the roof) and were aired by skylights. The extractor hood made it possible to build open kitchens in apartments, too, where both high ceilings and skylights were not possible.

The re-integration of the kitchen and the living area went hand in hand with a change in the perception of cooking: increasingly, cooking was seen as acreative and sometimes social act instead of work. And there was a rejection by younger home-owners of the standard suburban model of separate kitchens and dining rooms found in most 1900-1950 houses.

Many families also appreciated the trend towards open kitchens, as it made it easier for the parents to supervise the children while cooking and to clean up spills.

The enhanced status of cooking also made the kitchen a prestige object for showing off one's wealth or cooking professionalism. Some architects have capitalized on this "object" aspect of the kitchen by designing freestanding "kitchen objects". However, like their precursor, Colani's "kitchen satellite", such futuristic designs are exceptions.

Another reason for the trend back to open kitchens (and a foundation of the "kitchen object" philosophy) is changes in how food is prepared. Whereas prior to the 1950s most cooking started out with raw ingredients and a meal had to be prepared from scratch, the advent of frozen meals and pre-preparedconvenience food changed the cooking habits of many people, who consequently used the kitchen less and less.

For others, who followed the "cooking as a social act" trend, the open kitchen had the advantage that they could be with their guests while cooking, and for the "creative cooks" it might even become a stage for their cooking performance.

The "Trophy Kitchen" is equipped with very expensive and sophisticated appliances which are used primarily to impress visitors and to project social status, rather than for actual cooking.

### Ventilation

The ventilation of a kitchen, in particular a large restaurant kitchen, poses certain difficulties that are not present in the ventilation of other kinds of spaces. In particular, the air in a kitchen differs from that of other rooms in that it typically contains grease, smoke and odours.

## MATERIALS

The Frankfurt Kitchen of 1926 was made of several materials depending on the application. The built-in kitchens of today use particle boards or MDF, decorated with veneers, in some cases also wood. Very few manufacturers produce home built-in kitchens from stainless-steel. Until the 1950s, steel kitchens were used by architects, but this material was displaced by the cheaper particle board panels sometimes decorated with a steel surface.

## DOMESTIC KITCHEN PLANNING

**Fig.** Kitchen in Vietnam before a lunch.

**Fig.** Food over a kitchen.

Domestic (or residential) kitchen design *per se* is a relatively recent discipline. The first ideas to optimize the work in the kitchen go back to Catharine Beecher's *A Treatise on Domestic Economy* (1843, revised and republished together with her sister Harriet Beecher Stowe as *The American Woman's Home* in 1869).

Beecher's "model kitchen" propagated for the first time a systematic design based on early ergonomics. The design included regular shelves on the walls, ample work space, and dedicated storage areas for various food items. Beecher even separated the functions of preparing food and cooking it altogether by moving the stove into a compartment adjacent to the kitchen.

Christine Frederick published from 1913 a series of articles on "New Household Management" in which she analyzed the kitchen following Taylorist principles, presented detailed time-motion studies, and derived a kitchen design from them.

Her ideas were taken up in the 1920s by architects in Germany and Austria, most notably Bruno Taut, Erna Meyer, and Margarete Schütte-Lihotzky. A social housing project in Frankfurt (the *Römerstadt* of architect Ernst May) realized in 1927/8 was the breakthrough for her Frankfurt kitchen, which embodied this new notion of efficiency in the kitchen.

While this "work kitchen" and variants derived from it were a great success for tenement buildings, home owners had different demands and did not want to be constrained by a 6.4 m$^2$ kitchen.

Nevertheless, kitchen design was mostly ad-hoc following the whims of the architect. In the U.S., the "Small Homes Council", since 1993 the "Building Research Council", of the School of Architecture of the University of Illinois at Urbana-Champaign was founded in 1944 with the goal to improve the state of the art in home building, originally with an emphasis on standardization for cost reduction.

It was there that the notion of the *kitchen work triangle* was formalized: the three main functions in a kitchen are storage, preparation, and cooking (which Catharine Beecher had already recognized), and the places for these functions should be arranged in the kitchen in such a way that work at one place does not interfere with work at another place, the distance between these places is not unnecessarily large, and no obstacles are in the way. A natural arrangement is a triangle, with the refrigerator, the sink, and the stove at a vertex each. This observation led to a few common kitchen forms, commonly characterized by the arrangement of the kitchen cabinets and sink, stove, and refrigerator:

- A *single-file kitchen (or one-way galley)* has all of these along one wall; the work triangle degenerates to a line. This is not optimal, but often the only solution if space is restricted. This may be common in an attic space that is being converted into a living space, or a studio apartment.
- The *double-file kitchen (or two-way galley)* has two rows of cabinets at opposite walls, one containing the stove and the sink, the other the refrigerator. This is the classical work kitchen.

- In the *L-kitchen*, the cabinets occupy two adjacent walls. Again, the work triangle is preserved, and there may even be space for an additional table at a third wall, provided it does not intersect the triangle.
- A *U-kitchen* has cabinets along three walls, typically with the sink at the base of the "U". This is a typical work kitchen, too, unless the two other cabinet rows are short enough to place a table at the fourth wall.
- A *G-kitchen* has cabinets along three walls, like the U-kitchen, and also a partial fourth wall, often with a double basin sink at the corner of the G shape. The G-kitchen provides additional work and storage space, and can support two work triangles. A modified version of the G-kitchen is the *double-L*, which splits the G into two L-shaped components, essentially adding a smaller L-shaped island or peninsula to the L-kitchen.
- The *block kitchen (or island)* is a more recent development, typically found in open kitchens. Here, the stove or both the stove and the sink are placed where an L or U kitchen would have a table, in a free-standing "island", separated from the other cabinets. In a closed room, this does not make much sense, but in an open kitchen, it makes the stove accessible from all sides such that two persons can cook together, and allows for contact with guests or the rest of the family, since the cook does not face the wall any more. Additionally, the kitchen island's counter-top can function as an overflow-surface for serving buffet style meals or sitting down to eat breakfast and snacks.

In the 1980s, there was a backlash against industrial kitchen planning and cabinets with people installing a mix of work surfaces and free standing furniture, led by kitchen designer Johnny Grey and his concept of the "Unfitted Kitchen".

Modern kitchens often have enough informal space to allow for people to eat in it without having to use the formal dining room. Such areas are called "breakfast areas", "breakfast nooks" or "breakfast bars" if the space is integrated into a kitchen counter. Kitchens with enough space to eat in are sometimes called "eat-in kitchens".

## OTHER KITCHEN TYPES

Restaurant and canteen kitchens found in hotels, hospitals, educational and work place facilities, army barracks, and similar establishments are generally (in developed countries) subject to public healthlaws. They are inspected periodically by public-health officials, and forced to close if they do not meet hygienic requirements mandated by law.

**Fig.** A canteen kitchen

Canteen kitchens (and castle kitchens) were often the places where new technology was used first. For instance, Benjamin Thompson's "energy saving stove", an early-19th century fully closed iron stove using one fire to heat several pots, was designed for large kitchens; another thirty years passed before they were adapted for domestic use.

Today's western restaurant kitchens typically have tiled walls and floors and use stainless steel for other surfaces (workbench, but also door and drawer fronts) because these materials are durable and easy to clean. Professional kitchens are often equipped with gas stoves, as these allow cooks to regulate the heat more quickly and more finely than electrical stoves. Some special appliances are typical for professional kitchens, such as large installed deep fryers, steamers, or a bain-marie. (As of 2004, steamers — not to be confused with a pressure cooker — are beginning to find their way into domestic households, sometimes as a combined appliance of oven and steamer.)

**Fig.** The Food Technology room at Marling School in Stroud, Gloucestershire.

The fast food and convenience food trends have also changed the way restaurant kitchens operate. There's a trend for restaurants to only "finish" delivered convenience food or even just re-heat completely prepared meals, maybe at the utmost grilling, a hamburger, or a steak.

The kitchens in railway dining cars present special challenges: space is constrained, and, nevertheless, the personnel must be able to serve a great number of meals quickly. Especially in the early history of railways this required flawless organization of processes; in modern times, the microwave oven and prepared meals have made this task much easier. Galleys are kitchens aboard ships or aircraft (although the term *galley* is also often used to refer to a railroad dining car's kitchen).

On yachts, galleys are often cramped, with one or two burners fuelled by an LP gas bottle, but kitchens on cruise ships or large warships are comparable in every respect with restaurants or canteen kitchens. On passenger airliners, the kitchen is reduced to a merepantry, the only function reminiscent of a kitchen is the heating of in-flight meals delivered by a cateringcompany. An extreme form of the kitchen occurs in space, *e.g.*, aboard a Space Shuttle (where it is also called the "galley") or the International Space Station. The astronauts' food is generally completely prepared, dehydrated, and sealed in plastic pouches, and the kitchen is reduced to a rehydration and heating module.

Outdoor areas in which food is prepared are generally not considered to be kitchens, even though an outdoor area set up for regular food preparation, for instance when camping, might be called an "outdoor kitchen". Military camps and similar temporary settlements of nomads may have dedicated kitchen tents. In schools where home economics (HE) or food technology (previously known as "domestic science") are taught, there will be a series of kitchens with multiple equipment (similar in some respects to laboratories) solely for the purpose of teaching. These will consist of six to twelve workstations, each with their own oven, sink, and kitchen utensils.

## KITCHEN TYPES BY REGION

**Fig.** A Tibetan kitchen

### Japan

Kitchens in Japan are called Daidokoro. Daidokoro is the place where food is prepared in a Japanese house. Until the Meiji era, a kitchen was also called *kamado* and there are many sayings in the Japanese language that involve kamado as it was considered the symbol of a house and the term could even be used to mean "family" or "household" (similar to the English word "hearth"). When separating a family, it was called *Kamado wo wakeru,* which means "divide the stove". *Kamado wo yaburu* (lit. "break the stove") means that the family was bankrupt.

**Tibet**

Tibetan kitchens may be very different from what western kitchens are. They use different items.

## ACCESSIBLE KITCHEN APPLIANCES

The kitchen is the most interactive room in the house. People, work surfaces, appliances and tools - all work together several times a day to produce meals that are nutritious and tasty. Inappropriate placement or design of large kitchen appliances can be a nuisance, a burden or even an impossibility. However, with some planning, you can look for features in your new appliances or identify modifications to your kitchen design that can provide a much more agreeable place to work.

Begin with a personal assessment of the needs of those who will be working in the kitchen, from their physical requirements to the types of food they will be preparing. Some households will have very tall or very short cooks.

Some will have difficulty bending or stretching. Perhaps they cannot stand for very long, if at all. Still others will be using many small appliances to assist with preparation. Think about keeping the design flexible, as needs may very well change over time.

We know how important this topic is to you, so the staff at Dynamic Living, Inc. has done some extensive research on accessible kitchen appliances. Most of them can be found at local appliance stores or at building supply mega-stores like Home Depot or Lowe's.

### THE DISHWASHER

With push button controls or dials in the front, dishwashers are already fairly accessible appliances. Most dishwashers are at least 34" in height and fit under a standard 36" high counter, but "standards" don't well work for everybody.

For example, people in wheelchairs find it easier to work at a counter that has space underneath for the wheelchair, with a height that is reasonable from the seated position. For most, a 34" counter height is ideal. If the kitchen design requires the counter to remain at 34" where the dishwasher will be placed, our unique ADA Compliant Dishwasher is a terrific solution, because its 32.5" height fits comfortably under the counter.

What to do about the person who is very tall or has trouble bending? Try installing the dishwasher higher, as you would a wall oven. This raised approach makes loading and unloading dishes a whole lot easier. (A reader tip from O2BNNZ!)

Another design alternative is the use of a countertop electric dishwasher that sit on the counter next to the sink. Hook-up is a snap (no plumber needed!). If you need the counter space, a portable dishwasher can also be placed on a rolling cart, so it can be pushed out of the way when not in use. Because they use less water, these dishwashers are also terrific for those city dwellers who are not permitted to have multi-cycle dishwashers.

## THE STOVE

Several major appliance manufacturers, such as Jennair, GE and Frigidaire, are now designing burners and ovens with accessibility in mind. Knobs or push-button controls are in the front, so the user doesn't have to reach across hot burners. Ceramic cooktop units, or burners with a flat surface, allow persons who have little upper torso strength to easily slide pots and pans from one area to another. Pan holders can keep a pot in place for single-handed stirring.

A cooktop and separate wall-mounted oven offer more placement flexibility than a floor-standing range. The cooktop might have an open space underneath for the wheelchair, allowing them to maneuver pans to the burners more easily, but be sure the underneath of the cooktop is properly insulated to avoid burns. (You can also use this space to store a rolling table or rolling vegetable bins/storage.) Or place the cooktop on an island to allow access from more than one side. If you locate the cooktop near the sink, you can fill a pot or pan using the hand-held sprayer without having to move the container off the stove.

People in wheelchairs might prefer the stove to be closer to the floor, making it easier to reach inside. Other cooks prefer built-in ovens, commonly 30" above the floor, because they don't need to stoop or bend to inspect cooking food or to remove hot pans from the oven. Choose a self-cleaning oven for easy maintenance.

How the oven door opens is also important. For some, a door that pulls downward provides a very convenient transitional shelf. Still others might prefer a door that swings to the left or right, allowing them better access to the oven racks. Side swing door models are sold by Frigidaire and Gaggenau.

## REFRIGERATORS

Side-by-side refrigerators are the most convenient for everyone. Some refrigerators feature water and ice dispensers on the outside of the door that are easily accessible. GE has designed a refrigerator that is shallower in depth than traditional models making it much easier to reach for items at the back of the shelf!

Perhaps the best approach might be to install a smaller refrigerator, like an "office" sized unit, that could be raised on a table if needed. If freezer accessibility is an issue, a standalone upright freezer offers plenty of easy-to-reach storage.

## MICROWAVES

Microwave ovens have some terrific benefits and offer great cooking flexibility. They are safer and cheaper to operate than conventional ovens and turn off at a predetermined time, which is great for the forgetful cook. When placed on the counter, their side-swinging door allows for easy transfer of plates.

Although it is common to see a microwave above the stove or high on a wall, we do not recommend that. Such a position is harder to reach and more likely to encourage spills from hot containers. If you decide to mount one lower on a wall, consider including a pull out shelf below it for easier transition of dishes into and out of the oven.

Most microwaves have a touch pad for programming operation. These pads are terrific, unless you have low vision. Some companies, such as Whirlpool Corp., offer optional Braille controls or the touch pad can be marked with raised dots to help the low vision cook. Control panels with fewer buttons are easier to understand and a back lit display is much easier to see. You can still find simpler microwaves that have a timer dial rather than a touch pad. This allows for quick programming of cooking time by a clock-like rotation of the dial.

Look for a door release that can be pushed easily with a closed fist or some other part of the body and a front edge that does not have a lip that might hinder a smooth transfer of dishes.

## SMALLER CONVENIENCES

"Instant" hot water dispensers can provide great convenience for those who'd like quick access for coffee or soup, but have trouble lifting a kettle or reaching into a microwave. Please be careful about placement to prevent scalding accidents.

In-sink garbage disposers are a terrific way to dispose of food waste easily. Make sure the switch is located in an accessible position for you. If space permits, you might also consider adding a trash compactor as well. They can help eliminate excessive trips to empty the kitchen trash!

Many hours are spent in the kitchen. Think about safety and convenience and take a little time now to plan for current and changing needs. You'll enjoy the results for years to come '

# 2

# Kitchen Design: Meeting Everyone's Needs

Designing or modifying a kitchen that is accessible for a range of users can be challenging and requires some compromise. General principles can be applied to help achieve an accessible kitchen for most of the population. The three Australian Standards that can be useful for reference are *AS 1428.1, AS 1428.2 and AS 4299*.

Important features of kitchen design include:

- Adequate space for moving around the kitchen.
- Work surfaces and adequate storage at suitable heights.
- Appropriate kitchen appliances, easy to use knobs, handles and controls.
- Easy access to kitchen waste disposal facilities.
- Planning for the future and considering the changing needs of users.

Becoming familiar with Australian Standards and current relevant legislation may help in the design process. Legislation and appliances change over time and as technology improves. It is advisable to contact appropriate organisations and health professionals to discuss current appliances and fixtures in relation to your needs.

## THE ONE-WALL KITCHEN DESIGN

Very basic, the one-wall kitchen design is perfect for long and narrow kitchens. It's simple and, as far as kitchen remodels go, fairly inexpensive. While it does not utilize the classic kitchen triangle, its linear design still allows for unimpeded traffic flow. Counter space is at a premium. The one-wall kitchen design is not the best design, though. It can be improved with either the corridor or L-shape kitchen design plans—provided kichen square footage is available.

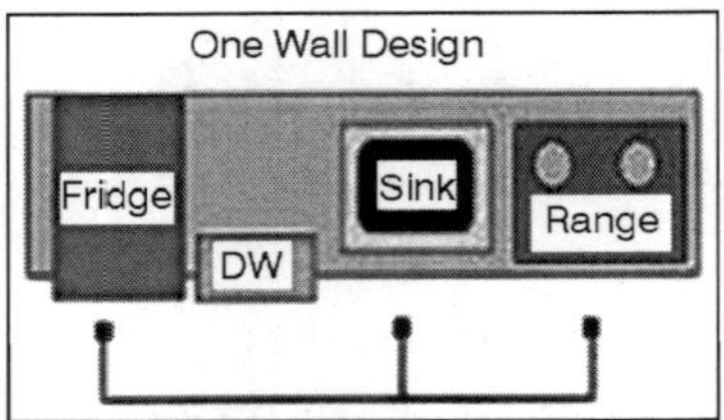


Most likely, everyone has at one point lived in a house or apartment with a corridor kitchen design.

### KITCHEN LAYOUT: CORRIDOR STYLE

With counters on both sides, the corridor style kitchen design is highly functional because it uses the classic kitchen triangle. This layout gives a bit more space for counters and cabinets, though crowding between the two main work spaces may be a problem. Still, the corridor-style kitchen design is a highly affordable and functional plan.

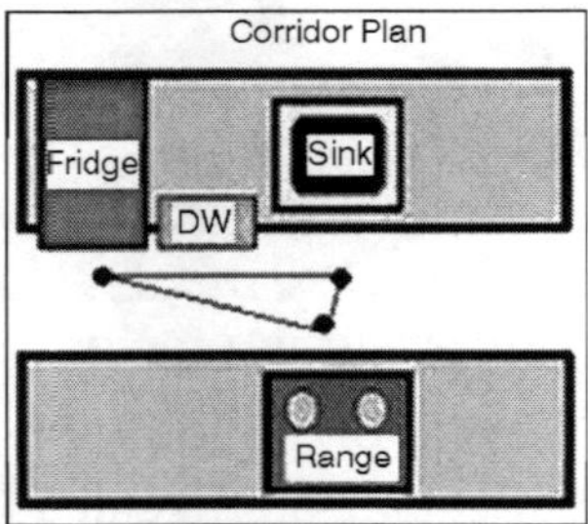


### THE L-SHAPED KITCHEN DESIGN PLAN

Along with the corridor plan, the L-shaped kitchen design plan is very popular, though this plan does away with the crowding problems found in the corridor plan. We still find the kitchen triangle, though the walk from range to refrigerator is longer.

This arrangement allows as much—and even a bit more—counter and cabinet space than the L-shaped design. The corner counter space is difficult to reach for food preparation, and is often used for storing mixers, toaster ovens, and other small appliances. Note that with the increased counter space, a double-sink can installed.

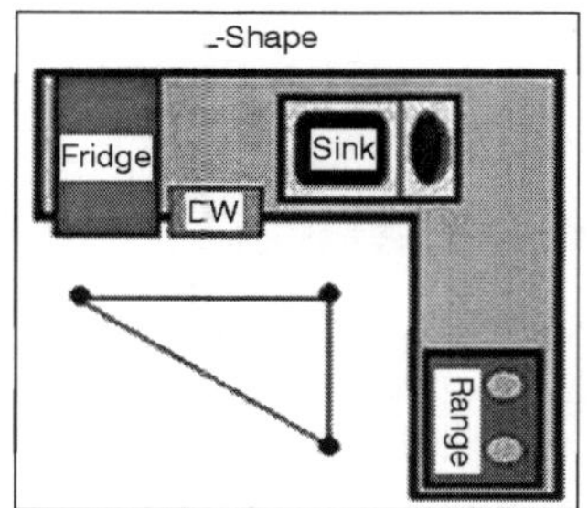


## THE DOUBLE-L KITCHEN DESIGN LAYOUT

A highly evolved kitchen design layout, the double-L allows for *two* workstations.

The smaller "L" has a cooktop and a second sink. The major cooking operations are focused on this area, while food prep goes on in the larger of the "L" spaces. This larger "L" also has tons of open counter space because the cooktop has been moved away.

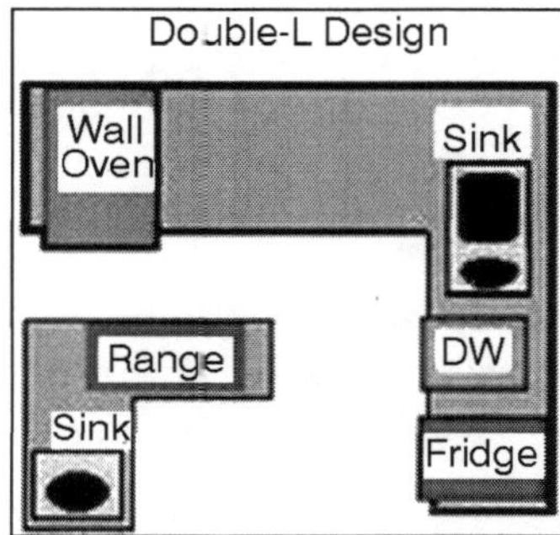


Note that not much space is gained for cabinets: the smaller "L" has only a short run along the wall for cabinets.

## THE U-SHAPE KITCHEN DESIGN LAYOUT

The U-shape kitchen design plan can be thought of as a corridor-shape plan—but with a closed end. The closed end gives extra room for a range or a sink.

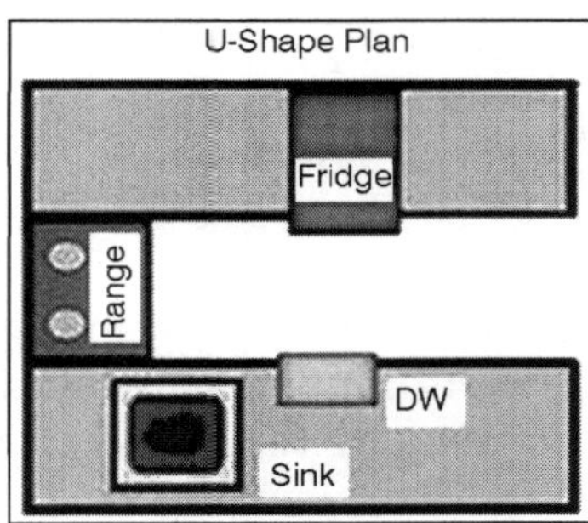

This arrangement maintains good workflow by means of the classic kitchen triangle. The closed end also provides plenty of space for extra cabinets.

## ORGANISATIONAL DESIGN

Organizing, the process of structuring human and physical resources in order to accomplish organizational objectives, involves dividing tasks into jobs, specifying the appropriate department for each job, determining the optimum number of jobs in each department, and delegating authority within and among departments. One of the most critical challenges facing lodging managers today is the development of a responsive organizational structure that is committed to quality.

The framework of jobs and departments that make up any organization must be directed toward achieving the organization's objectives. In other words, the structure of a lodging business must be consistent with its strategy.

Managers give structure to a hotel and lodging through job specialization, organization, and establishment of patterns of authority and span of control.

## JOB SPECIALIZATION

There are as many degrees of job specialization within the lodging industry as there are types of organizations, there are many types of organizations.

One extreme is the case of a hotel where the owner/operator is responsible for checking in the guests, servicing their needs, taking care of the housekeeping for the guest rooms, maintaining the building and grounds, and checking out the guests.

There is, to be sure, much to recommend this method of work. It is rewarding to have total control over a project from beginning to end, and many people find it motivating to the results of their efforts. However, as the demand for additional products or services increases it becomes more and more difficult for an individual to do his or her job well.

One benefit of the increased workload is increased revenue, which would enable the individual hotel operator to add housekeeping staff, one or more front desk agents to check in and check out the additional guests, and engineering and maintenance personnel to care for the building and grounds.

As a general rule, specialization increases worker productivity and efficiency. On the other hand, delegating jobs increases the need for managerial control and coordination.

Someone has to make sure that housekeeping staff come in after the painters have repainted a room not before! A crucial element of hotel and lodging management is coordinating the many specialized functions within hotels so that the organization runs smoothly.

Specialization has its own set of problems; it can result in workers performing the same tasks over and over again. A point can be reached where the degree of specialization so narrows a job's scope that the worker finds little joy or satisfaction in it. Signs of overspecialization include workers' loss of interest, lowered morale, increasing error rate, and reduction in service and product quality.

One solution to this problem is to modify jobs so that teams can perform them. Instead of a single guest room attendant being assigned to a group of rooms, a work team in a hotel housekeeping department might clean all of the rooms on a particular floor. Some establishments use teams regularly throughout the organization; others use teams more selectively. Teams can be directed by a manager or can be selfmanaged.

The idea behind self-managed work teams is for workers to become their own managers, which increases their self-reliance as well as develops a talent pool.

A concept called the quality circle is based on the belief that the people who actually do the work, rather than their managers, are the ones who are best able to identify, analyse, and correct problems they encounter. The idea originated in Japan in 1962. The quality circle is a group of employees, usually fewer than ten, who perform similar jobs and meet once per week to discuss their work, identify problems, and present possible solutions to those problems. For example, a quality circle might be formed among front desk agents. The group forwards its findings and proposals to management for evaluation and action. Quality circles are most successful when they are part of an organization- wide improvement effort. American business picked up on the quality circle concept in the mid-1970s.

## THE ORGANIZATION OF A LODGING ESTABLISHMENT

As their facilities grow in size, lodging managers are faced with the need to group certain jobs in order to ensure efficient coordination and control of activities. These job groupings are usually called departments. In general, departments might be grouped as front of the house (those departments in which employees have guest contact, such as front desk), and back of the house (where employees have little guest contact, such as accounting).

However, separating departments by function is the most common method of organizing a hotel or a lodging business. The departmental structures of a limited-service hotel, a full-service hotel with under 500 rooms, and a full-service hotel with over 500 rooms. There may be as few as 2 or as many as 50 employees in a particular department. In a very small lodging business, such as a bed-and-breakfast, the owner can supervise each department. However, as the lodging business increases in size it is most effective to create managerial positions within departments.

## ROOM DEPARTMENT

Typically, the rooms department includes reservations, the front office, housekeeping, and telephone or PBX. In smaller full-service hotels, security and engineering might also be included in the rooms department. Responsibilities of the rooms department include reservations, guest reception, room assignment, tracking the status of rooms, prompt forwarding of mail and phone messages, security, housekeeping of guest rooms and public spaces such as lobbies, and answering guests' questions. To perform these many duties effectively, the rooms department may be divided into a number of specialized subunits.

To complicate matters, in many instances these subunits are also referred to as departments. For example, the laundry department is responsible for cleaning and pressing all the hotel's linens and employee uniforms as well as guest laundry. Because of its specialized function, little of the knowledge and skills required to manage a laundry operation is transferable to other areas of hotel operations.

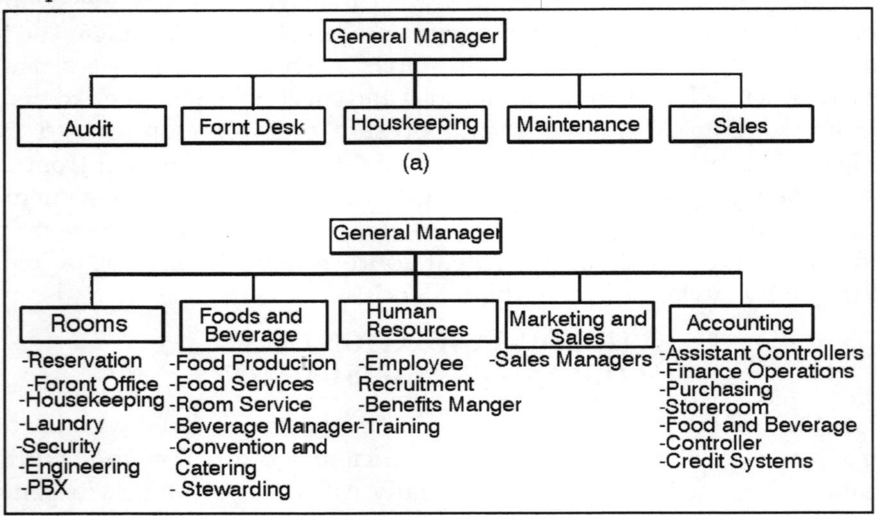


**Fig.** Department Structure in the Hotel and Lodging Industry: (a) Departments of a Limited-Servoce Hotel; (b) Departments of a Full-Service Hotel (Under 500 Rooms)

The front office is one of the most important departments in a hotel, as it often offers the only contact between guests and staff. A hotel's front office is where guests are greeted when they arrive, where they are registered and assigned to a room, and where they check out.

Usually, the telephone operator, other guest communications functions, and the bell staff or those employees responsible for delivering luggage and messages and attending to special guest requests also fall under the front office umbrella. The reservations department takes and tracks the hotel's future bookings. The housekeeping department is responsible for cleaning guest rooms and public spaces. Because of their specialized nature, the security and engineering departments are discussed in separate sections.

A great deal of interdependence exists among the subunits of the rooms department. For example, reservations must inform the front office of the number of presold rooms each day to ensure that a current inventory of salable rooms is always available. On the other hand, the front office must let reservations know whenever walk-in guests register. A similar level of cooperation is required between the front office and housekeeping. When a guest checks out, the front office must inform housekeeping so that the room may be cleaned.

Once a room is cleaned, housekeeping must inform the front office so that the room may be sold. Certain tasks within the rooms department must occur in a specific order. For example, housekeeping cannot properly provision a guest room if the laundry does not supply enough clean towels or bed sheets. Engineering cannot replace a defective light switch in a guest room if housekeeping does not report the problem. Effective management of this busy department calls for standardized plans, procedures, schedules, and deadlines, as well as frequent direct communication between the executives who manage the key operating units of the rooms department.

## SECURITY

The hotel and lodging business is vulnerable to security and safety problems. Problems can be created by guests, employees, or intruders. Security breaches can result in embezzlement, theft, arson, robbery, and even terrorism. Depending on the size of a hotel or a lodging establishment, the security function may be handled by a fully staffed department on site, contracted to an outside security company, or assigned to designated staff members or on-premises supervisory personnel in the rooms department. In a larger, full-service hotel, the director of security may report directly to the general manager. In smaller hotels, the security function might become a task of the rooms department.

## ENGINEERING

Typically, the engineering department's responsibilities include preventive maintenance; repair; replacement; improvement and modification to furniture, fixtures, and equipment (FFE); and ensuring uninterrupted provision of utilities (gas, electricity, water). Preventive maintenance involves routine checks and inspection of the key components of all equipment. Maintenance of recreational facilities may be part of the engineering department's responsibilities. In particular, swimming pools require extensive maintenance to ensure proper filtration and to prevent the accumulation of algae and other conditions unsuitable for swimming.

Prompt repair minimizes loss of productivity in other hotel operating departments and inconvenience to hotel guests. When a particular FFE has reached the end of its useful life and repair is no longer cost-effective, replacement is indicated. Improvement projects enhance the existing operation or reduce operating costs of the facility. Modification projects alter the existing operation to accommodate one or more new functions.

One hotel might have a large engineering staff that includes plumbers, carpenters, painters, electricians, and other technicians. Another might have maintenance personnel who have general knowledge and understanding of the hotel's operations but rely on outside contractors for specialized jobs. In larger, full-service hotels, engineering may be a separate department, with a director who reports directly to the resident manager.

## FOOD AND BEVERAGE DEPARTMENT

The primary function of the food and beverage department is to provide food and drink to a hotel's guests. In earlier times, when an inn had a single dining room that could hold a limited number of guests, this was a fairly simple task. Today, however, providing food and drink is much more complicated. A large hotel might well have a coffee shop, a gourmet restaurant, a poolside snack bar, room service, two banquet halls, and ten function rooms where food and beverages are served.

It might also have a lounge, a nightclub, and a lobby bar. On a busy day, it's quite likely that functions will be booked in many outlets at the same time. In addition, some outlets may have multiple events scheduled for a single day. There is great diversity in the types of activities performed by a food and beverage department, requiring a significant variety of skills on the part of its workers.

Because of the diversity of services provided, the food and beverage department is typically split into subunits. The executive chef, a person of considerable importance and authority in any full-service hotel, runs the food production, or kitchen, department. A variety of culinary specialists who are responsible for different aspects of food preparation report to the executive chef.

The actual serving of food in a large hotel's restaurants is usually the responsibility of a separate department, headed by the assistant food and beverage director. The food service department is composed of the individual restaurant and outlet managers, maitre d's, waiters, waitresses, and bus help.

Because of their special duties and concerns, many large hotels have a separate subunit that is responsible only for room service. Because of the high value and profit margins associated with the sale of alcoholic beverages, some hotels have a separate department that assumes responsibility for all outlets where alcoholic beverages are sold.

The person responsible for this department is the beverage manager. Most full-service hotels also do a considerable convention and catering business. The typical convention uses small function rooms for meetings and larger rooms for general sessions, trade shows, and banquets. As a hotel or lodging business increases the use of its facilities for conventions and meetings, it may form a separate convention services department.

The convention services department and its personnel are introduced to the client, a meeting planner, or an association executive by the marketing and sales department.

The convention services department then handles all of the client's meeting and catering requirements. Individually catered events include parties, wedding receptions, business meetings, and other functions held by groups. To provide for the unique needs of these types of customers, hotels often organize separate catering and convention departments.

Depending on the size of the hotel, the job of cleaning the food and beverage outlets themselves as well as of washing pots and pans, dishes, glasses, and utensils is often delegated to a subunit known as the stewarding department.

It is only through continuous cooperation and coordination that a hotel's food service function can be carried out effectively. A guest who is dining in a hotel restaurant requires the joint efforts of the kitchen, food service, beverage, and stewarding departments. A convention banquet cannot be held without the efforts of the convention and catering department along with the food production, beverage, and stewarding departments.

The sequence of events and cooperation required among the food and beverage staff is even more important than in the rooms department, thus increasing the importance of communication between managers and employees alike. Another challenge faced by management is the diversity of the employees in the food and beverage department; the dishwasher in the stewarding department is at a dramatically different level than the sous chef in the kitchen.

## MARKETING AND SALES DEPARTMENT

Coordination is not as important an issue in, the marketing and sales department which is generally much smaller than the food and beverage department. The primary responsibility of the sales managers who make up the marketing and sales department is sales, or the selling of the hotel facilities and services to individuals and groups. Sales managers sell rooms, food, and beverages to potential clients through advertising, attendance at association and conference meetings, and direct contacts.

The marketing and sales department is also removed from most of the day-to-day operational problems faced by other departments. The division of work among the sales managers is based on the type of customers a hotel is attempting to attract. Individual sales managers often specialize in corporate accounts, conventions, or tour and travel markets. Sales managers' accounts are sometimes subdivided along geographical lines into regional or national accounts. The sales staff of the largest full-service hotels usually does not exceed a dozen or so. These sales managers work more or less independently in their particular market segments.

## HUMAN RESOURCE DEPARTMENT

The human resources department serves no customers, books no business, and prepares no meals, yet it plays a vital role in a hotel's efficient operation. The three functions of the human resources department are employee recruitment, benefits administration, and training. The director of human resources is also expected to be an expert on federal and state Labour laws and to advise managers in other departments on these topics. The human resources department's major challenge is in its interactions with other hotel departments.

Although the human resources department recruits, interviews, and screens prospective employees, the final hiring decision rests within the department in which the potential employee will be working. The same is true of promotion and disciplinary decisions; the human resources department's input is, in most cases, limited to advice and interpretation of legal questions. The human resources department's effectiveness depends on its manager's ability to form effective working relationships with managers of other departments.

## ACCOUNTING DEPARTMENT

In many hotels, the accounting department combines staff functions and line functions, or those functions directly responsible for servicing guests. The accounting department's traditional role is recording financial transactions, preparing and interpreting financial statements, and providing the managers of other departments with timely reports of operating results. Other responsibilities, carried out by the assistant controller for finance, include payroll preparation, accounts receivable, and accounts payable.

Another dimension of the accounting department's responsibilities deals with various aspects of hotel operations, cost accounting, and cost control throughout the hotel. The two areas of central concern to the accounting department are rooms and food and beverage.

The accounting department's front office cashier is responsible for tracking all charges to guest accounts. At the close of each business day, which varies by hotel but typically occurs at midnight or after the bulk of guests' transactions have been completed, the night auditor is responsible for reconciling all guest bills with the charges from the various hotel departments. Although the front office cashier and the night auditor physically work at the front desk and, in the case of the cashier, have direct contact with guests, they are members of the accounting department and report to the assistant controller of operations.

The food and beverage department may be responsible for food preparation and service, but the accounting department is responsible for collecting revenues. The food and beverage controller and the food and beverage cashiers keep track of both the revenues and expenses of the food and beverage department. The food and beverage controller's job is to verify the accuracy and reasonableness of all food and beverage revenues.

In addition to tracking and preparing daily reports on the costs of the food and beverages used in the hotel, in many cases the accounting department is also responsible for purchasing and storeroom operations. Finally, the director of systems is responsible for designing the accounting and control systems used throughout the hotel.

The accounting department is anything but a passive staff unit contending with routine recordkeeping. The accounting department is also responsible for collecting and reporting most of a hotel's operational and financial statistics, which provide important data for decision making and budget preparation purposes.

The head of the accounting department may report not only to the hotel's general manager but also to the hotel chain's financial vice president or to the hotel's owner. The reason for this dual responsibility and reporting relationship is to afford the hotel corporation an independent verification of the financial and operating results of the hotel.

## GENERAL MANAGER

In addition to being in charge of overseeing all of the departments that we have discussed, the hotel's general manager (GM) is responsible for defining and interpreting the policies established by top management.

The general manager serves as a liaison to the hotel's owner or corporate parent, sets the overall strategic course of the hotel, sets hotel-wide goals, coordinates activities between departments, and arbitrates interdepartmental disputes.

It is common practice in a large, full-service hotel for a director of public relations to report directly to the GM. The GM also has corporate-level responsibilities, participates on civic boards and committees, and engages in industry-related activities such as serving on the local tourism commission or hotel-motel association.

In addition to possessing a high level of technical skill (i.e., a thorough understanding of each operating department in the hotel), the general manager must also be decisive, analytical, and skilled with both computers and people. He or she must be able to see the big picture and how all of the parts of the hotel fit into the overall organization.

## RESIDENT MANAGER

An executive may be promoted to relieve the general manager of some operational duties. This is often accomplished by elevating the duties and responsibilities of one particular department head without relieving that person of regular departmental duties. The title of this position is usually resident manager.

It is quite common (and logical) for the general manager to select the manager of the rooms department to be resident manager. Responsibilities of the resident manager include serving as acting GM in the GM's absence, representing the GM on interdepartmental hotel committees, and taking responsibility for important special projects such as major hotel renovations, VIP guests, and operating reports that require in-depth analysis for the regional or corporate offices.

## THE HOTEL STAFFING SYSTEM

Staffing, which is one of a hotel's most important management functions, is an ongoing challenge because of the high rate of employee and manager turnover. Full-service hotels can experience annual turnover rates in excess of 100 Per cent in certain employee classifications. Some managers consider an annual employee turnover rate of 33 Per cent low. (In other words, in a single year, one-third of a hotel's employees must be replaced.) At this rate, the entire hotel must be completely restaffed every three years. The higher the turnover rate, the larger the number of employees who must be replaced. For example, if a hotel with 450 employees has a 75 Per cent annual turnover rate, it will be completely restaffed every 16 months. Staffing is the responsibility of the human resources department.

In an attempt to reduce employee turnover, hotel and lodging businesses are giving increasing attention to job design, seeking to enhance those job characteristics that give the employee the greatest satisfaction and motivation. Good job design must take into account the needs of employees as well as the demands of the job.

Well-thought-out job design begins when management conducts a job analysis—that is, a thorough evaluation of the specific tasks performed for a particular job and the time required to perform them. Job analysis is an ongoing process, as many jobs change with improvements in technology and pressure to improve product quality.

The job analysis is the basis for the job description and job specification. A job description includes the job title, pay, a brief statement of duties and procedures, working conditions, and hours. The job specification is an outline of the qualifications necessary for a particular job.

In response to the limits of specialization, organizations can redesign jobs to improve coordination, productivity, and product quality while responding to an employee's needs for learning, challenge, variety, increased responsibility, and achievement. Such job redesign often involves job rotation, the systematic movement of employees from one job to another; job enlargement, an increase in the number of tasks an employee will do in the job; job enrichment, the attempt to give the employee more control over job-related activities; and flextime, a flexible work schedule that permits employee input in establishing work schedules. In team-driven job redesign, a concept similar to job rotation, employees can transfer back and forth among teams that provide different services or products.

Hotels recruit employees from a variety of sources. Newspapers and employee referrals are used to recruit nonskilled hourly employees. Supervisory and management employees generally are recruited through colleges and universities, promotions from within, professional associations, and management recruiters. Hotels that take more time in making their selections are more successful in retaining employees.

Discussions of employee training and development often concentrate on training techniques without giving a full explanation of what a hotel is trying to accomplish. As training and development impart job skills and educate employees, supervisors, and managers, they also improve current and future employee performance, which affects the bottom line. Effective training includes problem solving, problem analysis, quality measurement and feedback, and team building.

Performance evaluation, also called performance appraisal, is the systematic review of the strengths and weaknesses of an employee's performance. The major difficulty in a performance appraisal is quantifying those strengths and weaknesses. The performance of some jobs is easy to quantify, while for others it is more difficult. An important part of the appraisal process is a well-established job description, so that the employee and the supervisor have similar expectations.

Compensation includes the monetary and nonmonetary rewards that managers, supervisors, and employees receive for performing their jobs. In order to set compensation levels, the human resources department must periodically conduct job evaluations, which determine the value of the job to the hotel. Knowledge of the value of the job to the organization and of wage rates for each job classification allows the hotel to establish a fair compensation policy.

## CAREER PATHS AND OPPORTUNITIES

If you complete your course of study and graduate with a bachelor of science degree in hotel management, most likely you will enter the business at the managerial level. Along the way you will have learned that a successful manager provides clear direction, encourages open communication, coaches and supports people, provides objective recognition, establishes ongoing controls, follows up and gives subordinates feedback, selects the right people to staff the organization, understands the financial implications of decisions, encourages innovation and new ideas, gives subordinates clear-cut decisions when needed, and consistently demonstrates a high level of integrity.

There are three levels of management careers in the hotel or lodging business: first-line, middle, and top. First-line refers to those who have day-to-day contact with the guests and clients of a lodging business. The first-line manager oversees the work of the supervisors and line employees. In a hotel or lodging business, first-line positions may include assistant manager of housekeeping, assistant front office manager, and assistant restaurant manager. First-line managers are responsible for a hotel's basic work, such as checking guests in and out, making up the guests' rooms, and preparing and serving the meals. First-line managers are in daily or near-daily contact with line employees.

Middle management of most hotel or lodging businesses includes the department manager, general manager, and any position between those levels. Depending on the size of the hotel, the regional manager (who supervises the general managers of the hotels in his or her region) can also fall into this category. Unlike first-line managers, those in middle management plan, organize, lead, and control other managers' activities and are responsible for the performance of their departments.

Top management comprises a small group of managers such as the chief executive officer, president, or vice president. Top management is responsible for the performance of the entire hotel business as well as for supervision of the middle managers. The top manager is accountable to the owners of the financial resources used by the organization, such as the stockholders or executive board.

As you have already seen, there are numerous attractive careers in the hotel and lodging business.

*The following is one of the many paths your career might follow*:

- Assistant manager of the reservations department
- Reservations department manager
- Rooms department manager
- Resident manager
- General manager
- Regional manager

In a full-service hotel or lodging business, the movement from entry-level position to general manager might encompass 15 years. Career advancement in a limited-service hotel or lodging business can occur more rapidly. A career in a limited-service hotel or lodging establishment might commence at the assistant general manager level, with movement to general manager within three years and to district or regional manager within five to eight years. This accelerated pace is due in large part to the more restricted range of services the manager must master before advancing.

## KITCHEN LAYOUT

Good kitchen design begins with the main work areas—the cook top and oven, refrigerator and sink. Focus on fixtures designed with a range of users in mind and that are easily removed if extra manoeuvring space is needed. For people with a cognitive impairment, it may assist to use a simple, uncluttered design layout that may resemble something the person was familiar with in the past.

The distance between each main work area should allow sufficient room for easy day-to-day food preparation tasks. If it's too small, people may feel cramped. If too large, more energy is required for walking, lifting, carrying and cleaning.

For circulation space, an 'L' or 'U' shaped layout is preferable. If possible, make provision for dining space in the kitchen, using a table, counter or pull out board.

For people who need support when walking or standing, a corridor-style kitchen design allows them to make use of the bench tops on either side for support. Additional handrails can be installed along the sides of benches for extra assistance.

The maximum recommended space between the parallel bench tops is 1200 millimetres. Keep in mind that a corridor design does not provide wheelchair access should it be required later, nor does it meet the requirements of adaptable housing design.

The minimum comfortable manoeuvring space for a wheelchair user to make a 60 to 90 degree turn is 1500 millimetres wide and 1500 millimetres long in the direction of travel.

To make a 90 to 180 degree turn, the minimum space required is not less than 2070 millimetres in the direction of travel and not less than 1540 millimetres wide. Foot recesses of at least 290 millimetres high and 190 millimetres deep under cupboards are required to accommodate footplates. A compact kitchen design may work for a wheelchair user if the person does not need to turn around and is able to drive in and reverse out.

### DOORS AND WINDOWS

To maximise circulation space, doors to the kitchen should open out or slide. If the door must open into the kitchen, additional circulation space may be required inside the room. The minimum clear doorway width should be 850 millimetres. If designing for a wheelchair user, include extra width on the latch side of the door—this allows room for wheelchair footplates when the user reaches for the door handle. Additional width on the hinge side of the door is also recommended depending on the direction of approach to the doorway.

Windows can be located over the sink or the cook top and should be low enough for a wheelchair user to be able to see out. A remote control opening device may be necessary if the window is above bench height and out of reach.

## CHOICE OF MATERIALS

Materials selected for kitchen use should be easy to clean, durable and stain resistant. A section of heat resistant material next to hotplates can be useful for sliding saucepans and pots directly off the cook top.

Colour contrast is important for those with vision impairment or for planning ahead when building for an ageing resident. Choose anti-glare surfaces and colours that provide a 30% luminance contrast with each other. Contrast bench tops to cupboards and power points to their background. Horizontal surfaces should be a lighter colour than vertical surfaces.

Opt for appliances where the control buttons and the backgrounds have strong contrasting colours. Words and pictures on controls should be large, simple and contrasting to the background.

### Worktops

Everything should be in easy reach of both standing adults and wheelchair users.

Standing adults generally prefer bench heights of 850 millimetres to 900 millimetres. Wheelchair users often prefer 700 millimetres to 850 millimetres. A compromise height of 850 millimetres may be used but if this is not ideal—consider who uses the bench tops the most.

Consider providing multiple work surfaces at different heights, pull out worktops or height adjustable worktops that can be operated electrically or manually and incorporate an emergency stop for safety.

A bench depth of 600 millimetres is generally recommended, however, wheelchair users and people with limited reach may find this width difficult when cleaning or reaching for objects at the back of the bench. As a minimum, provide an unbroken bench sequence between the sink and cook top to assist with sliding items from one area to another. Bench edges and corners should be rounded for safety.

At least one work surface should provide a clear opening of 820 millimetres underneath to allow for the front approach of a wheelchair. Knee space under kitchen benches allows a person with limited standing tolerance to sit on a stool while preparing food.

### Sinks

Sinks should be placed centrally in the kitchen and ideally should be at the same level as the work surface and positioned towards the front of the work top. Sinks placed against an outside wall with a window above have access to convenient drainage and natural lighting. A sink unit or two single bowls located diagonally across a corner in the kitchen with knee space underneath gives easy access to the sink and to the counter on either side.

Standing adults and wheelchair users will prefer the sink at different heights. Options include a compromise fixed sink height, using a height adjustable sink or two sinks at different heights (if space permits). For people with limited reach, a narrow sink may be suitable.

Food preparation can be concentrated in a small area by choosing a single or one and-a-half bowl sink. For double bowls, consider a compact size without a drainer or a sink which features the option of fitting a chopping board and draining basket over one of the bowls.

A shallow sink provides greater knee space under the sink for wheelchair users, as does the selection of a P-trap with all waste pipes located against the back wall. The underside of the bowl and any exposed pipes should be insulated to protect users from burns. A slide out towel rail can be fixed to the side wall of the knee recess.

Any rubbish disposals or dishwashers should be easy to reach from the sink position.

**Storage**

Clutter can create confusion and make it harder to find things. Clean out drawers and cupboards regularly and discard the items that are no longer required.

Food, dishes and cooking utensils need to be within easy reach to minimise the time, work and effort expended in doing simple tasks. Frequently used items should be located on bench tops or stored between hip and shoulder height to minimise reaching and bending. Heavy pots and pans are best kept near the stove and sink.

High cupboards may be out of reach for wheelchair users or people with restricted shoulder movement. However, they should be included for other users. A shelf fitting that pulls down from the upper cupboard to the bench top may be useful in this instance.

Island benches or mobile storage units provide more workspace and storage to house tableware and cutlery. Removable cupboard modules underneath bench tops allow easy access to their contents. Other ideas include:

- Pull out pantry, drawers and units provide easy access to items stored at the back of draws and shelves and reduce the amount of extended reach required. Examples include an under-sink pull out unit for storing dishwashing equipment, cabinet interiors with pull out baskets, or an ironing board hidden in a draw that pulls out and unfolds for use.
- Drawer inserts or dividers arrange the contents of drawers, and can

include single or split-level, twin or diagonal cutlery dividers for storage of utensils.

- Mobile storage units can be moved to different task areas around the kitchen as required. These provide accessible storage and additional work surfaces.
- Revolving wire basket shelves rotate 360 degrees to allow easy access for cupboard corners. These should have a lip of no less than 50 millimetres.
- Clear plastic food storage containers allow their contents to be easily identified.
- A cookbook holder attached underneath an overhead cabinet keeps bench space free and allows more room for food preparation.
- A fold down plate rack attached at a comfortable bench height stores plates within easy reach.
- Cupboard doors should be easy to open and close. Cupboard items will be most accessible if the doors have extended hinges that open up to 180 degrees. Door knobs can come in a variety of sizes and shapes to suit the user. Handles should be of a design that enables opening with one hand. Consider D shaped or lever style handles. Glow in the dark or brightly coloured knobs may be useful for people with a visual impairment. Door handles should be fitted to the bottom of high cupboard doors, and at the top of low cupboard doors. Closing mechanisms should be soft roller catches, press release, magnetic catches or self-closing hinges.
- Label drawers and cupboards with their contents. Consider see-through cupboard doors or remove cupboard doors altogether.
- Consider installing a pantry. Pantry shelves should be U-shaped and shallow enough that stored items are within easy reach. For increased access, consider installing half doors with 180 degree hinges. Where space is restricted, a pre made, pull out pantry supported on heavy duty extension runners may be an option. This kind of fixture can be accessed from both sides.

**Taps**

Rotating taps can be difficult for many people to operate. Alternative options include:

- Seal valve system: replaces existing washers and enables taps to be turned off with minimal effort.
- Extended lever taps: are available in various lengths and can be operated without requiring a strong grip. To enable reach for a

wheelchair user, the lever handle must be a maximum of 300 millimetres from the front of the bench to the operable part of the tap (the centre line of the tap, or the end point of the level measure through its arc of movement).

- Ceramic disk quarter turn taps: do not have washers and only require a quarter turn (that is, turning the tap from full OFF to full ON is a ninety degree angle).
- Spring loaded taps: turn off automatically after a specific time.
- Foot or knee operated taps for those who cannot operate hand taps.
- Infra red sensor taps: activated by movement and don't need turning on or off. Consideration needs to be taken of the location of the sensor when building for unknown or multiple users to ensure that the sensor is not installed beyond the recommended reach range of the user.
- Child-proof taps: the tap handle is pushed in and turned simultaneously.
- Single lever mixing taps are useful, but may be confusing for some older people or those with intellectual disability.

If permitted by local water authorities and if a back flow prevention device is fitted, taps with retractable hose fittings in the spout are useful for filling pans or jugs on the adjacent bench, or buckets on the floor. Swivel spouts with a high reach are also useful for filling tall jugs and pots. A bench mounted instant boiling water tap is a convenient way to prepare hot drinks.

## Flooring

Choose a surface that is firm, durable, slip resistant and easy to keep clean (for example, resistant to grease). Choose a colour that contrasts to adjacent surfaces and avoid complex patterns that may cause visual confusion. Clean floors regularly. Avoid polishing the flooring surfaces because this will increase the risk of someone slipping.

Ideally, the flooring should be extended to each wall so that if a cupboard is removed, increased circulation space with suitable flooring is already in place. Sheet flooring such as vinyl, PVC, or cork and rubber combinations are available in slip resistant options. They are embedded with an abrasive material such as sand, aluminium oxide or fibreglass.

If tiles are preferred, select unglazed ceramic tiles. Smaller tiles provide extra slip resistance due to the increased area of grout. Tiles already treated with a slip resistant formula are available. If replacing an existing tiled floor proves too difficult or expensive, a slip resistant coating can be applied to an existing floor. These chemical applications etch the tile surface to improve traction. The appearance of the floor surface does not change.

Padded vinyl is available for those requiring cushioning in the floor, however, cushioned vinyl may not withstand wheelchair use.

**Switches**

Large rocker style switches for power and lights are generally the easiest to use and should have a minimum dimension of 30 millimetres by 30 millimetres.

Light switches should be located between 900 millimetres and 1100 millimetres above floor level. Ensure there are sufficient outlets to avoid the inconvenience of unplugging and plugging in appliances.

Power outlets on rear walls should be avoided because they are difficult to access. If sufficient knee space is provided under bench tops, wheelchair users may be able to reach power outlets on rear walls. If not, place the outlets on the side of a cupboard or on the front fascia.

## ELECTRICAL APPLIANCES

Electrical appliances with fewer control options are usually easier to manage. Control knobs should be located at the centre, front or side of the unit. Controls should be large, have clear markings and a central cross bar to make them easier to operate.

Dials and knobs with simple choices will be easier to manage, for example ON/OFF and HIGH/LOW knobs. For users with a visual impairment, a switch with spring or automatic return to the OFF position may be useful. Look for appliances that have safety features. Appliances that beep or switch off if left on are helpful.

Power point timers may be useful because they automatically switch appliances off at a pre-set time. Consider installing a stove cut-off device for users who may forget to turn off the stove.

**Dishwashers**

If incorporating a dishwasher, consider that while the ideal location is alongside the sink, it may not fit under a lowered bench top height and may need to be located at the end of the counter. Before buying a dishwasher, check the ease of opening, size and ease of controls and the accessibility of the detergent dispenser.

If the house is in an open plan style, or someone in the household has hearing impairment or sensory issues, consider a dishwasher with noise reduction features.

**Ovens, Cook Tops and Microwaves**

Under-counter ovens are generally not accessible or safe for people who have difficulty reaching or bending. Separate wall mounted ovens are more accessible because they can be installed at the right height so that the shelf that is used most is in line with the bench top.

Select ovens with hinged doors that open away from the adjoining work surface. An oven with a side-opening door through 180 degrees allows closer access for most users. The lower edge of the oven door should be approximately 760 millimetres from the floor to allow clearance for wheelchair access, and the opening of the oven should be placed at eye level so the person can see into the oven.

When an oven with a side-opening door is used, it is useful to install a pull-out shelf beneath the oven, or a heat resistant surface next to the oven. This will make it easy and safe for a person to remove hot items from the oven and for temporary placement of hot pots and pans.

Hotplates should be arranged in a staggered or half moon layout, flush with adjacent work surfaces to enable pots to be slid directly onto the bench space. If knee space is provided underneath the hotplate surface, consider the need for insulating material under the hotplate base to protect from radiating heat and accidental burns.

An electric cook top will reduce the risk of accidents from naked flames but may be a burn risk if the user cannot tell when the hotplate is warm. Gas provides instant, tangible heat and burners can be heard or gas odour detected if a hotplate is left on.

Sealed hotplates are easier to wipe clean than coil-style hotplates, but can create a hazard when sliding pots due to their raised profile.

Ventilator hoods should have separate buttons for an extractor fan and a light to improve visibility in the kitchen, especially over the stove.

Portable electric elements, electric fry pans, grills or woks can be used instead of a built-in cook top. Ceramic, convection and continuous trivet cook tops provide a flush work surface.

Microwave ovens should be located at bench height.

### Refrigerators

When selecting a refrigerator it is important to consider the ease of opening and accessibility of the shelving. For wheelchair users, the refrigerator should be positioned in a way that provides easy access to most of the shelves from a seated position. Consider a smaller side-by-side refrigerator and freezer or a combination fridge/freezer with the freezer underneath. Freezers with pull out storage drawers may be easier to access.

## LIGHTING

Kitchens should be well lit with an adequate, uniform level of room lighting. Good lighting will help minimise accidents, eyestrain and fatigue.

A central ceiling fitting provides general room lighting, but additional task-specific lighting should be considered, particularly over the sink, cook tops and food preparation areas in positions that avoid shadowing.

Consider the type of light fitting used (for example track lighting, fluorescent strips) and how easy it will be to replace burnt out bulbs.

# 3

# The Best (and Worst) Cookware Materials

With the wide range of cookware available on the market today, it is easy to see why consumers may be confused about which materials to look for. I am frequently asked about my opinion on various cookware materials, particularly regarding their safety and potential toxicity.

In addition to the health issues with various cookware, there are also differences in quality, durability, and ease of use that may influence your decision on what type of material to use. With all these different factors in mind, choosing the best cookware can be challenging.

While many popular brands and styles of pots and pans are perfectly safe and versatile in their uses, there are a few types that may pose health risks if used regularly. In this article, I will clear up any confusion about which types of pots and pans are safest and easiest to use for all types of cooking.

The following are my picks for the three best and three worst types of cookware.

## BEST MATERIALS

### Enamel

Enamel cookware is ideal for dishes where heat retention and balance are required. The best quality can be found in enameled cast iron, but enameled ceramic or steel are other great choices. It is one of the safest types of cookware that comes close to a non-stick surface, making it easy to use and clean up after cooking. The cooking surface is nonreactive, so there is no need to worry about dangerous chemicals or metals leaching into food.

Though it can take a long time to heat up, the heat is distributed evenly and is easily maintained, making it a versatile cookware material for many types of dishes. Enamel cookware can also easily go from stovetop to oven, so these pots and pans are great for slow cooking or braising.

The major downside of enamel cookware is it tends to be very expensive, particularly when made by a reputable brand like Le Creuset. That said, high quality enamel pots and pans can be a worthwhile investment, as they are extremely durable and will last for many years. I personally love my enamel cookware and use it on a regular basis to create many of my meals.

### Cast Iron

Cast iron is another popular and traditional style of cookware that has been used for hundreds of years. Cast iron is durable and provides great conductivity and heat retention. It is perfect for cooking dishes that need to go from stove-top to oven, and is excellent for searing meat. Cast iron tends to be far less expensive than enamel, but lasts just as long and can be used for a variety of recipes.People with iron overload should probably not use iron skillets, as inorganic iron can leach into the food, particularly when cooking with liquids and acidic ingredients like citrus or tomato. However, the amount of iron that is released into the food is generally safe for those who do not have any issues with excess iron.

Cast iron does require some extra effort in its maintenance. A cast iron pan should be seasoned by coating with an oil like coconut oil, tallow, or lard (do not use butter), and then putting it in a 300° oven for three hours. While it is heating, you should remove it at least three times to wipe it clean and re-grease it. Seasoning your cast iron cookware will help give it a natural nonstick coating and will prevent rusting. Never use soap on a seasoned cast iron pan, simply wipe it out with a nonabrasive sponge or washcloth, or use salt as an abrasive if extra cleaning is needed.

### Stainless Steel

Stainless steel can be used for any type of cooking, but is especially useful for quick dishes, browning meat, or for recipes that require gauging the color of a broth or a sauce. If you are just looking to sauté something quickly, stainless steel is your best choice. Stainless steel is great for quickly heating things up, is far less expensive than ceramic, and is easier to clean and maintain than cast iron.

Stainless steel can withstand dishwashers and abrasive cleansers without scratching or denting, so clean up is relatively painless. Stainless steel is quite durable, and even the less expensive brands will last a long time. Also, stainless steel is one of the few metal cookwares that are nonreactive, so the metal doesn't interact with the food or affect the final flavor of the dish.

One of the major drawbacks of using stainless steel for cooking is that many types can be prone to sticking if the cookware is not used correctly. It is important to add adequate oil to the pan, and allow it to get hot before adding the food, in order to minimize sticking. Unfortunately, compared to enamel and cast iron, stainless steel is not a great conductor of heat and doesn't distribute heat as evenly.

## WORST MATERIALS

### Teflon

If there is one cookware material I would never use, it's one with a non-stick plastic coating like Teflon. While non-stick cookware is a tempting purchase due to its inexpensive price point and easy clean up, the health risks from using this type of material for cooking overshadow any time or effort you may save in the kitchen.

Teflon, made of the chemical known as PFOA, is the most persistent synthetic chemical known to man, and is found in the blood of nearly every person tested. Animal studies have shown that PFOA causes cancer, liver damage, growth defects, immune system damage, and death in lab rats and monkeys. An EPA advisory panel reported that PFOA is a "likely carcinogen" in humans.

Besides just leaching chemicals into the food, Teflon cookware has also been shown to release dangerous chemicals into the air during use. Toxic fumes released from heated non-stick cookware has been shown to be deadly to birds, with many hundreds of birds dying every year from "Teflon toxicosis." Even more scary is that DuPont's own scientists have admitted that polymer fume fever in humans is possible at 662°F, a temperature easily exceeded when a pan is preheated on a burner or placed beneath a broiler.

There is no amount of time or stuck-on food that could be saved that would make up for the likely dangers that cooking with Teflon brings, and any cookware made with this toxic material should be thrown out immediately. It amazes me that this product is still allowed on the market, considering the warnings from the EPA about its toxicity.

## Aluminum

Aluminum cookware, while not as toxic as Teflon, may pose some health risks as well, and is not recommended for use in cooking. Aluminum cookware has been shown to leach a significant amount of aluminum into food during cooking, which could pose a toxicity threat.

This raises some concerns due to the effects of aluminum on the human nervous system and the hypothesized connection between aluminum exposures and Alzheimer's disease. Studies in animals show that the nervous system is a sensitive target of aluminum toxicity. While there is yet to be a scientific consensus on the dangers of low level aluminum ingestion, avoiding aluminum exposure in cooking is generally a good idea for optimal health.

Depending on the type of food cooked in aluminum cookware, levels of aluminum in the food will be highly varied. Leafy vegetables and acidic foods, such as tomatoes and citrus products, absorb the most aluminum during cooking. If you absolutely must use an aluminum pan, avoid cooking highly acidic or basic foods, and do not scrape the pan with a spatula or metal spoon.

## Copper

While copper may be a safer choice than Teflon or aluminum, I do not recommend using copper cookware due to leaching concerns. An excess of copper can cause a variety of health problems, many stemming from a copper-zinc imbalance.

Some symptoms of this imbalance include behavior disorders, depression, acne, eczema, headaches, and poor immune function to name a few. You can learn more about the symptoms of copper-zinc imbalance by listening to my podcast on the topic.

Most copper cookware these days is coated with stainless steel to improve durability and ease of cleaning. Despite this steel coating, copper should never be used to cook acidic food, since over time the acid can cause copper to leach into the food.

Older copper cookware may be coated with tin or nickel, which is unsafe for food use and should not be used for cooking. If you are unsure of the age of your copper pots and pans, it is probably safer to just discard them. Regardless of whether your pot is new or old, the risk of copper leaching into your food is still significant, so replacing your copper cookware with a safer alternative is recommended.

## Good Cookware is Worth the Investment

While enamel, cast iron, and stainless steel tend to be more expensive, they are durable, versatile, and safe. I feel it is worth investing a little extra money into high quality cookware, and I am confident these non-toxic kitchen tools will last you and your family a lifetime.

## COATED AND COMPOSITE COOKWARE

*Non-stick*

Steel or aluminum cooking pans can be coated with a substance such as polytetrafluoroethylene (PTFE) in order to minimize food sticking to the pan surface.

There are advantages and disadvantages to such a coating. Coated pans are easier to clean than most non-coated pans, and require little or no additional oil or fat to prevent sticking.

On the other hand, some sticking is needed to cause sucs to form, so a non-stick pan cannot be used where *e.g.* a pan sauce is desired. And non-stick pans must not be overheated.

Nonstick coatings tend to degrade over time. In order to preserve the coating, it is important never to use metal implements or harsh scouring pads or chemical abrasives when cleaning. There is a potential danger in the use of PTFE-based coatings: while decomposition of the coating does not occur at normal cooking temperatures (below about 465°F/240°C), overheating can produce decomposition products that are toxic to humans and fatal to birds. Unfortunately, overheating is relatively easy. Fortunately, there are alternatives such as seasoned or enameled cast iron.

The main difference in quality levels of the coatings is in the formulas of the liquid coating, the thickness of each layer and the number of layers used. Higher quality nonsticks use powdered ceramic or titanium mixed in with the nonstick to strengthen them and to make them more resistant to abrasion and deterioration. Some nonstick coatings containing hardening agents. Some coatings are high enough in quality that they pass the strict standards of the National Sanitation Foundation for approval for restaurant use.

*Enameled Cast Iron*

Enameled cast iron cooking vessels are made of cast iron covered with a porcelain surface. This creates a piece that has the heat distribution and retention properties of cast iron combined with a non-reactive, low-stick surface.

***Non-metallic Cookware***

Non-metallic cookware can be used in both conventional and microwave ovens. Non-metallic cookware typically can't be used on the stovetop, but some kinds of ceramic cookware, for example Corningware, are an exception.

*Ceramics*

Glazed ceramics, such as porcelain, provide a nonstick cooking surface. Some unglazed ceramics, such as terra cotta, have a porous surface that can hold water or other liquids during the cooking process, adding moisture in the form of steam to the food. Historically some glazes used on ceramic articles have contained high levels of lead, which can possess health risks.

*Glass*

Borosilicate glass, such as Pyrex, is safe at oven temperatures. The clear glass also allows for the food to be seen during the cooking process.

*Glass-ceramic*

Glass ceramic is used to make products such as Corningware, which have many of the best properties of both glass and ceramic cookware. While Pyrex can shatter if taken between extremes of temperature too rapidly, glass-ceramics can be taken directly from deep freeze to the stove top. Their near-zero coefficient of thermal expansion makes them almost entirely immune to thermal shock.

*Silicone*

Silicone bakeware is light, flexible, and able to withstand sustained temperatures of 675°F (360°C). It melts around 930°F (500°C), depending upon the fillers used. Its flexibility is advantageous in removing baked goods from the pan. This rubbery material is not to be confused with the silicone resin used to make hard, shatterproof children's dishware, which is not suitable for baking.

***Bakeware***

Bakeware is designed for use in the oven (for baking), and encompasses a variety of different styles of baking pans as cake pans, pie pans, and loaf pans.

- Cake pans include square pans, round pans, and speciality pans such as angel food cake pans and springform pans often used for baking cheesecake.
- Sheet pans, cookie sheets, and jelly-roll pans are bakeware with large flat bottoms.
- Pie pans are flat-bottomed flare-sided pans specifically designed for baking pies.

## METAL

Metal pots are made from a narrow range of metals because pots and pans need to conduct heat well, but also need to be chemically unreactive so that they do not alter the flavor of the food. Most materials that are conductive enough to heat evenly are too reactive to use in food preparation. In some cases (copper pots, for example), a pot may be made out of a more reactive metal, and then tinned or clad with another.

## ALUMINUM

Aluminum is a lightweight metal with very good thermal conductivity. It is resistant to many forms of corrosion. Aluminum is commonly available in sheet, cast, or anodized forms, and may be physically combined with other metals. Sheet aluminum is spun or stamped into form. Due to the softness of the metal it may be alloyed with magnesium, copper, or bronze to increase its strength. Sheet aluminum is commonly used for baking sheets, pie plates, and cake or muffin pans.

Deep or shallow pots may be formed from sheet aluminum. Cast aluminum can produce a thicker product than sheet aluminum, and is appropriate for irregular shapes and thicknesses. Due to the microscopic pores caused by the casting process, cast aluminum has a lower thermal conductivity than sheet aluminum, and is more expensive. Accordingly, cast aluminum cookware has become less common. It is used for Dutch ovens, heavyweight baking pans such as bundt pans, and wares such as ladles or handles where low thermal conductivity is desired.

Anodized aluminum has had the naturally occurring layer of aluminum oxide thickened by an electrolytic process to create a surface that is hard and non-reactive. It is used for sauté pans, stockpots, roasters, and Dutch ovens.

Uncoated and un-anodized aluminum can react with acidic foods to change the taste of the food.

Sauces containing egg yolks, or vegetables such as asparagus or artichokes may cause oxidation of non-anodized aluminum. Evidence has consistently linked aluminum exposure to neurodegenerative diseases such as Alzheimer's disease.

The Rondeau, Commenges et al article cited below states "These findings support the hypothesis that aluminum in drinking water is a risk factor for AD." (Alzheimer's disease)". The Alzheimer's Association states that "studies have failed to confirm any role for aluminum in causing Alzheimer's. [Today] few [experts] believe that everyday sources of aluminum pose any threat." According to Dr. Morton Walker on page 98 of his 1994 book "Toxic Metal Syndrome: How Metal Poisonings Can Affect Your Brain" the Alzhhimers Association has accepted funding from major players in the aluminum industry.

## STAINLESS STEEL

Stainless steel is an iron alloy containing a minimum of 11.5% chromium. Blends containing 18% chromium with either 8% nickel,called 18/8, or with 10% nickel, called 18/10, are commonly used for kitchen equipment. Stainless steel's virtues are resistance to corrosion, non-reactivity with either alkaline or acidic foods, and resistance to scratching and denting. Stainless steel's drawback for cooking use is that it is a relatively poor heat conductor and contains chromium; a toxic metal considered unsafe when ingested as metal particles. As a result, stainless steel cookware is generally made with a disk of copper or aluminum in or on the base to conduct the heat across the base.

## PROPERTIES

High oxidation-resistance in air at ambient temperature are normally achieved with additions of a minimum of 13% (by weight) chromium, and up to 26% is used for harsh environments.

The chromium forms a passivation layer of chromium(III) oxide ($Cr_2O_3$) when exposed to oxygen. The layer is too thin to be visible, and the metal remains lustrous. The layer is impervious to water and air, protecting the metal beneath. Also, this layer quickly reforms when the surface is scratched.

This phenomenon is called passivation and is seen in other metals, such as aluminium and titanium. Corrosion-resistance can be adversely affected if the component is used in a non-oxygenated environment, a typical example being underwater keel bolts buried in timber.

When stainless steel parts such as nuts and bolts are forced together, the oxide layer can be scraped off, causing the parts to weld together. When disassembled, the welded material may be torn and pitted, an effect known as galling.

This destructive galling can be best avoided by the use of dissimilar materials for the parts forced together, e.g. bronze and stainless steel, or even different types of stainless steels (martensitic against austenitic, etc.), when metal-to-metal wear is a concern. Nitronic alloys (trademark of Armco, Inc.) reduce the tendency to gall through selective alloying with manganese and nitrogen.

## APPLICATIONS

Stainless steel's resistance to corrosion and staining, low maintenance, relatively low cost, and familiar luster make it an ideal base material for a host of commercial applications. There are over 150 grades of stainless steel, of which fifteen are most common.

The alloy is milled into coils, sheets, plates, bars, wire, and tubing to be used in cookware, cutlery, hardware, surgical instruments, major appliances, industrial equipment, and as an automotive and aerospace structural alloy and construction material in large buildings. Storage tanks and tankers used to transport orange juice and other food are often made of stainless steel, due to its corrosion resistance and antibacterial properties. This also influences its use in commercial kitchens and food processing plants, as it can be steam-cleaned, sterilized, and does not need painting or application of other surface finishes.

Stainless steel is used for jewellery and watches. The most common stainless steel alloy used for this is 316L. It can be re-finished by any jeweller and will not oxidize or turn black.

Some firearms incorporate stainless steel components as an alternative to blued or parkerized steel. Some handgun models, such as the Smith and Wesson Model 60 and the Colt M1911 pistol, can be made entirely from stainless steel. This gives a high-luster finish similar in appearance to nickel plating; but, unlike plating, the finish is not subject to flaking, peeling, wear-off due to rubbing (as when repeatedly removed from a holster over the course of time), or rust when scratched.

Some automotive manufacturers use stainless steel as decorative highlights in their vehicles.

**Uses in Sculpture, Building Facades and Building Structures**

- Stainless steel was in vogue during the art deco period. The most famous example of this is the upper portion of the Chrysler Building (pictured). Some diners and fast-food restaurants use large ornamental panels, stainless fixtures and furniture. Owing to the durability of the material, many of these buildings retain their original appearance.
- The forging of stainless steel has given rise to a fresh approach to architectural blacksmithing in recent years.
- The Unisphere (pictured), constructed as the theme symbol of the 1964-4 World's Fair in New York City, is the world's largest global structure.
- The Gateway Arch (pictured) is clad entirely in stainless steel: 886 tons (804 metric tonnes) of 0.25 in (6.4 mm) plate, #3 finish, type 304 stainless steel.
- Type 316 stainless is used on the exterior of both the Petronas Twin Towers and the Jin Mao Building, two of the world's tallest skyscrapers.
- The Parliament House of Australia in Canberra has a stainless steel flagpole weighing over 220 tons.
- The aeration building in the Edmonton Composting Facility, the size of 14 hockey rinks, is the largest stainless steel building in North America.
- The United States Air Force Memorial has an austenitic stainless steel structural skin.
- The Atomium in Brussels, Belgium was renovated with stainless-steel cladding in a renovation completed in 2006; previously the spheres and tubes of the structure were clad in aluminium.
- The Cloud Gate sculpture by Anish Kapoor, in Chicago US.

## RECYCLING AND REUSE

Stainless steel is 100% recyclable. An average stainless steel object is composed of about 60% recycled material of which H"40% originates from end-of-life products and H"60% comes from manufacturing processes.Types of Stainless Steel

There are different types of stainless steels: when nickel is added, for instance, the austenite structure of iron is stabilized.

This crystal structure makes such steels non-magnetic and less brittle at low temperatures. For greater hardness and strength, more carbon is added. When subjected to adequate heat treatment, these steels are used as razor blades, cutlery, tools, etc.

Significant quantities of manganese have been used in many stainless steel compositions. Manganese preserves an austenitic structure in the steel as does nickel, but at a lower cost.

*Stainless steels are also classified by their crystalline structure:*

- *Austenitic*, or 300 series, stainless steels make up over 70% of total stainless steel production. They contain a maximum of 0.15% carbon, a minimum of 16% chromium and sufficient nickel and/or manganese to retain an austenitic structure at all temperatures from the cryogenic region to the melting point of the alloy. A typical composition of 18% chromium and 10% nickel, commonly known as 18/10 stainless, is often used in flatware. 18/0 and 18/8 are also available. Superaustenitic stainless steels, such as alloy AL-6XN and 254SMO, exhibit great resistance to chloride pitting and crevice corrosion due to high molybdenum content (>6%) and nitrogen additions, and the higher nickel content ensures better resistance to stress-corrosion cracking versus the 300 series.

  The higher alloy content of superaustenitic steels makes them more expensive. Other steels can offer similar performance at lower cost and are preferred in certain applications.. Low-carbon versions, for example 316L or 304L, are used to avoid corrosion problem caused by welding. Grade 316LVM is preferred where biocompatibility is required (such as body implants and piercings). The "L" means that the carbon content of the alloy is below 0.03%, which reduces the sensitization effect (precipitation of chromium carbides at grain boundaries) caused by the high temperatures involved in welding.

- Ferritic stainless steels generally have better engineering properties than austenitic grades, but have reduced corrosion resistance, due to the lower chromium and nickel content. They are also usually less expensive. They contain between 10.5% and 27% chromium and very little nickel, if any, but some types can contain lead. Most compositions include molybdenum; some, aluminium or titanium. Common ferritic grades include 18Cr-2Mo, 26Cr-1Mo, 29Cr-4Mo, and 29Cr-4Mo-2Ni. These alloys can be degraded by the presence of ? chromium, an intermetallic phase which can precipitate upon welding.

- Martensitic stainless steels are not as corrosion-resistant as the other two classes but are extremely strong and tough, as well as highly machineable, and can be hardened by heat treatment. Martensitic stainless steel contains chromium (12-14%), molybdenum (0.2-1%), nickel (0-<2%), and carbon (about 0.1-1%) (giving it more hardness but making the material a bit more brittle). It is quenched and magnetic.
- Precipitation-hardening martensitic stainless steels have corrosion resistance comparable to austenitic varieties, but can be precipitation hardened to even higher strengths than the other martensitic grades. The most common, 17-4PH, uses about 17% chromium and 4% nickel. There is a rising trend in Defence budgets to opt for an ultra-high-strength stainless steel when possible in new projects, as it is estimated that 2% of the US GDP is spent dealing with corrosion. The Lockheed-Martin Joint Strike Fighter is the first aircraft to use a precipitation-hardenable stainless steel-Carpenter Custom 465-in its airframe.
- Duplex stainless steels have a mixed microstructure of austenite and ferrite, the aim usually being to produce a 50/50 mix, although in commercial alloys the ratio may be 40/60. Duplex steels have improved strength over austenitic stainless steels and also improved resistance to localised corrosion, particularly pitting, crevice corrosion and stress corrosion cracking. They are characterised by high chromium (19-28%) and molybdenum (up to 5%) and lower nickel contents than austenitic stainless steels. Duplex grades are characterized into groups based on their alloy content and corrosion resistance. Lean duplex refers to grades such as UNS S32101, S32304, and S32003. The standard duplex is 22% chromium with S31803/S32205 known as 2205 being the most widely used. Super duplex refers to 25% chromium grades such as S32760 (Zeron 100), S32750 (2507), and S32550 (Ferralium). Hyper duplex refers to higher chromium grades such as S32906. The properties of duplex stainless steels are achieved with an overall lower alloy content than similar-performing super-austenitic grades, making them use cost-effective for many applications.

**Table. Comparison of Standardized Steels**

| EN-standard Steel no. k.h.s DIN | EN-standard Steel name | SAE grade | UNS |
|---|---|---|---|
| | | 440A | S44002 |
| 1.4112 | 440B | S44003 | |
| 1.4125 | 440C | S44004 | |
| | 440F | S44020 | |
| 1.4016 | X6Cr17 | 430 | S43000 |
| 1.4408 | G-X 6 CrNiMo 18-10 | 316 | |
| 1.4512 | X6CrTi12 | 409 | S40900 |
| | | 410 | S41000 |
| 1.4310 | X10CrNi18-8 | 301 | S30100 |
| 1.4318 | X2CrNiN18-7 | 301LN | N/A |
| 1.4307 | X2CrNi18-9 | 304L | S30403 |
| 1.4306 | X2CrNi19-11 | 304L | S30403 |
| 1.4311 | X2CrNiN18-10 | 304LN | S30453 |
| 1.4301 | X5CrNi18-10 | 304 | S30400 |
| 1.4948 | X6CrNi18-11 | 304H | S30409 |
| 1.4303 | X5CrNi18-12 | 305 | S30500 |
| | X5CrNi30-9 | 312 | |
| 1.4541 | X6CrNiTi18-10 | 321 | S32100 |
| 1.4878 | X12CrNiTi18-9 | 321H | S32109 |
| 1.4404 | X2CrNiMo17-12-2 | 316L | S31603 |
| 1.4401 | X5CrNiMo17-12-2 | 316 | S31600 |
| 1.4406 | X2CrNiMoN17-12-2 | 316LN | S31653 |
| 1.4432 | X2CrNiMo17-12-3 | 316L | S31603 |
| 1.4435 | X2CrNiMo18-14-3 | 316L | S31603 |
| 1.4436 | X3CrNiMo17-13-3 | 316 | S31600 |
| 1.4571 | X6CrNiMoTi17-12-2 | 316Ti | S31635 |
| 1.4429 | X2CrNiMoN17-13-3 | 316LN | S31653 |
| 1.4438 | X2CrNiMo18-15-4 | 317L | S31703 |
| 1.4539 | X1NiCrMoCu25-20-5 | 904L | N08904 |
| 1.4547 | X1CrNiMoCuN20-18-7 | | N/A S31254 |

## Stainless Steel Grades

### *Stainless Steel in 3D Printing*

Some 3D printing providers have developed proprietary stainless steel sintering blends for use in rapid prototyping. Currently available grades do not vary in properties significantly.

## STAINLESS STEEL FINISHES

Standard mill finishes can be applied to flat rolled stainless steel directly by the rollers and by mechanical abrasives. Steel is first rolled to size and thickness and then annealed to change the properties of the final material. Any oxidation that forms on the surface (scale) is removed by pickling, and a passivation layer is created on the surface. A final finish can then be applied to achieve the desired aesthetic appearance.

- *No*. 0: Hot rolled, annealed, thicker plates
- *No*. 1: Hot rolled, annealed and passivated
- *No*. 2D: Cold rolled, annealed, pickled and passivated
- *No*. 2B: Same as above with additional pass-through highly polished rollers
- *No*. 2BA: Bright annealed (BA or 2R) same as above then bright annealed under oxygen-free atmospheric conditions
- *No*. 3: Coarse abrasive finish applied mechanically
- *No*. 4: Brushed finish
- *No*. 5: Satin finish
- *No*. 6: Matte finish
- *No*. 7: Reflective finish
- *No*. 8: Mirror finish
- *No*. 9: Bead blast finish
- *No*. 10: heat coloured finish-wide range of electropolished and heat coloured surfaces

## BEAM (STRUCTURE)

A beam is a structural element that is capable of withstanding load primarily by resisting bending. The bending force induced into the material of the beam as a result of the external loads, own weight and external reactions to these loads is called a bending moment.

Beams generally carry vertical gravitational forces but can also be used to carry horizontal loads (i.e., loads due to an earthquake or wind). The loads carried by a beam are transferred to columns, walls, or girders, which then transfer the force to adjacent structural compression members. In Light frame construction the joists rest on the beam.

Beams are characterized by their profile (the shape of their cross-section), their length, and their material. In contemporary construction, beams are typically made of steel, reinforced concrete, or wood. One of the most common types of steel beam is the I-beam or wide-flange beam (also known as a "universal beam" or, for stouter sections, a "universal column"). This is commonly used in steel-frame buildings and bridges. Other common beam profiles are the C-channel, the hollow structural section beam, the pipe, and the angle.

## STRUCTURAL CHARACTERISTICS

Internally, beams experience compressive, tensile and shear stresses as a result of the loads applied to them. Typically, under gravity loads, the original length of the beam is slightly reduced to enclose a smaller radius arc at the top of the beam, resulting in compression, while the same original beam length at the bottom of the beam is slightly stretched to enclose a larger radius arc, and so is under tension.

The same original length of the middle of the beam, generally halfway between the top and bottom, is the same as the radial arc of bending, and so it is under neither compression nor tension, and defines the neutral axis. The beam is exposed to shear stress. There are some reinforced concrete beams that are entirely in compression.

These beams are known as prestressed concrete beams, and are fabricated to produce a compression more than the expected tension under loading conditions. High strength steel tendons are stretched while the beam is cast over them.

Then, when the concrete has begun to cure, the tendons are released and the beam is immediately under eccentric axial loads. This eccentric loading creates an internal moment, and, in turn, increases the moment carrying capacity of the beam. They are commonly used on highway bridges.

The primary tool for structural analysis of beams is the Euler–Bernoulli beam equation. Other mathematical methods for determining the deflection of beams include "method of virtual work" and the "slope deflection method". Engineers are interested in determining deflections because the beam may be in direct contact with a brittle material such as glass. Beam deflections are also minimized for aesthetic reasons. A visibly sagging beam, though structurally safe, is unsightly and to be avoided. A stiffer beam (high modulus of elasticity and high second moment of area) produces less deflection.

Mathematical methods for determining the beam forces (internal forces of the beam and the forces that are imposed on the beam support) include the "moment distribution method", the force or flexibility method and the direct stiffness method.

### General shapes

Most beams in reinforced concrete buildings have rectangular cross sections, but the most efficient cross section is a universal beam. The fact that most of the material is placed away from the neutral axis (axis of symmetry in case of universal beam) increases the second moment of area of the beam which in turn increases the stiffness.

A universal beam is only the most efficient shape in one direction of bending: up and down looking at the profile as an I. If the beam is bent side to side, it functions as an H where it is less efficient. The most efficient shape for both directions in 2D is a box (a square shell) however the most efficient shape for bending in any direction is a cylindrical shell or tube. But, for unidirectional bending, the universal (I or wide flange) beam is superior.

Efficiency means that for the same cross sectional area (Volume of beam per length) subjected to the same loading conditions, the beam deflects less.

Other shapes, like L (angles), C (Channels) or tubes, are also used in construction when there are special requirements.

## ARGON OXYGEN DECARBURIZATION

Argon oxygen decarburization (AOD) is a process primarily used in stainless steel making and other high grade alloys with oxidizable elements such as chromium, aluminum, etc. After initial melting the metal is then transferred to an AOD vessel where it will be subjected to three steps of refining; decarburization, reduction, and desulphurization. AOD was invented in 1954 by Praxair.

### Decarburization

Prior to the step Decarburization one more step should be taken into consideration i.e De-siliconization which is very important factor for refractory lining and further processing.

The decarburization step is controlled by ratios of oxygen to argon or nitrogen to remove the carbon from the metal bath. The ratios can be done in any number of phases to facilitate the reaction. The gases are usually blown through a top lance (oxygen only) and tuyeres in the sides/bottom (oxygen with an inert gas shroud). The stages of blowing remove carbon by the combination of oxygen and carbon forming CO gas.

$$3CO_{(gas)} \cdot 2Cr_{(bath)} \dagger Cr_2O_{3(slag)} \cdot 3C_{(bath)}$$

To drive the reaction to the forming of CO the partial pressure of CO is lowered using argon or nitrogen. Since the AOD vessel isn't externally heated, the blowing stages are also used for temperature control. The burning of oxygen increases the bath temperature.

### Reduction

After a desired carbon and temperature level have been reached the process moves to reduction. Reduction recovers the oxidized elements such as Cr from the slag. To achieve this, alloy additions are made with elements that have a higher affinity for oxygen than Cr, using either a Silicon alloy or Aluminum. The reduction mix also includes lime (CaO) and fluorspar ($CaF_2$). The addition of lime and fluorspar help with driving the reduction of $Cr_2O_3$ and managing the slag, keeping the slag fluid and volume small.

### Desulphurization

Desulphurization is achieved by having a high lime concentration in the slag and a low oxygen activity in the metal bath.

$$S_{(bath)} \cdot CaO_{(slag)} \dagger CaO_{(slag)} \cdot Cas_{(slag)} \cdot O_{(bath)}$$

So, additions of lime are added to dilute sulfur in the metal bath. Also, aluminum or silicon maybe added to remove oxygen. Other trimming alloy additions might be added at the end of the step. After sulfur levels have been achieved the slag is removed from the AOD vessel and the metal bath is ready for tapping. The tapped bath is then either sent to a stir station for further chemistry trimming or to a caster for casting.

## MARINE GRADE STAINLESS

Marine grade stainless is a stainless steel preferred for use in marine environments to avoid pitting corrosion. The AISI number grade is 316 and refers to the chromium content.

The salinity contained with the oceans acts as a catalyst to the rusting process, therefore a higher quality stainless steel is used on marine vessels. While the steel is not completely rust-proof, the alloy is more resistant than household stainless steels, and hence more expensive.

Fire trucks manufactured in the United States are made with Marine Grade stainless steel.Very few countries and mills make marine grade stainless. Japan, Germany and South Korea are three.

## RAZOR BLADE STEEL

Razor blade steel, also known as razor steel, is special type of stainless steel designed specifically to be used as a razor blade. Its defining characteristics are its chemical composition and shape.

### Chemical Composition

Razor blade steel is a martensitic stainless steel with a composition of chromium between 12 and 14.5%, a carbon content of approximately 0.6%, and the remainder iron and trace elements.

### Shape

The United States International Trade Commission defines that the shape of the material must be flat rolled coils that are not more than 23 mm (0.91 in) in width. The thickness cannot exceed 0.266 mm (0.0105 in).

## ROUGING

Rouging refers to a form of corrosion found in stainless steel. It can be due to iron contamination of the stainless steel surface due to welding of ferrous steel for support columns, or other temporary means, which when welded off, leave a low chromium area.

*The are three classes of rouging*: Class I, Class II, and Class III.

Class I - stainless steel surface and the Cr/Fe ratio of the metal surface beneath such deposits usually remain unaltered. Class II - Iron particles originating in-situ on unpassivated or improperly passivated stainless steel surfaces. By their formation the Cr/Fe ratio of the metal surface is altered. Class III - Iron oxide (or scale) which forms on surfaces in high temperature steam systems. The Cr/Fe ratio of the protective film is usually altered.

### STAINLESS STEEL SOAP

A stainless steel soap is a piece of stainless steel, usually in the shape of a soap bar. Its purpose is to neutralize or reduce strong odours from the hands, present from handling odorous ingredients such as garlic, onion or fish. The shape of a soap bar is purely decorative and any piece of stainless steel, such as a spoon, can be used for the same purpose.

In the absence of plausible chemical explanations of why this may work, or experiments using controls, it is unknown whether the stainless steel soap is actually effective.

Stainless steel soaps are often advertised for use with water; so it is likely that sulfurous compounds either dissolve directly in the water or their removal is catalyzed by the steel, if indeed the odor removal is measurably greater with stainless steel than any other substance.

Stainless steel consists of mainly iron and chromium, and contains a thin layer of chromium (III) oxide on its surface. Metal oxides are Lewis acids and readily catalyze oxidations. Iron and chromium oxides can be used as oxidation catalysts, effective for industrial-scale oxidation of odorous reduced sulfur compounds at a temperature of 180 C.

For this to occur to begin with, the compounds must adsorb on the metal oxide surface. Chromium(III) may also act as an adsorbent only. Another plausible explanation is that a thin layer of grease, containing the odorous compounds, is rubbed off mechanically onto the steel surface. There are similar applications, such as stainless steel discs in shoes and dishwashers, that claim to absorb odors.

## CARBON STEEL

Carbon steel cookware can be rolled or hammered into very thin sheets of material, while still maintaining high strength and heat resistance. This allows for rapid and high heating. Carbon steel does not conduct heat as well as other materials, but this may be an advantage for woks and paella pans, where one portion of the pan is intentionally kept at a different temperature than the rest. Like cast iron, carbon steel must be seasoned before use. Rub a fat (lard is recommended) on the cooking surface only and heat the cookware over the stovetop. The process can be repeated if needed. Over time, the cooking surface will become dark and nonstick. Carbon steel is often used for woks and crêpe pans.

## COPPER

In classical Western cooking, pots are formed with thick copper sheets with a thin inner layer of tin. The copper provides the best thermal conductivity of common metals and therefore results in even heating. Copper is reactive with acidic foods, discovered with the discovery of tomatoes in the new world and subsequent introduction to old world copper pots. The tin lining prevents the copper from reacting with acidic foods. The products resulting from the reaction causes copper toxicity.

The lead-free and cadmium-free tin lining is susceptible to tin pest. In some cases unlined copper is desirable, for instance in the preparation of meringues and foams. Copper pots are expensive and require retinning, and when made with thick copper plates are heavy. With modern metallurgical techniques, such as cladding, copper is incorporated into the constructions of cookware, often as an enclosed heat spreading disk.

### HISTORY

#### Copper Age

Copper, as native copper, is one of the few metals to occur naturally as an un-compounded mineral. Copper was known to some of the oldest civilizations on record, and has a history of use that is at least 10,000 years old. Some estimates of copper's discovery place this event around 9000 BC in the Middle East.

A copper pendant was found in what is now northern Iraq that dates to 8700 BC. It is probable that gold and meteoritic iron were the only metals used by humans before copper. By 5000 BC, there are signs of copper smelting: the refining of copper from simple copper compounds such as malachite or azurite. Among archaeological sites in Anatolia, Çatal Höyük (~6000 BC) features native copper artifacts and smelted lead beads, but no smelted copper.

Can Hasan (~5000 BC) had access to smelted copper but the oldest smelted copper artifact found (a copper chisel from the chalcolithic site of Prokuplje in Serbia) has pre-dated Can Hasan by 500 years. The smelting facilities in the Balkans appear to be more advanced than the Anatolian forges found at a later date, so it is quite probable that copper smelting originated in the Balkans. Investment casting was realised in 4500–4000 BC in Southeast Asia.

Copper smelting appears to have been developed independently in several parts of the world. In addition to its development in the Balkans by 5500 BC, it was developed in China before 2800 BC, in the Andes around 2000 BC, in

Central America around 600 AD, and in West Africa around 900 AD. Copper is found extensively in the Indus Valley Civilization by the 3rd millennium BC. In Europe, Ötzi the Iceman, a well-preserved male dated to 3300–3200 BC, was found with an axe with a copper head 99.7% pure. High levels of arsenic in his hair suggest he was involved in copper smelting. Over the course of centuries, experience with copper has assisted the development of other metals; for example, knowledge of copper smelting led to the discovery of iron smelting.

In the Americas production in the Old Copper Complex, located in present day Michigan and Wisconsin, was dated back to between 6000 to 3000 BC.

## Bronze Age

Alloying of copper with zinc or tin to make brass or bronze was practiced soon after the discovery of copper itself. There exist copper and bronze artifacts from Sumerian cities that date to 3000 BC, and Egyptian artifacts of copper and copper-tin alloys nearly as old. In one pyramid, a copper plumbing system was found that is 5000 years old.

The Egyptians found that adding a small amount of tin made the metal easier to cast, so copper-tin (bronze) alloys were found in Egypt almost as soon as copper was found. Very important sources of copper in the Levant were located in Timna valley and Faynan .

By 2000 BC, Europe was using bronze. The use of bronze became so widespread in Europe approximately from 2500 BC to 600 BC that it has been named the Bronze Age.

The transitional period in certain regions between the preceding Neolithic period and the Bronze Age is termed the Chalcolithic ("copper-stone"), with some high-purity copper tools being used alongside stone tools. Brass (copper-zinc alloy) was known to the Greeks, but only became a significant supplement to bronze during the Roman empire.

During the Bronze Age, one copper mine at Great Orme in North Wales, extended for a depth of 70 metres. At Alderley Edge in Cheshire, carbon dates have established mining at around 2280 to 1890 BC (at 95% probability).

## Antiquity and Middle Ages

In Greek, the metal was known by the name *chalkos*. Copper was a very important resource for the Romans, Greeks and other ancient peoples. In Roman times, it became known as *aes Cyprium* . From this, the phrase was simplified to *cuprum,* hence the English *copper*. Copper was associated with the goddess Aphrodite/Venus in mythology and alchemy, owing to its lustrous beauty, its ancient use in producing mirrors, and its association with Cyprus, which was sacred to the goddess. In astrology, alchemy the seven heavenly bodies known to the ancients were associated with seven metals also known in antiquity, and Venus was assigned to copper.

Britain's first use of brass occurred around the 3rd–2nd century BC. In North America, copper mining began with marginal workings by Native Americans. Native copper is known to have been extracted from sites on Isle Royale with primitive stone tools between 800 and 1600.

Copper metallurgy was flourishing in South America, particularly in Peru around the beginning of the first millennium AD. Copper technology proceeded at a much slower rate on other continents. Africa's major location for copper reserves is Zambia. Copper burial ornamentals dated from the 15th century have been uncovered, but the metal's commercial production did not start until the early 1900s.Australian copper artifacts exist, but they appear only after the arrival of the Europeans; the aboriginal culture apparently did not develop their own metallurgical abilities.

Crucial in the metallurgical and technological worlds, copper has also played an important cultural role, particularly in currency. Romans in the 6th through 3rd centuries BC used copper lumps as money. At first, just the copper itself was valued, but gradually the shape and look of the copper became more important. Julius Caesar had his own coins, made from a copper-zinc alloy, while Octavianus Augustus Caesar's coins were made from Cu-Pb-Sn alloys.

The gates of the Temple of Jerusalem used Corinthian bronze made by depletion gilding. Corinthian bronze was most prevalent in Alexandria, where alchemy is thought to have begun. In ancient India (before 1000 BC), copper was used in the holistic medical science Ayurveda for surgical instruments and other medical equipment. Ancient Egyptians (~2400 BC) used copper for sterilizing wounds and drinking water, and as time passed, (~1500 BC) for headaches, burns, and itching.

Hippocrates (~400 BC) used copper to treat leg ulcers associated with varicose veins. Ancient Aztecs fought sore throats by gargling with copper mixtures.

Copper is also the part of many rich stories and legends, such as that of Iraq's Baghdad Battery. Copper cylinders soldered to lead, which date back to 248 BC to 226 AD, resemble a galvanic cell, leading people to believe this may have been the first battery. This claim has so far not been substantiated.

The Bible also refers to the importance of copper: "Men know how to mine silver and refine gold, to dig iron from the earth and melt copper from stone".

**Modern Period**

The Great Copper Mountain was a mine in Falun, Sweden, that operated for a millennium from the 10th century to 1992. It produced as much as two thirds of Europe's copper needs in the 17th century and helped fund many of Sweden's wars during that time. It was referred to as the nation's treasury; Sweden had a copper backed currency.

Throughout history, copper's use in art has extended far beyond currency. Vannoccio Biringuccio, Giorgio Vasari and Benvenuto Cellini are three Renaissance sculptors from the mid 1500s, notable for their work with bronze. From about 1560 to about 1775, thin sheets of copper were commonly used as a canvas for paintings. Silver plated copper was used in the pre-photograph known as the daguerreotype. The Statue of Liberty, dedicated on October 28, 1886, was constructed of copper thought to have come from French-owned mines in Norway.

Plating was a technology that started in the mid 1600s in some areas. One common use for copper plating, widespread in the 1700s, was the sheathing of ships' hulls. Copper sheathing could be used to protect wooden hulled ships from algae, and from the shipworm "Teredo navalis", a saltwater clam. The ships of Christopher Columbus were among the earliest to have this protection. The Norddeutsche Affinerie in Hamburg was the first modern electroplating plant starting its production in 1876.

In 1801 Paul Revere established America's first copper rolling mill in Canton, Massachusetts. In the early 1800s, it was discovered that copper wire could be used as a conductor, but it wasn't until 1990 that copper, in oxide form, was discovered for use as a superconducting material. The German scientist Gottfried Osann invented powder metallurgy of copper in 1830 while determining the metal's atomic weight. Around then it was also discovered that the amount and type of alloying element (e.g. tin) would affect the tones of bells, allowing for a variety of rich sounds, leading to bell casting, another common use for copper and its alloys.

Flash smelting, was developed by Outokumpu in Finland and first applied at the Harjavalta plant in 1949. The process makes smelting more energy efficient and is today used for 50% of the world's primary copper production.

Copper has been pivotal in the economic and sociological worlds, notably disputes involving copper mines. The 1906 Cananea Strike in Mexico dealt with issues of work organization. The Teniente copper mine (1904–1951) raised political issues about capitalism and class structure. Japan's largest copper mine, the Ashio mine, was the site of a riot in 1907. The Arizona miners' strike of 1938 dealt with American Labour issues including the "right to strike".

## CHARACTERISTICS

### Colour

Copper has a reddish, orangish, or brownish colour because a thin layer of tarnish (including oxides) gradually forms on its surface when gases (especially oxygen) in the air react with it. But pure copper, when fresh, is actually a pinkish or peachy metal. Copper, osmium (blueish) and gold (yellow) are the only three elemental metals with a natural colour other than gray or silver. The usual gray colour of metals depends on their "electron sea" that is capable of absorbing and re-emitting photons over a wide range of frequencies. Copper has its characteristic colour because of its unique band structure. By Madelung's rule the 4s subshell should be filled before electrons are placed in the 3d subshell but copper is an exception to the rule with only one electron in the 4s subshell instead of two.

The energy of a photon of blue or violet light is sufficient for a *d* band electron to absorb it and transition to the half-full *s* band. Thus the light reflected by copper is missing some blue/violet components and appears red. This phenomenon is shared with gold which has a corresponding 5s/4d structure. In its liquefied state, a pure copper surface without ambient light appears somewhat greenish, a characteristic shared with gold. When liquid copper is in bright ambient light, it retains some of its pinkish luster. When copper is burnt in oxygen it gives off a black oxide.

**Group 11 of the Periodic Table**

Copper occupies the same family of the periodic table as silver and gold, since they each have one s-orbital electron on top of a filled electron shell which forms metallic bonds. This similarity in electron structure makes them similar in many characteristics. All have very high thermal and electrical conductivity, and all are malleable metals. Among pure metals at room temperature, copper has the second highest electrical and thermal conductivity, after silver.

**Occurrence**

Copper can be found as native copper in mineral form (for example, in Michigan's Keweenaw Peninsula). It is a polycrystal, with the largest single crystals measuring 4.4×3.2×3.2 cm. Minerals such as the sulfides: chalcopyrite ($CuFeS_2$), bornite ($Cu_5FeS_4$), covellite ($CuS$), chalcocite ($Cu_2S$) are sources of copper, as are the carbonates: azurite ($Cu_3(CO_3)_2(OH)_2$) and malachite ($Cu_2CO_3(OH)_2$) and the oxide: cuprite ($Cu_2O$).

**Mechanical Properties**

Copper is easily worked, being both ductile and malleable. The ease with which it can be drawn into wire makes it useful for electrical work in addition to its excellent electrical properties.

Copper can be machined, although it is usually necessary to use an alloy for intricate parts, such as threaded components, to get really good machinability characteristics.

Good thermal conduction makes it useful for heatsinks and in heat exchangers. Copper has good corrosion resistance, but not as good as gold. It has excellent brazing and soldering properties and can also be welded, although best results are obtained with gas metal arc welding.

Copper is normally supplied, as with nearly all metals for industrial and commercial use, in a fine grained polycrystalline form. Polycrystalline metals have greater strength than monocrystalline forms, and the difference is greater for smaller grain (crystal) sizes. The reason is due to the inability of stress dislocations in the crystal structure to cross the grain boundaries.

## Electrical Properties

At 59.6×10 S/m copper has the second highest electrical conductivity of any element, just after silver. This high value is due to virtually all the valence electrons (one per atom) taking part in conduction. The resulting free electrons in the copper amount to a huge charge density of 13.6×10 C/m.

This high charge density is responsible for the rather slow drift velocity of currents in copper cable (drift velocity may be calculated as the ratio of current density to charge density).

For instance, at a current density of 5×10 A/m (typically, the maximum current density present in household wiring and grid distribution) the drift velocity is just a little over S! mm/s.

## Corrosion

### *Contact with Other Metals*

Copper should not be in direct mechanical contact with metals of different electropotential (for example, a copper pipe joined to an iron pipe), especially in the presence of moisture, as the completion of an electrical circuit (for instance through the common ground) will cause the juncture to act as an electrochemical cell (like a single cell of a battery).

The weak electrical currents themselves are harmless but the electrochemical reaction will cause the conversion of the iron to other compounds, eventually destroying the functionality of the union. This problem is usually solved in plumbing by separating copper pipe from iron pipe with some non-conducting segment (usually plastic or rubber).

### *Solutions*

Copper does not react with water, but it slowly reacts with atmospheric oxygen forming a layer of brown-black copper oxide. In contrast to the oxidation of iron by wet air, this oxide layer stops the further, bulk corrosion. A green layer of copper carbonate, called verdigris, can often be seen on old copper constructions, such as the Statue of Liberty.

Copper reacts with hydrogen sulfide- and sulfide-containing solutions, forming various copper sulfides on its surface. In sulfide-containing solutions, copper is less noble than hydrogen and will corrode. This is observed in everyday life when copper metal surfaces tarnish after exposure to air containing sulfur compounds. Copper is slowly dissolved in oxygen-containing ammonia solutions because ammonia forms water-soluble complexes with copper. Copper reacts with a combination of oxygen and hydrochloric acid to form a series of copper chlorides. Copper(II) chloride (green/blue) when boiled with copper metal undergoes a symproportionation reaction to form white copper(I) chloride.

### Germicidal Effect

Copper is germicidal, via the oligodynamic effect. For example, brass doorknobs disinfect themselves of many bacteria within a period of eight hours. Antimicrobial properties of copper are effective against MRSA, Escherichia coli and other pathogens. At colder temperatures, longer times are required to kill bacteria.

Copper has the intrinsic ability to kill a variety of potentially harmful pathogens. On February 29, 2008, the United States EPA registered 275 alloys, containing greater than 65% nominal copper content, as antimicrobial materials. Registered alloys include pure copper, an assortment of brasses and bronzes, and additional alloys.

EPA-sanctioned tests using Good Laboratory Practices were conducted in order to obtain several antimicrobial claims valid against: methicillin-resistant *Staphylococcus aureus* (MRSA), *Enterobacter aerogenes, Escherichia coli* O157: H7 and *Pseudomonas aeruginosa.*

The EPA registration allows the manufacturers of these copper alloys to legally make public health claims as to the health effects of these materials. Several of the aforementioned bacteria are responsible for a large portion of the nearly two million hospital-acquired infections contracted each year in the United States.

Frequently touched surfaces in hospitals and public facilities harbor bacteria and increase the risk for contracting infections. Covering touch surfaces with copper alloys can help reduce microbial contamination associated with hospital-acquired infections on these surfaces.

### Isotopes

Copper has 29 distinct isotopes ranging in atomic mass from 52 to 80. Two of these, Cu and Cu, are stable and occur naturally, with Cu comprising approximately 69% of naturally occurring copper.

The other 27 isotopes are radioactive and do not occur naturally. The most stable of these is Cu with a half-life of 61.83 hours. The least stable is Cu with a half-life of approximately 75 ns. Unstable copper isotopes with atomic masses below 63 tend to undergo â decay, while isotopes with atomic masses above 65 tend to undergo â decay. Cu decays by both â and â.

Cu, Cu, Cu, Cu, and Cu each have one metastable isomer. Cu has two isomers, making a total of 7 distinct isomers. The most stable of these is Cu with a half-life of 3.75 minutes. The least stable is Cu with a half-life of 360 ns.

## PRODUCTION

### Output

Most copper ore is mined or extracted as copper sulfides from large open pit mines in porphyry copper deposits that contain 0.4 to 1.0% copper. Examples include: Chuquicamata in Chile and El Chino Mine in New Mexico. The average abundance of copper found within crustal rocks is approximately 68 ppm by mass, and 22 ppm by atoms. In 2005, Chile was the top mine producer of copper with at least one-third world share followed by the USA, Indonesia and Peru, reports the British Geological Survey.

### Reserves

Copper has been in use at least 10,000 years, but more than 95% of all copper ever mined and smelted has been extracted since 1900. As with many natural resources, the total amount of copper on Earth is vast (around 10 tons just in the top Kilometre of Earth's crust, or about 5 million years worth at the current rate of extraction). However, only a tiny fraction of these reserves is economically viable, given present-day prices and technologies. Various estimates of existing copper reserves available for mining vary from 25 years to 60 years, depending on core assumptions such as the growth rate.

Copper is a finite resource, but it can be recycled. Recycling is a major source of copper in the modern world. As consumption in India and China increases, copper supplies are becoming scarcer.

The copper price has quintupled from the 60-year low in 1999, rising from US$0.60 per pound (US$1.32/kg) in June 1999 to US$3.75 per pound (US$8.27/kg) in May 2006, where it dropped to US$2.40 per pound (US$5.29/kg) in February 2007 then rebounded to US$3.50 per pound (US$7.71/kg = £3.89 = €5.00) in April 2007. By early February 2009, however, weakening global demand and a steep fall in commodity prices since the previous year's highs had left copper prices at US$1.51 per pound.

The Intergovernmental Council of Copper Exporting Countries (CIPEC), defunct since 1992, once tried to play a similar role for copper as OPEC does for oil, but never achieved the same influence, not least because the second-largest producer, the United States, was never a member. Formed in 1967, its principal members were Chile, Peru, Zaire, and Zambia.

## APPLICATIONS

Copper is malleable and ductile and is a good conductor of both heat and electricity.

The purity of copper is expressed as 4N for 99.99% pure or 7N for 99.99999% pure. The numeral gives the number of nines after the decimal point when expressed as a decimal (e.g. 4N means 0.9999, or 99.99%). Copper is often too soft for its applications, so it is incorporated in numerous alloys.

For example, brass is a copper-zinc alloy, and bronze is a copper-tin alloy.It is used extensively, in products such as:

**Piping**

- Including water supply.
- Used extensively in refrigeration and air conditioning equipment because of its ease of fabrication and soldering, as well as high conductivity to heat.

*Electrical applications*:

- Copper wire
- Oxygen-free copper
- Electromagnets
- Printed circuit boards
- Lead free solder, alloyed with tin
- Electrical machines, especially electromagnetic motors, generators and transformers
- Electrical relays, electrical busbars and electrical switches
- Vacuum tubes, cathode ray tubes, and the magnetrons in microwave ovens
- Wave guides for microwave radiation
- Integrated circuits, increasingly replacing aluminium because of its superior electrical conductivity
- As a material in the manufacture of computer heat sinks, as a result of its superior heat dissipation capacity to aluminium

**ARCHITECTURE AND INDUSTRY**

- While electrical applications use oxygen-free copper, unalloyed copper used in architectural applications is the lower-purty Phosphorus Deoxidized Copper (also called Cu-DHP).
- Copper has been used as water-proof roofing material since ancient times, giving many old buildings their greenish roofs and domes. Initially copper oxide forms, replaced by cuprous and cupric sulfide, and finally by copper carbonate. The final carbonate patina (termed verdigris) is highly resistant to corrosion.
- Statuary: The Statue of Liberty, for example, contains 179,220 pounds (81.29 metric tons) of copper.
- Alloyed with nickel, e.g. cupronickel and Monel, used as corrosive resistant materials in shipbuilding.

- Watt's steam engine firebox due to superior heat dissipation.
- Copper compounds in liquid form are used as a wood preservative, particularly in treating original portion of structures during restoration of damage due to dry rot.
- Copper wires may be placed over non-conductive roofing materials to discourage the growth of moss. (Zinc may also be used for this purpose.)
- Copper is used to prevent a building being directly struck by lightning. High above the roof, copper spikes (lightning rods) are connected to a very thick copper cable which leads to a large metal plate underneath the ground. The voltage is dispersed throughout the ground harmlessly, instead of destroying the main structure.

## HOUSEHOLD PRODUCTS

- Copper plumbing fittings and compression tubes.
- Doorknobs and other fixtures in houses.
- Roofing, guttering, and rainspouts on buildings.
- In cookware, such as frying pans.
- Some older flatware: (knives, forks, spoons) contains some copper if made from electroplated nickel silver (EPNS).
- Sterling silver, if it is to be used in dinnerware, must contain a few Per cent copper.
- Copper water heating cylinders
- Copper range hoods
- Copper bath tubs
- Copper counters
- Copper sinks
- Copper slug tape

## COINAGE

- As a component of coins, often as cupronickel alloy, or some form of brass or bronze.
- Countries all contain copper: European Union (euro), United States, United Kingdom (sterling), Australia and New Zealand.
- U.S. nickels are 75.0% copper by weight and only 25.0% nickel.

## ALLOYS

Numerous copper alloys exist, many with important historical and contemporary uses. Speculum metal and bronze are alloys of copper and tin. Brass is an alloy of copper and zinc. Monel metal, also called cupronickel, is an alloy of copper and nickel. While the metal "bronze" usually refers to copper-tin alloys, it also is a generic term for any alloy of copper, such as aluminium bronze, silicon bronze, and manganese bronze. Copper is one of the most important constituents of carat silver and gold alloys and carat solders used in the jewelry industry, modifying the colour, hardness and melting point of the resulting alloys.

## COMPOUNDS

Common oxidation states of copper include the less stable copper(I) state, Cu; and the more stable copper(II) state, Cu, which forms blue or blue-green salts and solutions. Under unusual conditions, a 3+ state and even an extremely rare 4+ state can be obtained. Using old nomenclature for the naming of salts, copper(I) is called *cuprous*, and copper(II) is *cupric*. In oxidation copper is mildly basic.

Copper(II) carbonate is green from which arises the unique appearance of copper-clad roofs or domes on some buildings. Copper(II) sulfate forms a blue crystalline pentahydrate which is perhaps the most familiar copper compound in the laboratory. It is used as a fungicide, known as Bordeaux mixture.

There are two stable copper oxides, copper(II) oxide (CuO) and copper(I) oxide ($Cu_2O$). Copper oxides are used to make yttrium barium copper oxide ($YBa_2Cu_3O_{7-g}$) or YBCO which forms the basis of many unconventional superconductors.

- *Copper(I) compounds*: Copper(I) chloride, copper(I) bromide, copper(I) iodide, copper(I) oxide.
- *Copper(II) compounds*: Copper(II) acetate, copper(II) carbonate, copper(II) chloride, copper(II) hydroxide, copper(II) nitrate, copper(II) oxide, copper(II) sulfate, copper(II) sulfide, copper(II) tetrafluoro-borate, copper(II) triflate.
- *Copper(III) compounds, rare*: potassium hexafluoro-cuprate ($K_3CuF_6$)
- *Copper(IV) compounds, extremely rare*: caesium hexafluorocuprate ($Cs_2CuF_6$)

### Tests for copper(II) ion

Adding an aqueous solution of sodium hydroxide will form a blue precipitate of copper(II) hydroxide.

*The ionic equation is*:

$$Cu\ (aq) + 2\ OH\ (aq)\ \dagger\ \ Cu(OH)_2\ (s)$$

The full equation shows that the reaction is due to hydroxide ions deprotonating the hexaaquacopper(II) complex:

$$[Cu(H_2O)_6] (aq) + 2 OH(aq) \dagger \; Cu(H_2O)_4(OH)_2 (s) + 2 H_2O (l)$$

Adding ammonia solution (aqueous ammonia) causes the same precipitate to form. Upon adding excess ammonia, the precipitate dissolves, forming a deep blue ammonia complex, tetraamminecopper(II):

$$Cu(H_2O)_4(OH)_2 (s) + 4 NH_3 (aq) \dagger \; [Cu(H_2O)_2(NH_3)_4] (aq) + 2 H_2O (l) + 2 OH (aq)$$

A more delicate test than ammonia is potassium ferrocyanide, which gives a brown precipitate with copper salts.

## BIOLOGICAL ROLE

Copper is essential in all plants and animals. The human body normally contains copper at a level of about 1.4 to 2.1 mg for each kg of body weight. Copper is distributed widely in the body and occurs in liver, muscle and bone.

Copper is transported in the bloodstream on a plasma protein called ceruloplasmin. When copper is first absorbed in the gut it is transported to the liver bound to albumin. Copper metabolism and excretion is controlled delivery of copper to the liver by ceruloplasmin, where it is excreted in bile.

Copper is found in a variety of enzymes, including the copper Centres of cytochrome c oxidase and the enzyme superoxide dismutase (containing copper and zinc). In addition to its enzymatic roles, copper is used for biological electron transport. The blue copper proteins that participate in electron transport include azurin and plastocyanin. The name "blue copper" comes from their intense blue colour arising from a ligand-to-metal charge transfer (LMCT) absorption band around 600 nm.

Most molluscs and some arthropods such as the horseshoe crab use the copper-containing pigment hemocyanin rather than iron-containing hemoglobin for oxygen transport, so their blood is blue when oxygenated rather than red.

It is believed that zinc and copper compete for absorption in the digestive tract so that a diet that is excessive in one of these minerals may result in a deficiency in the other. The RDA for copper in normal healthy adults is 0.9 mg/day.

On the other hand, professional research on the subject recommends 3.0 mg/day. Because of its role in facilitating iron uptake, copper deficiency can often produce anemia-like symptoms. Conversely, an accumulation of copper in body tissues are believed to cause the symptoms of Wilson's disease in humans.

Chronic copper depletion leads to abnormalities in metabolism of fats, high triglycerides, non-alcoholic steatohepatitis (NASH), fatty liver disease and poor melanin and dopamine synthesis causing depression and sunburn. Food rich in copper should be eaten away from any milk or egg proteins as they block absorption.

### Toxicity

Toxicity can occur from eating acidic food that has been cooked with copper cookware. Cirrhosis of the liver in children (Indian Childhood Cirrhosis) has been linked to boiling milk in copper cookware. The Merck Manual states that recent studies suggest that a genetic defect is associated with this cirrhosis.

Since copper is actively excreted by the normal body, chronic copper toxicosis in humans without a genetic defect in copper handling has not been demonstrated. However, large amounts (gram quantities) of copper salts taken in suicide attempts have produced acute copper toxicity in normal humans. Equivalent amounts of copper salts (30 mg/kg) are toxic in animals.

### Miscellaneous Hazards

The metal, when powdered, is a fire hazard. At concentrations higher than 1 mg/L, copper can stain clothes and items washed in water.

## RECYCLING

Copper is 100% recyclable without any loss of quality whether in a raw state or contained in a manufactured product. Copper is the third most recycled metal after iron and aluminium. It is estimated that 80% of the copper ever mined is still in use today.

Insulated wire is also commonly recycled once the insulation is stripped off. High purity copper scrap is directly melted in a furnace and the molten copper is deoxidized and cast into billets, or ingots. Lower purity scrap is usually refined to attain the desired purity level by an electroplating process in which the copper scrap is dissolved into a bath of sulfuric acid and then electroplated out of the solution.

# COPPER KITCHEN ACCESSORIES

Kitchen is the most important place of any home. The term kitchen accessories is commonly used containing several things used for the process of making or cooking food.

Now a days, copper is an important part of the kitchenware

- Copper kitchen accessories

*Serve Dual Purposes*:

- After using them when they become old than they can be reused as decorative showpieces.
- Copper kitchen accessories can furnish your kitchen providing an epicure touch.

## DESIGN

A vast range of copper kitchen accessories are available in the market such as copper canisters, copper burner covers, copper cookie cutters, copper funnels, copper graters and shredders, copper oil cans and many more.

Each one of them has its own classifications and types. As compared to earlier times the use of copper utensils has increased tremendously.

Available in a variety of shapes, sizes and varied price ranges these accessories are best and ideal that fit the needs of each and everyone. Copper is a well known oldest metal and copper kitchen accessories are available in various forms.

## TYPES

*There are various types of kitchen accessories available in the market*:

- Copper Burner Covers
- Copper Canisters
- Copper Cookie Cutters
- Copper Funnels
- Copper Graters and Shredders
- Copper Oil Cans

### Copper Burner Covers

Copper Burner covers always enhance the kitchen decor. They are very useful and functional.

*Features*:

- Copper burner covers are manufactured in such a way that they can be fitted to electric or gas burners
- Each end of the burner covers contain metal handles. Those handles are easy to take off or on

*Utility*:

- Copper Burner covers are both purposeful and decorative items
- To hide the messy electric or gas stoves burner covers are really useful
- Copper burner covers are also used in a stove decoration
- Large burner covers can be kept on table. One can set flowers or keep salt shakers on it for good show
- Small covers can be used to keep hot pot on it above the dinning table

### Copper Canisters

Canisters are usually a storage container, especially a box or can.

*Features*:

- Canisters are usually cylindrical

- Copper canisters have extra large capacity of storage
- Copper canisters are lacquered to resist tarnishing
- Copper canisters have nickel lining

*Utility*:

- Canisters are used to store dry foodstuffs or cooking
- 
- Ingredients such as flour or sugar
- Copper canisters are good to preserve freshness of food articles

**Copper Cookie Cutters**

Copper cookie or biscuit cutters are very much in use nowadays for cookie lovers.

*Features*:

- Copper cookie cutters are made from pure and heavy gauge copper
- Copper coated cookie cutters are very sturdy and long lasting
- They are fastened by rivets
- Some cookie cutters have handles. Few cookie cutters are open.
- Copper cookie cutters are found in different shapes and sizes.

*Utility*:

Copper cookie cutters are also used to cut pastries.

**Copper Funnels**

Copper funnels are an important day to day use kitchenware.

*Features*:

- Funnels are conical in shape.
- Copper funnels have a small hole and a narrow tube.
- Copper funnels are made in such a that they can resist tarnishing.
- Copper funnels are long lasting.

*Utility*:

Funnels are used to channel the flow of a substance into a small mouthed container.

**Copper Graters and Shredders**

Copper graters and shredders are very useful accessory in a kitchenware.

*Features*:

- Copper graters and shredders are sturdy
- They are hand held tools
- Graters and shredders have holes for grating and shredding

*Types*: There are various types of copper graters and shredders according to their designs and use.

- There is a four sided box graters with sharp edged large holes. They are useful for shredding soft cheeses like cheddar or mozzarella or vegetables.
- Graters having small holes with sharp teeth are used for grating hard cheeses.
- Graters with fine holes are used for grating zest or fresh ginger.
- Graters with wide and sharp slots are used for slicing soft cheeses or vegetables.
- Rotary graters transform nuts or chunks or hard cheese or chocolate into fine particles with the turn of a crank.

*Utility*: It is mainly used for grating and shredding food items into small particles.

**Copper Oil Cans**

*Product Overview*: Oil cans are also known as oil dispenser. Copper oil cans are very purposeful and appealing.

*Features*:

- Copper oil cans are made of solid copper.
- Copper oil cans are lined with nickel.
- Copper oil cans are lacquered to tarnishing.
- They are available in different shapes and sizes.

*Utility*: Oil cans are used as oil storage.

## FEATURES

*Some of the features and uses served by copper kitchen accessories are*:

- Represents high-society value.
- R and D shows that copper has medicinal value.
- Used to work out versatile applications of kitchenware.
- Excellent looks.
- Outstanding heat conduction property.
- Secure from humidity as well oxidation.

Copper kitchen accessories are very much recognized and appreciated in families all across worldwide. Kitchen accessories include a large medley of copper kitchenware.

Main utility of them is to solve the various purposes of the kitchen other than cooking. Due to the positive effect of copper on human health and body, families prefer more copper kitchen accessories everywhere.

## COPPER TABLEWARES

Copper tablewares are very popular. Since ages, copper has been linked with the culture and tradition of India and so has the Copper Tablewares. Commonly the term tableware refers to several items including utensils and tablecloth holders that are a part of dining table. Tableware consists of dishes, glassware, cutlery and eating utensils like knives, forks and spoons used to set a table for eating a meal; nature, variety and number of objects of tableware varies from culture to culture and from meal to meal.

Copper tableware has set a new trend in the tableware and dining industry. The buyers nowadays want utility along with aesthetic value of the product. Appealing designs and wide variety of copper tableware gives a better choice to the buyer. Using copper table ware is a vogue nowadays and its utility is unquestionable. Its appearance is very soothing and eye catching.

### UTILITY OF THE COPPER TABLEWARES

Using copper table ware is a vogue nowadays and its utility is unquestionable. Its appearance is very soothing and eye catching.

### FEATURES OF COPPER TABLEWARES

There are many important features associated with copper table ware. *Some of them are*:

- Copper is a good conductor of heat and hence it shortens the cooking time.
- In order to make cooking safer, stainless steel and nickel lining are also added with the copper. This makes copper tableware more attractive.
- Metals like Chromium, nickel etc. are usually added with copper to form alloys. Alloying of copper makes it stronger, harder, corrosion resistive and more electrically as well as thermally conductive. All these are desirable attributes of a copper tableware.

### VARIETY OF TABLEWARES

*To name a few of these*:

- Copper Cheese Shakers
- Copper Ice Cream Cups
- Copper Jugs
- Copper Mugs and Tumblers
- Copper Platter

- Copper Salt and Pepper Sets
- Copper Toothpick Holders
- Copper Trays

**Copper Cheese Shakers**

To add a cheesy taste to any food item cheese shakers are the best choice for the buyer.

*Features*:

- It is made of solid copper.
- Shakers have brass handles, plaque and bottom trim.
- *They may have*:
  - Hammered finish
  - Patina finish
- Copper cheese shakers have nickel lining.

*Utility*: Cheese shakers are mainly used to shake cheese.

## COPPER JUGS

Copper jugs are indispensable in the copper table ware.

*Features*:

- *Copper jugs are mainly available in two finishes*:
  - Hammered finish
  - Patina finish
- Copper jugs are available in different sizes and shapes

*Utility of Copper Jugs*: Since ancient times, copper jugs are widely used and they give healthy impact to human body.

*They can be used for following purposes*:

- *Ceremonial purposes*: Nowadays in various ceremonies copper jugs are widely used.
- *Regular household purposes*: It is always being in the use of regular household purpose for serving drinks.
- *Antique show piece*: It is sometimes used as an antique show piece for its traditional looks.
- *Health purpose*: By the recommendation of Ayurveda, from the ancient period of time it is believed that water kept overnight in copper jugs, when drunk in the morning ensures with good health.

While its helpful property gives healthy impact to the human body on the other hand its elegant look provides sound effect to the human mind.

## COPPER MUGS AND TUMBLERS

Copper mugs and tumblers for its trendy and elegant looks are rapidly capturing todays market.

- Copper mugs may have different finishes:
  - Patina finish
  - Hammered finish
- Copper mugs can be with or without handles
- They can be with the wide range of sizes and shapes

*Types*: There are various kinds of mugs are available in copper tableware collection.

- Travel mugs
- Beer mugs and tumblers
- Beverage mugs
- Coffee mugs

*Utility*:

- Copper mugs and tumblers are customizable and made for popular give ways at trade shows, promotions, holidays and other events
- These also serve the purpose of day to day use

## COPPER ICE CREAM CUPS

Ice cream cups are used for serving ice-cream. Elegant copper ice-cream cups are a must at every party.

*Features*:

- They are normally sold in sets of six
- Ice cream tumblers are adorned with beautiful designs and finishes
- *Finishes usual for these sets are*:
  - Hammered finish
  - Patina finish

*Utility*:

- Ice cream cups are used for serving ice-cream
- Copper ice-cream cups are also for its appealing design used as a show piece in crockery collection
- These cups are available in different sizes and shapes

## COPPER MUGS AND TUMBLERS

Copper mugs and tumblers for its trendy and elegant looks are rapidly capturing todays market.

- Copper mugs may have different finishes:
  - Patina finish
  - Hammered finish
- Copper mugs can be with or without handles
- They can be with the wide range of sizes and shapes

### Types

There are various kinds of mugs are available in copper tableware collection.

- Travel mugs
- Beer mugs and tumblers
- Beverage mugs
- Coffee mugs etc

*Utility*:

- Copper mugs and tumblers are customizable and made for popular give ways at trade shows, promotions, holidays and other events
- These also serve the purpose of day to day use

## COPPER SALT AND PEPPER SETS

Copper table ware collection is incomplete without copper salt and pepper shaker. To add pinch of salt and pepper to any delicacy according to our choice salt and pepper shaker are indispensable.

*Features*:

- Copper salt and pepper shakers have hammered finish.
- They are lacquered to resist tarnishing.
- Copper and pepper Shakers have nickel lining.
- They can be found with or without handles. Handles of this copper made shaker's may be available in brass.
- To give good support sometimes its base may be made of brass.
- They are different kinds of Copper salt and pepper sets with various sizes.

### Type of the Product

*There are lot more in the collection of the copper salt and pepper shaker like*:

- Copper retro style of salt and pepper shaker set
- Copper retro art deco salt and pepper shaker
- Clear pleated glass salt and pepper shaker copper
- Wood salt and pepper shaker with copper
- Antique Embossed Copper salt and pepper shaker
- Salt and pepper sets in a shape of chess piece, copper
- Copper stove salt and pepper sets

*Other Types of shakers*:

- The metal and lining used in a salt and pepper shaker, we can find two different types of salt and pepper shaker:

- One kind of shaker is made of shiny copper and brass combination with nickel lining.
- Another type of shaker is manufactured again from copper-brass combination with tin lining.

*Utility*: Salt and pepper shakers are used to sprinkle salt and pepper to any food item.

## COPPER PLATTER

Ravishing looks and multifarious utility have made Copper platters very much in choice to the today's customer.

*Features*:

- *Copper platters are available in different finishes such as*:
  - Hammered finish
  - Patina finish
- *Copper platters are generally lacquered to resist tarnishing*:
- *Utility*: A platter is large shallow dish or plate, used usually for serving foods. Top quality design and well polished copper platter also looks good as a kitchen hanging.

### Types

*Different kinds of copper platters are*:

- Wall hanging copper plate
  - Floral copper plate
  - Copper wall plate
  - Glazed copper plate with pine cone engraving
  - Copper platter with Egyptian motif
  - Isocuates, the 18th Century copper plate engraving
- *Other types of Copper Platter*:
  - Copper Hand hammer plate with patina finish. It is found in different sizes
  - There is another kind of plate for keeping salad. Metals used for this plate are copper and brass with nickel lining
  - Another type of salad plate is made of copper and brass with tin lining.

## COPPER TOOTHPICK HOLDERS

Copper toothpick holder has become very fashionable due to its rugged looks. Not only to avoid any inconvenience but keeping tooth pick holder in a table is a vogue nowadays.

*Features*:

- Tooth pick holders are crafted out of hammered copper sheets.

- Lining material used here is the nickel.
- They may be lacquered to resist tarnishing.
- These trendy tablewares are processed to two types of finishes:
  - patina finish
  - hammered finish

**Types**

This ornate tooth pick holder is pretty looking for its leafy scrolls all over the body and its filigree work. It is around 2.5" tall. The speciality of this toothpick holder is that one cherub is sitting next to the holder.

*Utility*:

- Tooth pick holder is used for keeping tooth pick in it.
- Appealing shaped copper tooth pick holder can also be used as a decoration.

**COPPER TRAYS**

New kind of a design and beautiful outlook due to copper have made trays mind boggling for any class.

*Features*:

- Copper trays are made of solid copper
- Finishes for copper trays are normally:
  - Plain patina finish
  - Hammered finish
- Copper trays are usually available in their natural, uncoated finish
- Serving trays may be powder coated, in order to match the crockery and decor
- They may come in different sizes and shapes
- Copper trays may be plain or may have beautiful designs and motifs engraved on them

**Types**

Copper trays are not just for serving foods and drink but also serve as decorative items.

*Some examples are*:

- "Tiesselinck" copper tray
- "Roy croft" copper tray

*There are also lot many other collection in the world of copper tray*:

- One kind of tray is found with a frame of oak. In this tray copper is hand beaten. Its size (approximately 14"-17") is such that it is sufficient to serve the purpose of tea tray

- There is a rectangular tray made only of copper with shiny finish
- Another kind of rectangular tray is found with shiny finish. But it is manufactured from both copper and brass
- There are two types of oval tray. One is called oval rice tray and another is oval tray with etching. Both are made of copper with shiny finish
- Hexagonal tray with shiny finish is also very attractive in a range of copper table ware. It is found in copper and brass make
- There is a copper made tray which is yellow in colour. It is known as fine engraved yellow copper tray
- There is another kind of yellow copper tray available. It is usually known as yellow copper tray with Oasis motive in relief

*Utility*:

- Copper trays are used to serve foods and drinks
- Well designed copper trays are also used as a wall hanging and in home decor

## CAST IRON

Cast iron cookware is slow to heat, but once at temperature provides even heating. Cast iron can also withstand very high temperatures, making cast iron pans ideal for searing.

Being a reactive material, cast iron can have chemical reactions with high acid foods such as wine or tomatoes. In addition, some foods (such as spinach) cooked on bare cast iron will turn black. Cast iron is a porous material that rusts easily.

As a result, it typically requires seasoning before use. Seasoning creates a thin layer of oxidized fat over the iron that coats and protects the surface, and prevents sticking.

Enameled cast iron cookware was developed by Le Creuset. In 1934, Le Creuset also solved the problem of excessive evaporation and scorching when using the cast iron Dutch ovens during cooking, by creating the enameled cast iron doufeu.

## BRASS

Food and Beverage department refers to Production, Service and Kitchen Stewarding. This is the third most energy-consuming department next to engineering and laundry which accounts for 20 to 25% of total energy consumed by the hotel. F&B uses energy in the form of electricity (for lighting and electrical cooking equipment's), Liquefied Petroleum Gas, Natural gas, Coal and solid fuel. FandB service department includes all restaurants, bar, lounge, clubs, room service, banquets and out door catering and contributes around 15% to 30% of the total hotel financial turnover.

## ENVIRONMENTAL IMPACTS

F&B department consumes enormous amount of resource at all the three levels of operation that is production, service and cleanliness. It also generates disproportionate amount of waste, which has adverse environmental impacts, some of them are:

**Table. Significant Environmental Aspects and Impacts – F&B Production Various activities in F&B Production**

| Various activities in F&B Production | Aspects | Environmental Impact | Significant Aspect |
|---|---|---|---|
| Receiving and storing of food item in kitchen | Generation of waste paper, jute bags, cloth bags, cartons, glass bottles, metal tins and plastics | Land pollution | Plastic waste |
| Production of food items in kitchen | Generation of smoke, vapors, ash and heat and possibility of overuse of cooking fuel | Air pollution | Oil and grease vapors |

**Table. Significant Environmental Aspects and Impacts – FandB Service (including Kitchen Stewarding)**

# 4

# Cookware and Bakeware

## INTRODUCTION

Cookware and bakeware are types of food preparation containers commonly found in a kitchen. Cookware comprises cooking vessels, such as saucepans and frying pans, intended for use on a stove or range cooktop. Bakeware comprises cooking vessels intended for use inside an oven. Some utensils are both cookware and bakeware.

**Fig.** Various baking pans

The choice of material for cookware and bakeware items has a significant effect on the item's performance (and cost), particularly in terms of thermal conductivity and how much food sticks to the item when in use. Some choices of material also require special pre-preparation of the surface - known as seasoning - before they are used for food preparation.

Both the cooking pot and lid handles can be made of the same material, but will mean that when picking up or touching either of these parts oven gloves will need to be worn. In order to avoid this, handles can be made of non heat conducting materials, for example bakelite, plastic or wood. It is best to avoid hollow handles because they are difficult to clean or to dry.

A good cooking pot design has an 'overcook edge' this is where the lid lies on. The lid has a dripping edge that avoids condensation fluid from dripping off when handling the lid (taking it off and holding it 45°) or putting it down.

## HISTORY

The history of cooking vessels before the development of pottery is minimal due to the limited archaeological evidence. The earliest pottery vessels, dating from 19,2000–20,000 BP, were discovered in Xianrendong Cave, Jiangxi, China.

The pottery may have been used as cookware, manufactured by hunter-gatherers.Harvard University archaeologist Ofer Bar-Yosef reported that "When you look at the pots, you can see that they were in a fire." It is also possible to extrapolate likely developments based on methods used by latter peoples.

Among the first of the techniques believed to be used by stone age civilizations were improvements to basic roasting. In addition to exposing food to direct heat from either an open fire or hot embers it is possible to cover the food with clay or large leaves before roasting to preserve moisture in the cooked result. Examples of similar techniques are still in use in many modern cuisines.

Of greater difficulty was finding a method to boil water. For people without access to natural heated water sources, such as hot springs, heated stones could be placed in a water-filled vessel to raise its temperature (for example, a leaf-lined pit or the stomach from animals killed by hunters). In many locations the shells ofturtles or large mollusks provided a source for waterproof cooking vessels. Bamboo tubes sealed at the end with clay provided a usable container in Asia, while the inhabitants of the Tehuacan Valley began carving large stone bowls that were permanently set into a hearth as early as 7,000 BC.

According to Frank Hamilton Cushing, native American cooking baskets used by the Zuni (Zuñi) developed from mesh casings woven to stabilize gourd water vessels. He reported witnessing cooking basket use byHavasupai in 1881. Roasting baskets covered with clay would be filled with wood coals and the product to be roasted. When the thus fired clay separated from the basket, it would become a usable clay roasting pan in itself. This indicates a steady progression from use of woven gourd casings to waterproof cooking baskets to pottery.

Other than in many other cultures, native Americans used and still use the heat source inside the cookware. Cooking baskets are filled with hot stones and roasting pans with wood coals. Native Americans would form a basket from large leaves to boil water, according to historian and novelist Louis

L'Amour. As long as the flames did not reach above the level of water in the basket, the leaves would not burn through.

The development of pottery allowed for the creation of fireproof cooking vessels in a variety of shapes and sizes. Coating the earthenware with some type of plant gum, and later glazes, converted the porous container into a waterproof vessel. The earthenware cookware could then be suspended over a fire through use of a tripod or other apparatus, or even be placed directly into a low fire or coal bed as in the case of the pipkin. Ceramics conduct heat poorly, however, so ceramic pots must cook over relatively low heats and over long periods of time. However, most ceramic pots will crack if used on the stovetop, and are only intended for the oven.

The development of bronze and iron metalworking skills allowed for cookware made from metal to be manufactured, although adoption of the new cookware was slow due to the much higher cost. After the development of metal cookware there was little new development in cookware, with the standard Medieval kitchen utilizing a cauldron and a shallow earthenware pan for most cooking tasks, with a spit employed for roasting.

By the 17th century, it was common for a Western kitchen to contain a number of skillets, baking pans, a kettle and several pots, along with a variety of pot hooks and trivets. Brass or copper vessels were common in Asia and Europe, whilst iron pots were common in the American colonies. Improvements in metallurgy during the 19th and 20th centuries allowed for pots and pans from metals such as steel, stainless steel and aluminium to be economically produced.

## COOKWARE MATERIALS

### Natural Clay

Natural clay has been used to make cookware from before dated history. Pots and pans made with this material are durable (some could last a lifetime or more)and are non-reactive. Pure clay harvested from the earth has no heavy metals and is inert and does not react to the food being cooked. Clay pots and pans are slow conductors of heat when they are new and unused, but get stronger and conduct heat much faster as they get used. Heat is also conducted evenly in this material. They can be used for both cooking on stove-tops and for baking in the oven.

### Metal

Metal pots are made from a narrow range of metals because pots and pans need to conduct heat well, but also need to be chemically unreactive so that they do not alter the flavor of the food. Most materials that are conductive enough to heat evenly are too reactive to use in food preparation. In some cases (copper pots, for example), a pot may be made out of a more reactive metal, and then tinned or clad with another.

**Aluminium**

Aluminium is a lightweight metal with very good thermal conductivity. It is resistant to many forms of corrosion. Aluminium is commonly available in sheet, cast, or anodized forms, and may be physically combined with other metals.

**Fig.** An anodized aluminium sauté pan

Sheet aluminium is spun or stamped into form. Due to the softness of the metal it may be alloyed with magnesium, copper, or bronze to increase its strength. Sheet aluminium is commonly used for baking sheets, pie plates, and cake or muffin pans. Deep or shallow pots may be formed from sheet aluminium.

Cast aluminium can produce a thicker product than sheet aluminium, and is appropriate for irregular shapes and thicknesses. Due to the microscopic pores caused by the casting process, cast aluminium has a lower thermal conductivity than sheet aluminium. It is also more expensive. Accordingly, cast aluminium cookware has become less common. It is used for Dutch ovens, heavyweight baking pans such as bundt pans, and wares such as ladles or handles where low thermal conductivity is desired.

Anodized aluminium has had the naturally occurring layer of aluminium oxide thickened by an electrolytic process to create a surface that is hard and non-reactive. It is used for sauté pans, stockpots, roasters, and Dutch ovens.

Uncoated and un-anodized aluminium can react with acidic foods to change the taste of the food. Sauces containing egg yolks, or vegetables such as asparagus or artichokes may cause oxidation of non-anodized aluminium.

Aluminium exposure has been suggested as a risk factor for neurodegenerative diseases such as Alzheimer's disease. The Rondeau, Commenges *et al.*article cited below states "These findings support the hypothesis that aluminium in drinking water is a risk factor for AD." (Alzheimer's disease)". The Alzheimer's Association states that "studies have failed to confirm any role for aluminium in causing Alzheimer's. [Today] few [experts] believe that everyday sources of aluminium pose any threat."

**Fig.** Copper saucepans, Vaux-le-Vicomtecastle.

## Copper

In classical Western cooking, pots are formed with thick copper sheets with a thin inner layer of tin. The copper provides the best thermal conductivity of common metals and therefore results in even heating. Copper is reactive with acidic foods, which can result in copper toxicity. This was discovered in the new world when tomatoes were cooked in old world copper pots.

A tin lining prevents copper from reacting with acidic foods. Lead-free and cadmium-free tin linings are susceptible to tin pest. In some cases unlined copper is desirable, for instance in the preparation of meringues and foams. Copper pots are expensive, require re-tinning and, when made with thick copper plates, are heavy. With modern metallurgical techniques, such as cladding, copper is incorporated into the constructions of cookware, often as an enclosed heat spreading disk.

## Cast iron

**Fig.** Cast-iron

Cast iron cookware is slow to heat, but once at temperature provides even heating. Cast iron can also withstand very high temperatures, making cast iron pans ideal for searing. Being a reactive material, cast iron can have chemical reactions with high acid foods such as wine or tomatoes. In addition, some foods (such as spinach) cooked on bare cast iron will turn black.

Cast iron is a porous material that rusts easily. As a result, it typically requires seasoning before use. Seasoning creates a thin layer of oxidized fat over the iron that coats and protects the surface, and prevents sticking.

Enameled cast iron cookware was developed in the 1920s. In 1934, the French company Cousancesdesigned the enameled cast iron Doufeu to reduce excessive evaporation and scorching in cast iron Dutch ovens. Modeled on old braising pans in which glowing charcoal was heaped on the lids (to mimic two-fire ovens), the Doufeu has a deep recess in its lid which instead is filled with ice cubes.

This keeps the lid at a lower temperature than the pot bottom. Further, little notches on the inside of the lid allow the moisture to collect and drop back into the food during the cooking. Although the Doufeu (literally, "gentlefire") can be used in an oven (without the ice, as a casserole), it is chiefly designed for stove top use.

**Carbon Steel**

**Fig.** Carbon steel

Carbon steel cookware can be rolled or hammered into very thin sheets of material, while still maintaining high strength and heat resistance. This allows for rapid and high heating. Carbon steel does not conduct heat as well as other materials, but this may be an advantage for woks and paella pans, where one portion of the pan is intentionally kept at a different temperature than the rest.

Like cast iron, carbon steel must be seasoned before use. Rub a fat on the cooking surface only and heat the cookware over the stovetop. The process can be repeated if needed.

Over time, the cooking surface will become dark and nonstick. Carbon steel will easily rust if not seasoned and should be stored seasoned to avoid rusting. Carbon steel is often used for woks and crêpe pans.

**Non-stick**

Steel or aluminum cooking pans can be coated with a substance such as polytetrafluoroethylene (PTFE) in order to minimize food sticking to the pan surface.

**Fig.** Teflon coated frying pan

There are advantages and disadvantages to such a coating. Coated pans are easier to clean than most non-coated pans, and require little or no additional oil or fat to prevent sticking.

On the other hand, some sticking is needed to cause sucs to form, so a non-stick pan cannot be used where a pan sauce is desired. And non-stick pans must not be overheated. Nonstick coatings tend to degrade over time. In order to preserve the coating, it is important never to use metal implements or harsh scouring pads or chemical abrasives when cleaning.

There is a potential danger in the use of PTFE-based coatings: while decomposition of the coating does not occur at normal cooking temperatures (below about 465 °F/240 °C), overheating, particularly likely when heating an empty pan, can produce decomposition products that are toxic to humans and fatal to birds.

The main difference in coating quality is due to the formulas of the liquid coating, the thickness of each layer and the number of layers used.Higher-quality non-stick cookware use powdered ceramic or titanium mixed with the non-stick material to strengthen them and to make them more resistant to abrasion and deterioration. Some non-stick coatings contain hardening agents. Some coatings are high enough in quality that they pass the strict standards of the National Sanitation Foundation for approval for restaurant use.

**COATED AND COMPOSITE COOKWARE**

**Enameled Cast Iron**

Enameled cast iron cooking vessels are made of cast iron covered with a porcelain surface. This creates a piece that has the heat distribution and retention properties of cast iron combined with a non-reactive, low-stick surface.

## Enamel Over Steel

The enamel over steel technique creates a piece that has the heat distribution of carbon steel and a non-reactive, low-stick surface. Such pots are much lighter than most other pots of similar size, are cheaper to make than stainless steel pots, and do not have the rust and reactivity issues of cast iron or carbon steel.

Enamel over steel is ideal for large stockpots and for other large pans used mostly for water-based cooking. Because of its light weight and easy cleanup, enamel over steel is also popular for cookware used while camping.

## Clad aluminium or Copper

Cladding is a technique for fabricating pans with a layer of heat conducting material, such as copper or aluminium, covered by a non-reactive material, such as stainless steel. Some pans feature a copper or aluminium layer that extends over the entire pan rather than just a heat-distributing disk on the base.

Aluminium pans are typically clad on both their inside and the outside surfaces, providing both a stainless cooking surface and a stainless surface to contact the cooktop. Copper is typically clad on its interior surface only, leaving the more attractive copper exposed on the outside of the pan.

Some high-end cookware uses a dual-clad process, with a thin stainless layer on the cooking surface, a thick core of aluminium to provide structure and heat diffusion, and a thin layer of copper on the outside of the pot that provides additional diffusion and the "look" of a copper pot. This provides much of the functionality of tinned-copper pots for a fraction of the price.

## Other Non-metallic Cookware

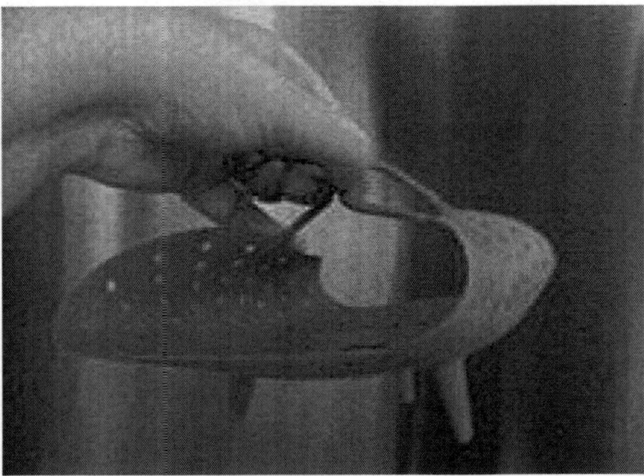

**Fig.** Silicone food steamer to be placed in a pot of boiling water.

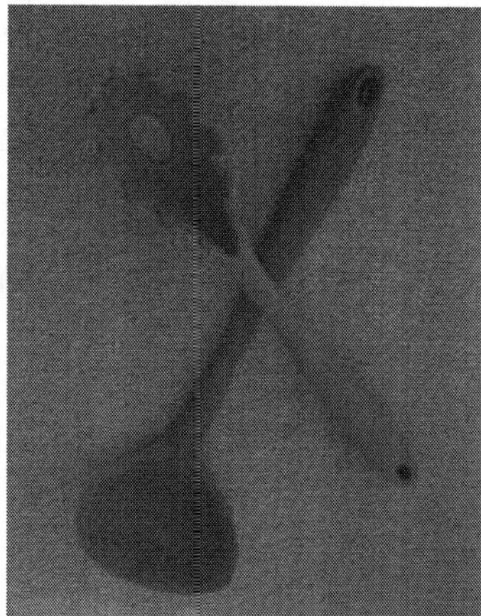

**Fig.** Silicone ladles.

Non-metallic cookware can be used in both conventional and microwave ovens. Non-metallic cookware typically can not be used on the stovetop, although Corningware and Pyroflam are some exceptions.

**Ceramics**

Glazed ceramics, such as porcelain, provide a nonstick cooking surface. Historically some glazes used on ceramic articles contained levels of lead, which can possess health risks; although this is not a concern with the vast majority of modern ware. Some pottery can be placed on fire directly.

**Glass**

Borosilicate glass is safe at oven temperatures. The clear glass also allows for the food to be seen during the cooking process. However, it can't be used on a stovetop, as it cannot cope with stovetop temperatures.

**Glass-ceramic**

Glass ceramic is used to make products such as Corningware and Pyroflam, which have many of the best properties of both glass and ceramic cookware. While Pyrex can shatter if taken between extremes of temperature too rapidly, glass-ceramics can be taken directly from deep freeze to the stove top. Their very low coefficient of thermal expansion makes them less prone immune to thermal shock.

**Stone**

a natural stone can be used to diffuse heat for indirect grilling or baking, as in a baking stone or pizza stone, or the French *pierrade*.

**Silicone**

Silicone bakeware is light, flexible and able to withstand sustained temperatures of 360 °C (675 °F). It melts around 500°C (930°F), depending upon the fillers used. Its flexibility is advantageous in removing baked goods from the pan. This rubbery material should not to be confused with the silicone resin used to make hard, shatterproof children's dishware, which is not suitable for baking.

## TYPES OF COOKWARE AND BAKEWARE

The size and shape of a cooking vessel is typically determined by how it will be used. Cooking vessels are typically referred to as "pots" and "pans," but there is great variation in their actual shapes. Most cooking vessels are roughly cylindrical.

### COOKWARE

"Saucepan" redirects here. For the unofficial Australian astronomic term, see Pavo (constellation).

"Caldero" redirects here. For the geological term, see Caldera.

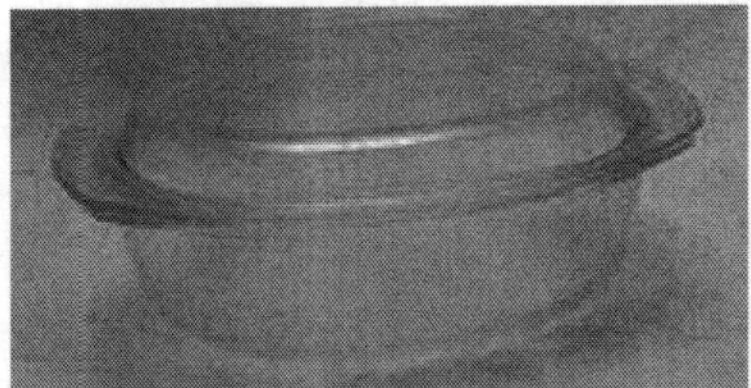

**Fig.** A Pyrex chicken roaster.

**Fig.** Römertopf.

**Fig.** A Passover brownie cake baked in a Wonder Pot.

**Fig.** Large and small skillets.

**Fig.** Electric griddle with temperature control.

**Fig.** A copper saucepot (stainless lined, with cast iron handles).

**Fig.** Angel Food Cake pan.

**Fig.** A springform pan with pizza.

**Fig.** A gugelhupf from Alsace,Unterlinden Museum.

- Braising pans and roasting pans (also known as braisers and roasters) are large, wide and shallow, to provide space to cook a roast (chicken, beef or pork). They typically have two loop or tab handles, and may have a cover. Roasters are usually made of heavy gauge metal so that they may be used safely on a cooktop following roasting in an oven. Unlike most other cooking vessels, roasters are usually rectangular or oval. There is no sharp boundary between braisers and roasters - the same pan, with or without a cover, can be used for both functions. In Europe, a clay roaster (Swedish: *Lergryta,* German: *Römertopf,* Slovene: *Rimski lonec*) is still popular because it allows roasting without adding grease or liquids. This helps preserve flavor and nutrients. Having to soak the pot in water for 15 minutes before use is a notable drawback.
- Casserole pans (for making casseroles) resemble roasters and Dutch ovens, and many recipes can be used interchangeably between them. Depending on their material, casseroles can be used in the oven or on the stovetop. Casseroles are commonly made of glazed ceramics or Pyrex.
- Dutch ovens are heavy, relatively deep pots with a heavy lid, designed to re-create oven conditions on the stovetop or campfire. They can be used for stews, braised meats, soups and a large variety

of other dishes that benefit from low heat, slow cooking. Dutch ovens are typically made from cast iron and are sized by volume.

- A Wonder Pot is an Israeli invention that acts as a Dutch oven but is made of aluminium. It consists of three parts: an aluminium pot shaped like a Bundt pan, a hooded cover perforated with venting holes, and a thick, round, metal disc with a centre hole that is placed between the Wonder Pot and the flame to disperse heat.
- Frying pans, frypans or skillets provide a large flat heating surface and shallow sides, and are best for pan frying. Frypans with a gentle, rolling slope are sometimes called omelette pans. Grill pans are frypans that are ribbed, to let fat drain away from the food being cooked. Frypans and grill pans are generally sized by diameter (20–30 cm).
- Spiders are skillets with three thin legs to keep them above an open fire. Ordinary flat-bottomed skillets are also sometimes called spiders, though the term has fallen out of general use.
- Griddles are flat plates of metal used for frying, grilling and making pan breads such as pancakes, injera,tortillas, chapatis and crepes. Traditional iron griddles are circular, with a semicircular hoop fixed to opposite edges of the plate and rising above it to form a central handle. Rectangular griddles that cover two stoveburners are now also common, as are griddles that have a ribbed area that can be used like a grill pan. Some have multiple square metal grooves enabling the contents to have a defined pattern, similar to a waffle maker. Like frypans, round griddles are generally measured by diameter (20–30 cm).
- In Scotland, griddles are referred to as girdles. In some Spanish speaking countries, a similar pan is referred to as a comal. Crepe pans are similar to griddles, but are usually smaller, and made of a thinner metal.
- Both griddles and frypans can be found in electric versions. These may be permanently attached to a heat source, similar to a hot plate.
- Saucepans (or just "pots") are vessels with vertical sides about the same height as their diameter, used forsimmering or boiling. Saucepans generally have one long handle. Larger pots of the same shape generally have two handles close to the sides of the pot (so they can be lifted with both hands), and are called sauce-pots or soup pots (3–12 litres). Saucepans and saucepots are measured by volume (usually 1–8 l). While saucepots often resemble Dutch ovens in shape, they do not have the same heat capacity characteristics. Very small saucepans used for heating milk

are referred to as milk pans, such saucepans usually have a lip for pouring the heated milk.

- Ironically, the saucepan is not the ideal vessel to use for making sauces. It is more efficient to use saucepans with sloping sides, called Windsor pans, or saucepans with rounded sides, called sauciers. These provide quicker evaporation than straight sided pans, and make it easier to stir a sauce while reducing.
- Sauté pans, used for sauteing, have a large surface area and low sides to permit steam to escape and allow the cook to toss the food. The word "sauté" comes from the French verb "sauter", meaning to jump. Saute pans often have straight vertical sides, but may also have flared or rounded sides.
- Stockpots are large pots with sides at least as tall as their diameter. This allows stock to simmer for extended periods of time without reducing too much. Stockpots are typically measured in volume (6-36 l). Stock pots come in a large variety of sizes to meet any need from cooking for a family to preparing food for a banquet. A specific type of stockpot exists for lobsters, and an all-metal stockpot usually called a caldero is used in Hispanic cultures to cook rice.
- An MEC Clay pot or pan is an American line of pots and pans made from non-reactive clay. They are unglazed and can be used both on the stove-top and in the oven. They can also cook in the slow cooker. The lids lock steam and since they are made from a non-reactive raw material they are considered to be ideal for nutritious cooking.
- Woks are wide, roughly bowl-shaped vessels with one or two handles at or near the rim. This shape allows a small pool of cooking oil in the centre of the wok to be heated to a high temperature using relatively little fuel, while the outer areas of the wok are used to keep food warm after it has been fried in the oil. In the Western world, woks are typically used only for stir-frying, but they can actually be used for anything from steaming todeep frying.

**Bakeware**

Bakeware is designed for use in the oven (for baking), and encompasses a variety of different styles of baking pans as cake pans, pie pans, and Bread pans.

- Cake tins (or cake pans in the US) include square pans, round pans, and speciality pans such as angel food cake pans and springform pans often used for baking cheesecake. Another type of cake pan is a muffin tin, which can hold multiple smaller cakes.

- Sheet pans, cookie sheets, and Swiss roll tins are bakeware with large flat bottoms.
- Pie pans are flat-bottomed flare-sided tins specifically designed for baking pies.

References


- Beard, James (1975). *The Cooks' Catalogue.* et al. Harper & Row. ISBN 0-06-011563-7.
- Kattumuri, Miriam (Dec 2009). "What is Clay pot cooking". Retrieved 19 December 2013.
- Bridge, Fred; Tibbetts, Jean F. (1991). *The Well-Tooled Kitchen.* William Morrow and Company. ISBN 0-688-08135-5.
- Houlihan, Jane; Thayer, Kris; Klien, Jennifer (May 2003). "Canaries in the Kitchen: Teflon Toxicosis". Environmental Working Group. Retrieved 21 April 2010.
- Reay Tannahill (1988). *Food in History.* Crown Publishers. ISBN 0-517-57186-2.
- Williams, Chuck (1986). *The Williams-Sonoma Cookbook and Guide to Kitchenware.* Random House. ISBN 0-394-54411-0.


## USABLE COOKWARE AND BAKEWARE MATERIALS

### NON-STICK SURFACE

**Fig.** Food in a non-stick pan

A non-stick surface is a surface engineered to reduce the ability of other materials to stick to it. Non-stick cookware is a common application, where the non-stick coating allows food to brown without sticking to the pan. Non-stick is often used to refer to surfaces coated with polytetrafluoroethylene (PTFE), which is sold under the brand name "Teflon." In recent years, however, other coatings have been marketed as non-stick, such as anodized aluminium, ceramics, silicone, enameled cast iron, and seasoned cast iron.

## HISTORY

### Ancient Greece

The Mycenaean Greeks might have used non-stick pans to make bread more than 3,000 years ago. Mycenaean ceramic griddles had one smooth side and one side covered with tiny holes. The bread was probably placed on the side with the holes, since the dough tended to stick when cooked on the smooth side of the pan. The holes seemed to be an ancient non-sticking technology, ensuring that oil spread quite evenly over the griddle.

### Modern Development

The modern non-stick pans were made using a coating of Teflon (polytetrafluoroethylene or PTFE). PTFE was invented serendipitously by Roy Plunkettin 1938, while working for a joint venture of the DuPont company.

The substance was found to have several unique properties, including very good corrosion resistance and the lowest coefficient of friction of any substance yet manufactured. PTFE was used first to make seals resistant to the uranium hexafluoride gas used in the Manhattan Project during World War II and was regarded as a military secret. Dupont registered the Teflon trademark in 1944 and soon began planning for post-war commercial use of the new product.

By 1951 Dupont had developed applications for Teflon in commercial bread and cookie-making; however the company avoided the market for consumer cookware due to potential problems associated with release of toxic gases if stove-top pans were overheated in inadequately ventilated spaces. Marc Grégoire, a French engineer, had begun coating his fishing gear with Teflon to prevent tangles. His wife Colette suggested using the same method to coat her cooking pans. The idea was successful and a French patent was granted for the process in 1954. The Tefal company was formed in 1956 to manufacture non-stick pans.

Not all modern non-stick pans use Teflon; other non-stick coatings have become available. For example, a mixture of titanium and ceramic can besandblasted onto the pan surface, and then fired to 2,000 °C (3,630 °F).

## PTFE AND SIMILAR COMPOUNDS

Polytetrafluoroethylene (PTFE) is a synthetic fluoropolymer used in various applications including non-stick coatings. Non-stick coating systems often include a special treatment of the substrate. For example, Whitford Corporation's *Excalibur* consists of three layers of PTFE over a metallic substrate which is first grit-blasted to roughen it, then electric-arc sprayed with a proprietary stainless steel alloy. According to Whitford, the irregular surface promotes adhesion of the PTFE and also resists abrasion of the PTFE.

### Health Concerns

When pans are overheated beyond approximately 350 °C (660 °F) the PTFE coating begins to dissociate, releasing byproducts (PFOA) which can causepolymer fume fever in humans and can be lethal to birds. Concerns have been raised over the possible negative effects of using PTFE-coated cooking pans.

Processing of PTFE in the past used to include Perfluorooctanoic acid (PFOA) as an emulsifier, however PFOA is a persistent organic pollutant and poses both environmental and health concerns, and is now being phased out of use in PTFE processing.

## USES AND LIMITATIONS

With other types of pans, some oil or fat is required to prevent hot food from sticking to the pan's surface. Food does not have the same tendency to stick to a non-stick surface; pans can be used with less, or no, oil, and are easier to clean, as residues do not stick to the surface.

Utensils used with PTFE-coated pans can scratch the coating, if the utensils are harder than the coating; this can be prevented by using non-metallic (usually plastic or wood) cooking tools.

According to writer Tony Polombo pans that are not non-stick are better for producing pan gravy, because the fond (the caramelized drippings that stick to the pan when meat is cooked) sticks to them, and can be turned into pan gravy by deglazing them—dissolving them in liquid.

# BEANPOT

**Fig.** Three-quart, one-quart (antique), and half-pint (souvenir) beanpots

A beanpot is a deep, wide-bellied, short-necked vessel used to cook bean-based dishes. Beanpots are typically made of ceramic, though pots made of other materials, like cast iron, can also be found. The relatively narrow mouth of the beanpot minimizes evaporation and heat loss, while the deep, wide, thick-walled body of the pot facilitates long, slow cooking times.

Beanpots are traditionally associated with New England, in particular Boston, Massachusetts. This association is evident in the nickname Beantown, and the use of the name *beanpot* for Boston events such as the Beanpot ice hockey tournament.

Beanpots resemble the Indian *handi* and the Spanish, Mexican or Native American *olla,* and may be related to the latter vessel. Unlike the German *Römertopf* and the Japanese *donabe,* they are typically glazed both inside and out, and so cannot be used for clay pot cooking.

## CHIP PAN

**Fig.** A cast iron chip pan with an aluminium basket being used to fry chips.

A chip pan is a deep-sided cooking pan used for deep-frying. Chip pans are named for their traditional use in frying chips (called "French fries" in the USA) .

Today, they are made from either aluminium or stainless steel, although in the past were commonly made from cast iron. A basket is placed inside the pan, to lower the chips into the hot cooking oil, and to raise them once cooked.

Chip pans are commonly used in the United Kingdom, although are slowly being outmoded by deep fryers.

### MANUFACTURE

Chip pans are commonly manufactured through a spinning process, as the metal used is malleable. The lid is typically stamped out by a die in a heavy press.

### HEALTH ISSUES

Repeated heating of oil is believed to greatly increase the free radicals in the oil, leading to a higher risk of heart disease.

## OIL BURNS

Injuries, particularly to children, caused by the hot oil from a chip pan falling on them are a common cause of hospital admission in the UK.

## FIRE HAZARD

Chip pans are well known for being a fire hazard. In the UK, chip pan fires are the largest cause of fire-related injuries in the home, such that several local fire brigades have offered a "chip pan amnesty", trading old chip pans for a deep fryer.

By comparison, electric deep fryers feature circuitry and design features (such as thermostat-controlled internal heating elements) that prevent the oil from being heated to the point of ignition. Boil-overs and splattering can still occur for the usual reasons, but the fire danger is largely eliminated.

Chip pans are the most common cause of house fires in the United Kingdom, with around 12,000 chip pan fires every year, 1,100 of them considered serious.

These fires result in over 4,600 injuries, and 50 deaths per year. British Fire Brigades frequently issue warnings and advice, urging households to switch to a safer means of cooking chips, and advising that unless the fire is easily contained to leave the fire to the emergency services.

Cooking oil fires (US class K, Europe class F) burn hotter than other typical combustible liquids, rendering the standard class B extinguisher ineffective. Class F fire extinguishers use saponification to put out chip pan fires by spraying an alkaline solution which reacts with the fat to make a non-flammablesoap. However, these extinguishers are generally only available in industrial and commercial kitchens.

The dangers of oil or fat fires (generally flammable substances less dense than water) are well known in industrial processes. Attempts to extinguish oil fires with water result in a boilover: an extremely hazardous condition whereby the flaming oil is violently expelled from the container. These fires result from either heating the oil to its autoignition point or by oil splattering onto the heat source.

# SHEET PAN

Sheet pans, baking trays or baking sheets are flat, rectangular metal pans used in an oven. They are often used for baking bread rolls, pastries and flat products such as cookies, sheet cakes, and swiss rolls.

These pans, like all bakeware, can be made of a variety of materials, but are primarily aluminum or stainless steel. The most basic sheet pan is literally a sheet of metal.

Common additional features that may be found in sheet pans include a lip on one or more edges to prevent food from sliding off, handles to aid in placing the pan into the oven, and removing it again, or a layer of insulation or air (air bake pan) designed to protect delicate food from burning.

**Fig.** A baker aboard a United States aircraft carrier places a hot sheet pan full of bread rolls on to a cooling rack

## TYPES AND SIZES

A sheet pan that has a continuous lip around all four sides may be called a jelly roll pan. A pan that has at least one side flat, so that it is easy to slide the baked product off the end, may be called a cookie sheet.

Professional sheet pans used in commercial kitchens typically are made of aluminum, with a 1 in (2.5 cm) raised lip around the edge, and in the United States come in standard sizes.

The full-size sheet pan is 26 by 18 in (66 by 46 cm), which is too large for most home ovens. A two thirds sheet pan (also referred to as a three quarter size sheet pan) is 21 by 15 in (53 by 38 cm). A half sheet pan is 18 by 13 in (46 by 33 cm); quarter sheets are 9 by 13 in (23 by 33 cm).

The half sheet is approximately the same size as mass-market baking sheets found in supermarkets, and the quarter sheet is a common size for rectangular, single-layer cakes. Other commercial kitchen equipment, such as cooling racks, ovens, and shelving, is made to fit these standard pans.

## BAIN-MARIE

**Fig.** A bain-marie on a stovetop

A bain-marie (pronounced: [b[Þ ma i]; also known as a water bath or double boiler in English) is a piece of equipment used in science, industry, and cooking to heat materials gently and gradually to fixed temperatures, or to keep materials warm over a period of time.

### Description

**Fig.** Schematic of an improvised double boiler, as used in outdoor cooking

The bain-marie comes in a wide variety of shapes, sizes, and types, but traditionally is a wide, cylindrical, usually metal container made of three or four basic parts: a handle, an outer (or lower) container that holds the working liquid, an inner (or upper), smaller container that fits inside the outer one and which holds the material to be heated or cooked, and sometimes a base underneath. Under the outer container of the bain-marie (or built into its base) is a heat source.

Typically the inner container is immersed about halfway into the working liquid.

The smaller container, filled with the substance to be heated, fits inside the outer container, filled with the working liquid (usually water), and the whole is heated at, or below, the base, causing the temperature of the materials in both containers to rise as needed. The insulating action of the water helps to keep contents of the inner pot from boiling or scorching.

When the working liquid is water and the bain-marie is used at sea level, the maximum temperature of the material in the lower container will not exceed 100 degrees Celsius (212 F), the boiling point of water at sea level. Using different working liquids (oils, salt solutions, etc.) in the lower container will result in different maximum temperatures.

## ALTERNATIVES

A contemporary alternative to the traditional, liquid-filled bain-marie is the electric "dry-heat" bain-marie,heated by elements below both pots. The dry-heat form of electric bains-marie often consumes less energy, requires little cleaning, and can be heated more quickly than traditional versions. They can also operate at higher temperatures, and are often much less expensive than their traditional counterparts.

Electric bains-marie can also be wet, using either hot water or vapor, or steam, in the heating process. The open, bath-type bain-marie heats via a small, hot-water tub (or "bath"), and the vapour-type bain-marie heats with scalding-hot steam.

## CULINARY APPLICATIONS

**Fig.** An improvised bain-marie being used to melt chocolate

- Chocolate can be melted in a bain-marie to avoid splitting and caking onto the pot. Specialdessert bains-marie have a thermally insulated container and are used as a chocolatefondue.
- Cheesecake is often baked in a bain-marie to prevent the top from cracking in the centre.

- Custard may be cooked in a bain-marie to keep a crust from forming on the outside of the custard before the interior is fully cooked. In the case of the crème brûlée, placing the ramekins in a roasting pan and filling the pan with hot water until it is 1/2 to 2/3 of the way up the sides of the ramekins transfers the heat to the custard gently, which prevents the custard from curdling. The humidity from the steam that rises as the water heats helps keep the top of the custard from becoming too dry.
- Classic warm sauces, such as Hollandaise and beurre blanc, requiring heat to emulsify the mixture but not enough to curdle or "split" the sauce, are often cooked using a bain-marie.
- Some charcuterie such as terrines and pâtés are cooked in an "oven-type" bain-marie.
- Thickening of condensed milk, such as in confection-making, is done easily in a bain-marie.
- Controlled-temperature bains-marie can be used to heat frozen breast milk before feedings.
- Bains-marie can be used in place of chafing dishes for keeping foods warm for long periods of time, where stovetops or hot plates are inconvenient or too powerful.
- A bain-marie can be used to re-liquify hardened honey by placing a glass jar on top of any improvised platform sitting at the bottom of a pot of gently boiling water.
- In Australia bain-maries are used in take-away stores to keep warm foods such as cheese-sausages, wing-dings, chiko rolls, crumbed sausages, toasted sandwiches, burgers and dim-sims.

## ORIGIN

**Fig.** An alchemical *balneum Mariae*, or Mary's bath, from *Coelum philosophorum*, Philip Ulstad, 1528, Chemical Heritage Foundation

Bains-marie were originally developed for use in the practice of alchemy, when alchemists needed a way to heat materials slowly and gently. In that early form of chemical science, it was believed by many that the best way to heat certain materials was to mimic the supposed natural processes, occurring in the Earth's core, by which precious metals were believed to be germinated.

The name comes from the medieval-Latin term *balneum* (or *balineum*) *Mariae*—literally, *Mary's bath*—from which the French *bain de Marie,* or *bain-marie,* is derived. There are many theories as to how the name*Marie* came to be associated with this equipment:

- The device's invention has been popularly attributed to Mary the Jewess, an ancient alchemist traditionally; according to *The Jewish Alchemists,* Maria the Jewess was an ancient alchemist who lived in Alexandria. Mythical traditions have suggested that she was Miriam, the sister of Moses.
- Alternatively, according to culinary writer Giuliano Bugialli, the term comes from the Italian *bagno maria,* named after Maria de' Cleofa, who developed the technique in Florence in the sixteenth century., but earlier mentions (e.g. by Arnold de Villanova in the fourteenth century) seem to invalidate that attribution.
- Finally, some consider the name a reference to the Virgin Mary, whose proverbial gentleness can be likened to the gentleness of this cooking technique.

## DUTCH OVEN

**Fig.** Dutch oven from the 1890s. Note the evidence of ashes on the lid

A Dutch oven is a thick-walled (usually cast iron but also ceramic and clay) cooking pot with a tight-fitting lid. Dutch ovens have been used as cooking vessels for hundreds of years. They are called casserole dishes in

English speaking countries other than the USA ("casserole" means "pot" in French), and *cocottes* in French. They are similar to both the Japanese *tetsunabe* and the *Saè*, a traditional Balkan cast-iron oven, and are related to the South AfricanPotjie and the Australian Bedourie oven.

## HISTORY

### Early European history

During the late 17th century, the Dutch system of producing these cast metal cooking vessels was more advanced than the English system. The Dutch used dry sand to make their molds, giving their pots a smoother surface. Consequently, metal cooking vessels produced in the Netherlands were imported into Britain.

In 1704, an Englishman named Abraham Darby decided to go to the Netherlands to observe the Dutch system for making these cooking vessels. Four years later, back in England, Darby patented a casting procedure similar to the Dutch process and began to produce cast-metal cooking vessels for Britain and her new American colonies. Thus the term "Dutch oven" has endured for over 300 years, since at least 1710.

### American history

Over time, the Dutch oven used in the American colonies began to change. The pot became shallower and legs were added to hold the oven above the coals. A flange was added to the lid to keep the coals on the lid and out of the food.

The cast-iron cookware was loved by colonists and settlers because of its versatility and durability. It could be used for boiling, baking, stews, frying,roasting, and just about any other use. The ovens were so valuable that wills in the 18th and 19th centuries frequently spelled out the desired inheritor of the cast iron cookware. For example, Mary Ball Washington (mother of President George Washington) specified in her will, dated 20 May 1788, that one-half of her "iron kitchen furniture" should go to her grandson, Fielding Lewis, and the other half to Betty Carter, a granddaughter. Several Dutch ovens were among Mary's "iron kitchen furniture."

When the young American country began to spread westward across the North American continent, so did the Dutch oven. A Dutch oven was among the gear Lewis and Clark carried when they explored the great American Northwest in 1804–1806.

The pioneers who settled the American West also took along their Dutch ovens. In fact, a statue raised to honor the Mormon handcart companies who entered Utah's Salt Lake Valley in the 1850s proudly displays a Dutch oven hanging from the front of the handcart. The Dutch oven is also the official state cooking pot of Texas, Utah and Arkansas.

Mountain men exploring the great American frontier used Dutch ovens into the late 19th century. Dutch oven cooking was also prominent among those who took part in the western cattle drives that lasted from the mid-19th century into the early 20th century.

**Dutch history**

**Fig.** A Dutch oven, or braadpan, as it is used in the Netherlands today.

In the Netherlands, a Dutch oven is called a braadpan. The design most used today is a black (with blue inside)enameled steel pan, that is suitable for gas and induction heating. The model was introduced in 1891 by BK, a well known Dutch manufacturer of cookware. Cheaper and lighter in weight, it proved to be a revolution in the kitchen. A braadpan is mainly used for frying meat only, but it can also be used for making traditional stewssuch as hachee. Cast iron models exist, but are used less frequently.

## TYPES OF DUTCH OVENS

### Camping

A camping, cowboy, or chuckwagon Dutch oven has three legs, a wire bail handle, and a slightly concave, rimmed lid so that coals from the cooking fire can be placed on top as well as below. This provides more uniform internal heat and lets the inside act as an oven. These ovens are typically made of bare cast iron, although some are aluminum. Dutch ovens are often used in Scouting outdoor activities.

## COOKWARE DESCENDED FROM DUTCH OVENS

### Bedourie Oven

In Australia, a bedourie camp oven is a steel cookpot shaped and used like a Dutch oven. Named after Bedourie, Queensland, the Bedourie ovens were developed as a more robust (non-breakable) alternative to the more fragile cast iron Dutch ovens.

## Potjie

**Fig.** A cast iron *potjie* on a fire

In South Africa, a potjie /pÈTjkiÐ/, directly translated "pottle or little pot" from Afrikaans or Dutch, is unlike most other Dutch ovens, in that it is round bottomed. Traditionally, it is a single cast, cast iron pot, reinforced with external double or triple circumscribing ribs, a wire handle for suspending the pot, and three short legs for resting the pot. It is similar in appearance to a cauldron.

It has a cast iron lid with a recessed convex contour to allow for hot coals to lay on top, so that the pot may also be heated from above, and a handle. When the vessel is to be stored long term, care must be taken to avoid rust forming, this is accomplished by coating it in a non-toxic oil, such as cooking oil.

This act ensures that the vessel remains in a seasoned state. "Potjie" can also refer to the technique of cooking *potjiekos*. Among the recipes which require a potjie, there is one for a type of bread called "potbrood", which literally means "pot bread".

Among the South African indigenous peoples (specifically Zulus) these pots also became known as phutupots, after a popular food prepared in it. The larger pots are normally used for large gatherings e.g. Funerals or weddings to prepare large quanties of food. Wooden spoons referred to as Kombe in the Tsonga language are used for mixing and stirring.

This tradition originated in the Netherlands during the Siege of Leiden and was brought to South Africa by Dutch immigrants. It persisted over the years with the Voortrekkers and survives today as a traditionalAfrikaner method of cooking. It is still in common use by South African campers, both domestic and international.

## USE IN COOKING

Dutch ovens are well suited for long, slow cooking, such as in making roasts, stews, and casseroles.

When cooking over a campfire, it is possible to use old-style lipped cast iron Dutch ovens as true baking ovens, to prepare biscuits, cakes, breads, pizzas, and even pies. A smaller baking pan can be placed inside the ovens, used and replaced with another as the first batch is completed. It is also possible to stack Dutch ovens on top of each other, conserving the heat that would normally rise from the hot coals on the top. These stacks can be as high as 5 or 6 pots.

## SEASONING AND CARE

### Bare Cast Iron

Americans traditionally season their iron Dutch ovens like other cast-iron cookware.

After use Dutch ovens are typically cleaned like other cast iron cookware: with boiling water and a brush, and no or minimal soap. After the oven has been dried, it should be given a thin coating of cooking oil to prevent rusting. Whether that should be a vegetable fat or an animal fat (such as lard) is hotly contested. Saturated fats are more stable than polyunsaturated fats, which tend to go rancid more quickly.

Where possible, a cleaned and freshly oiled Dutch oven should be stored in a clean, dry location with the lid ajar or off to promote air circulation and to avoid the smell and taste of rancid oil. If the Dutch oven must be stored with the lid on, a paper towel or piece of newspaper should be placed inside the oven to absorb any moisture.

With care, after much use the surfaces of the Dutch oven will become dark black, very smooth, shiny and non-stick. With proper care, a Dutch oven will provide long service.

### Enameled Ovens

Enameled ovens do not need to be seasoned before use. However, they lose some of the other advantages of bare cast iron. For example, deep frying is usually not recommended in enameled ovens; the enamel coating is not able to withstand high heat, and is best suited for water-based cooking.

Enameled ovens can usually be cleaned like ordinary cookware, and some brands can be put in the dishwasher.

# FOOD PROCESSOR

A food processor is a kitchen appliance used to facilitate repetitive tasks in the preparation of food. Today, the term almost always refers to an electric-motor-driven appliance, although there are some manual devices also referred to as "food processors".

**Fig.** An electric food processor

**Fig.** A crank-operated food processor

Food processors are similar to blenders in many ways. The primary difference is that food processors use interchangeable blades and disks (attachments) instead of a fixed blade. Also, their bowls are wider and shorter, a more appropriate shape for the solid or semi-solid foods usually worked in a food processor.

Usually, little or no liquid is required in the operation of the food processor, unlike a blender, which requires some amount of liquid to move the particles around the blade.

## HISTORY

One of the first electric food processors was the Starmix, introduced by German company Electrostar in 1946. Although the basic unit resembled a simple blender, numerous accessories were available, including exotic attachments for slicing bread, milk centrifuges and ice cream bowls. In a time when electric motors were expensive, they also developed the piccolo, where the food processor's base unit could drive a vacuum cleaner. In the

1960s, Albrecht von Goertz designed the Starmix MX3 food processor. Although the entire company was rebranded as Starmix in 1968 following the success of the processors, they later focused on vacuum cleaners and electric hand-dryers and the last mixer was produced around the year 2000.

In France, the idea of a machine to process food began when a catering company salesman, Pierre Verdun, observed the large amount of time his clients spent in the kitchen chopping, shredding and mixing. He produced a simple but effective solution, a bowl with a revolving blade in the base. In 1960, this evolved into Robot-Coupe, a company established to manufacture commercial "food processors" for the catering industry. In the late 1960s, a commercial food processor driven by a powerful commercial induction motor was produced. The Magimix food processor arrived from France in the UK in 1974, beginning with the Model 1800. Then, a UK company Kenwood Limitedstarted their own first Kenwood Food Processor, 'processor de- luxe,' in 1979.

Carl Sontheimer introduced this same Magimix 1800 food processor into North America in 1973 under the Cuisinart brand, as America's first domestic food processor. Sontheimer contracted with a Japanese manufacturer to produce new models in 1977 in order to immediately launch his new Japanese-made food processor in 1980 when his contract with Robot-Coupe expired.

## FUNCTIONS

Food processors normally have multiple functions, depending on the placement and type of attachment or blade. These functions normally consist of:

- Slicing/chopping vegetables
- Grinding items such as nuts, seeds (e.g. spices), meat, or dried fruit
- Shredding or grating cheese or vegetables
- Pureeing
- Mixing and kneading doughs

## DESIGN AND OPERATION

The base of the unit houses a motor which turns a vertical shaft. A bowl, usually made of transparent plastic, fits around the shaft. Cutting blades can be attached to the shaft; these fit so as to operate near the bottom of the bowl. Shredding or slicing disks can be attached instead; these spin near the top of the bowl. A lid with a "feed tube" is then fitted onto the bowl.

The feed tube allows ingredients to be added while chopping, grinding or pureeing. It also serves as a chute through which items are introduced to shredding or slicing disks. A "pusher" is provided, sized to slide through the feed tube, protecting fingers.

Almost all modern food processors have safety devices which prevent the motor from operating if the bowl isn't properly affixed to the base or if the lid is not properly affixed to the bowl.

## KARAHI

**Fig.** A wok sits next to a karahi on a Western-style stove. Note that the flat-bottomed karahi (right) sits on an ordinary burner cover, while the round-bottomed wok balances in a wok-ring. Karahi often have round (loop-shaped) handles.

A karahi is a type of thick, circular, and deep cooking-pot (similar in shape to a wok) used in Indian,Pakistani, Bangladeshi and Nepalese cuisine. Traditionally made out of cast iron, karahi look like woks with steeper sides. Today they can be made of stainless steel, copper, and non-stick surfaces, both round and flat-bottomed.

### USE

Karahi serve for the shallow or deep frying of meat, potatoes, sweets, and snacks such assamosa and fish and also for Indian papadums, but are most noted for the simmering of stewsor posola, which are often named *karahi* dishes after the utensil.

### KARAHI DISHES

**Fig.** A small decorative karahi (left) and handi (right) used to serve Indian food.

**Fig.** A karahi in a Pakistani restaurant

Stews prepared in a karahi include chicken karahi, mutton karahi (made with goat meat) and dumba karahi (made with lamb meat) and also karahi paneer (a vegetarian version). Prepared in a reduced tomato and green-chilli base, a karahi is a popular late-night meal in Pakistani cuisine, usually ordered by the kilogram and consumed with naan.

A *balti,* based on the food of Baltistan, is another dish cooked in a karahi.

An inverted karahi is used to cook Rumali Rotis.

## KETTLE

**Fig.** A stainless steel kettle

A kettle, sometimes called a tea kettle or teakettle, is a type of pot, typically metal, specialized for boilingwater, with a lid, spout and handle, or a small kitchen appliance of similar shape that functions in a self-contained manner. Kettles can be heated either by placing on a stove, or by their own internal electric heating element in the appliance versions.

## HISTORY

**Fig.** Norwegian cast iron kettle.

The first kettles were used in ancient Mesopotamia for purposes other than cooking. Over time these artistically decorated earthenware containers became more frequently utilized in the kitchen. In China, kettles were typically made of iron and were placed directly over an open flame. Travelers used the kettles to boil fresh water to make it suitable for drinking.

The word *kettle* originates from Old Norse *ketill* "cauldron". The Old English spelling was *cetel* with initial *che*-[t?] like 'cherry', Middle English (and dialectal) was *chetel,* both come (together with German *Kessel* "cauldron") ultimately from Germanic **katilaz,* that was borrowed from Latin *catillus,* diminutive form of *catinus* "deep vessel for serving or cooking food", which in various contexts is translated as "bowl", "deep dish", or "funnel".

The development of kettles was in direct correlation with the evolution of the modern stove.

### Electric kettle

**Fig.** Swan electric kettle in brass, an early electric kettle at the Museum of Liverpool.

In the latter part of the 1800s, electric kettles were introduced as an alternative to stove top kettles. In 1893 the Crompton and Co. firm ofEngland started featuring electric kettles in their catalogue. The early electric kettles were quite primitive as theheating element couldn't be immersed in the water. Instead, a separate compartment underneath the water storage area in the kettle was used to house the electric heating element. The design was inefficient even relative to the conventional stove-top kettles of the time.

In 1922, the problem was finally solved by Leslie Large, an engineer working at Bulpitt & Sons of Birminghamwho designed an element of wire wound around a core and sheathed in a metal tube. As this element could be immersed directly into the water it made the new electric kettle much more efficient than stovetop kettles.

In 1955, the newly founded British company Russell Hobbs brought out its stainless steel K1 model as the first fully automatic kettle. A thermostat, triggered by the rising steam as the water would come to boil, would flex, thereby cutting off the current.

Modern kettles include a variety of technological advancements. Some electric kettles are cordless with illumination capabilities. Whistling kettles are equipped with lightweight dynamics and heat-resistant handles.

## STOVETOP KETTLES

**Fig.** A stovetop kettle on a gas burner; this type, without a lid, is filled through the spout

A stovetop kettle is a roughly pitcher-shaped metal vessel used to heat water on a stovetop or hob. Kettles usually have a handle on top, a spout, and a lid. Sometimes stove-mounted kettles also have a steam whistlethat indicates when the water has reached boiling point. In whistling tea kettles, when the steam building up in the container of the kettle tries to escape, it causes vibrations to occur within the chamber. As the speed of the releasing steam increases, the vibrations become louder, causing a whistle. Some whistling kettles have an actual whistle on a cover at the end of the spout.

The most popular stovetop kettles are made with stainless steel. This is due to the lightweight nature of the kettle, in addition to the bright finish and durability. The crack-resistant nature of the kettle also makes it easier to clean.

Kettles can also be made from copper, iron, aluminum, polished chrome or ceramic.

A kettle has two principal advantages over a saucepan for heating water: the enclosed nature of a kettle reduces heat losses and leads to quicker boiling, and the exclusive use of the kettle for water means that hot drinks cannot be contaminated by grease spots or food residues left if saucepans are not meticulously washed.

## ELECTRIC KETTLES

Electric kettles were introduced as a means to boil water without the necessity of a stove top. They are normally constructed of durable plastic or steel (with a plastic handle) and powered by mains electricity. In modern kettles the heating element is typically fully enclosed, with a power rating of 2 - 3 kW. In countries with 110V mains electricity, kettles may be less powerful to avoid drawing too much current and requiring a very thick supply wire.

In modern designs, once the water has reached boiling point, the kettle automatically deactivates, preventing the water from boiling away and damaging the heating element. A bimetallic strip thermostat is commonly used as the automatic shut-off mechanism. The thermostat is isolated from the water in the kettle and is instead heated by the steam created when the water boils, which is directed through a duct onto the bimetallic strip. This allows the thermostat to be coarsely calibrated, which in turn allows the kettle to function normally at a wide range of altitudes. A consequence of this design is that the kettle may fail to deactivate if the lid is left open, due to an insufficient amount of steam being ducted onto the bimetallic strip.

Jug kettles became popular in the late 20th century. They have a more upright design and are more economical to use, since small amounts of water, enough for only one cup, can be boiled while still keeping the element covered.

In the United States an electric kettle may sometimes be referred to as a hot pot.

# PRESSURE COOKING

**Fig.** A pressure cooker: the regulator is a weight on a nozzle next to the handle on the lid

Pressure cooking is the process of cooking food, using water or other cooking liquid, in a sealed vessel—known as a *pressure cooker*, which does not permit air or liquids to escape below a pre-set pressure. Pressure cookers are used for cooking food more quickly than conventional cooking methods, which also saves energy.

Pressure cookers heat food quickly because the internal steam pressure from the boiling liquid causessaturated steam (or "wet steam") to bombard and permeate the food. Thus, higher temperature water vapour (i.e., increased energy), which transfers heat more rapidly compared to dry air, cooks food very quickly.

Pressure cooking allows food to be cooked with greater humidity and higher temperatures than possible with conventional boiling or steaming methods. In an ordinary non-pressurised cooking vessel, the boiling point of water is 100 °C (212 °F) at standard pressure; the temperature of food is limited by the boiling point of water because excess heat causes boiling water to vaporize into steam. In a sealed pressure cooker, the boiling point of water increases as the pressure rises, resulting in superheated water. At a pressure of 15 psi (pounds per square inch) above the existing atmospheric pressure, water in a pressure cooker can reach a temperature of up to 121 °C (250 °F), depending on altitude.

Pressure is created initially by boiling a liquid such as water or broth inside the closed pressure cooker. The trapped steam increases the internal pressure and temperature. After use, the pressure is slowly released so that the vessel can be safely opened.

Pressure cooking can be used to quickly simulate the effects of long braising or simmering.

Almost any food which can be cooked in steam or water-based liquids can be cooked in a pressure cooker.

## HISTORY

**Fig.** A pressure cooker manufactured by Georg Gutbrod, Stuttgart, in about 1864

In 1679, French physicist Denis Papin, better known for his studies on steam, invented the *steam digester* in an attempt to reduce the cooking time of food. His airtight cooker used steam pressure to raise the water's boiling point, thus resulting in a much quicker cooking. In 1681, Papin presented his invention to the Royal Society of London, but his invention was treated as a scientific study. They granted him permission to become a member of the society afterwards.

In 1864, Georg Gutbrod of Stuttgart began manufacturing pressure cookers made of tinned cast iron.

In 1919, Spain granted a patent for the pressure cooker to Jose Alix Martínez from Zaragoza. Martínez named it the *olla exprés* (literally "express cooking pot") under patent number 71143 in the *Boletín Oficial de la Propiedad Industrial*.

In 1938, Alfred Vischler presented his invention, the *Flex-Seal Speed Cooker*, in New York City. Vischler's pressure cooker was the first one designed for home use, and its success led to competition among American and European manufacturers. At the 1939 New York World's Fair, National Presto Industries, known as the "National Pressure Cooker Company" at the time, introduced its own pressure cooker.

## VARIANTS

Large pressure cookers are often called *pressure canners* in the United States because of their capacity to hold jars used in canning. Pressure canners are specifically designed for home canning, whereas ordinary pressure cookers are not recommended for canning due to the risk of botulism poisoning, because pressure canners hold heat and pressure for much longer than ordinary pressure cookers and these factors are a critical part of the total processing time required to destroy harmful microorganisms. An *autoclave* is a type of pressure cooker used by laboratories and hospitals to sterilize equipment. *Pressure fryers* are used for deep fat frying under pressure — note that ordinary pressure cookers are not suitable for pressure frying. In the food industry, pressure cookers are often referred to as *retorts* or *canning retorts*.

## DESIGN

### Parts

Portable pressure cookers consist of all or most of these basic component parts, depending on the manufacturer and model of pressure cooker:

Pan:

- Metal pan body
- Pan handles, usually one each on opposite ends, for carrying the cooker with both hands

Lid:

- Lid handle, usually with a locking device button or slider which "clicks" shut
- Gasket (also known as a "sealing ring") which seals the cooker airtight
- Steam vent with a pressure regulator on top (either a weight or spring device) which maintains the pressure level in the pan
- Pressure indicator pin, for showing the presence or absence of any pressure, however slight
- Safety devices on the lid

Accessories

- Steamer basket
- Trivet for keeping the steamer basket above liquid
- Metal divider, for separating different foods in the steamer basket e.g. vegetables

Pressure cookers are typically made of aluminum (aluminium) or stainless steel. Aluminum pressure cookers may be stamped, polished, or anodized, but are unsuitable for the dishwasher. They are cheaper, but the aluminium is reactive to acidic foods (changes the flavour) and less durable than stainless steel pressure cookers.

Higher-quality stainless steel pressure cookers are made with heavy, three-layer, or copper-clad bottoms (heat spreader) for uniform heating because stainless steel has lower thermal conductivity. Most modern stainless steel cookers are dishwasher safe, although some manufacturers may recommend washing by hand. Some pressure cookers have a non-stick interior.

A gasket or sealing ring, made from either rubber or silicone, forms a gas-tight seal that does not allow air or steam to escape between the lid and pan. Normally, the only way steam can escape is through a regulator on the lid while the cooker is pressurized. If the regulator becomes blocked, a safety valveprovides a backup escape route for steam.

To seal the gasket, some pressure cookers have a lid lock with flanges, similar to a bayonet-style lens mount, that works by placing the lid on the pot and twisting it about 30° to lock it in place.

Other cookers, particularly the larger types used for home canning, have over-sized oval lids. With such cookers, one inserts the lid at an angle, then turns the lid to align it with the pot opening on top because the lid is larger than the opening.

A spring arrangement straddles the top of the cooker and holds the lid in place. While cooking, the internal pressurized steam keeps the lid tightly in place, preventing accidental removal.

Because of the forces that pressure cookers must withstand, they are usually heavier than conventional pots of similar size.

## GENERATIONS

There are three generations of pressure cookers:

### First generation

**Fig.** Super cocotte décor SEB, 1973. Aluminium body, polyamide lacquered with an embossed aluminium lid and a stainless steel stirrup. On display at the Musée gallo-romain de Fourvière, Lyon. 18/10.

Also known as "old type" pressure cookers, these operate with a weight-modified or "jiggly" valve, which releases pressure during operation. Some people might consider them loud or very loud because the weight-modified valve operates similarly to the piston in a steam engine.

They typically offer only one pressure level—with the exception of some newer "old style" pressure cookers that allow the operator to change the weight of the weight-modified valve.

Even today, many of the less expensive modern pressure cookers (such as those manufactured and marketed by Presto) are basically variants on the First Generation cookers, albeit with new safety features, such as a mechanism which prevents the cooker from being opened by any means once it comes to pressure, until it is entirely de-pressurized.

### Second Generation

Also known as "new" or "latest generation" pressure cookers, these operate with a spring-loaded valve that is often hidden from view in a proprietary mechanism. This generation is characterized by two or more pressure settings.

Some of these pressure cookers do not release any steam during operation (non-venting) and instead use a rising indicator with markings to show the pressure level. These only release steam when the pan is opened, or as a safety precaution if the heat source is not reduced enough when the pan reaches the required cooking pressure.

Others use a dial that the operator can advance by a few clicks (which adjusts a spring underneath) to change the pressure setting or release pressure; these release steam during operation (venting).

### Electric Pressure Cookers

Electric pressure cookers are called "third generation" pressure cookers by their manufacturers. These include an electric heat source that is automatically regulated to maintain the operating pressure. They also include a spring-loaded valve (as described above). Two or more pressure settings are available on this type of pressure cooker, along with features such as a timer and a setting to keep food warm. However, this pressure cooker type cannot be opened with a cold water quick-release method and should be operated with caution when releasing vapour through the valve, especially while cooking foamy foods and liquids (lentils, beans, grains, milk, gravy, etc.).

## PRESSURE SETTINGS

Most pressure cookers have a cooking (operating) pressure setting of 13 - 15 psi. The 15 psi standard cooking pressure was determined by the United States Department of Agriculture in 1917. At this pressure, water boils at 121 °C (250 °F) (described in vapour pressure of water article). In other countries (e.g. those in Europe), different pressure units are used, hence 15 psi is rounded to 1 bar, 100 kPa or 1 kg/cm.

The higher temperature causes food to cook faster; cooking times can typically be reduced to one-third of the time for conventional cooking methods.The actual cooking time also depends on the pressure release method used after timing and the thickness and density of the food, since thicker (and denser) foods take longer to cook. Meat joints and some other foods like sponge puddings and Christmas puddings are typically timed according to their weight. Frozen foods need extra cooking time to allow for thawing.

When pressure cooking at 15 psi, approximate cooking times are one minute for shredded cabbage, ten minutes for potatoes cut into one-inch pieces (steamed or boiled) and three minutes for fresh green beans. If the pressure is released naturally after timing, cooking times are even shorter. Food cooks more quickly when cut into smaller pieces.

Some recipes may require cooking at lower than 15 psi; many pressure cookers have 2 or more selectable pressure settings or weights.

### Non-standard Pressure Settings

Some pressure cookers have a lower *maximum* pressure than the industry standard 15 psi or can be adjusted to different pressures for some recipes; cooking times will increase or decrease accordingly. This is typically done by having different regulator weights or different pressure settings. If the recipe is devised for 15 psi and the pressure cooker does not reach 15 psi, the cooking time will need increasing slightly to compensate. Electric pressure cookers operate below 15 psi.

## OPERATION

### Liquid

Pressure cooking always requires liquid. Pressure cooking cannot be used for cooking methods that produce little steam such as roasting, pan frying, ordeep frying. However, Kentucky Fried Chicken restaurants use a combination of pressure cooking and frying, with special pressure fryers in which chicken juices supply the water. Cooking time is reduced substantially, but the breading texture is much softer (less crispy) than deep-fried chicken since moisture remains in the breading. Thick sauces do not contain enough liquid to vaporize and create pressure, so they usually burn onto the interior base of the pressure cooker after prolonged heating. Sauces should normally be thickened after pressure cooking.

### Bringing to Pressure (Stove top Pressure Cookers)

Food is placed inside the pressure cooker with a small amount of water or other liquid (e.g., stock). Food is either cooked in the liquid or above the liquid to be steamed; the latter method prevents the transfer of flavours from the liquid.

The lid is closed, the pressure setting is chosen and the pressure cooker is placed on a stove on the highest heat. For pressure cookers with a weight, the weight is placed over the steam vent pipe while steam is being emitted, to ensure the air inside has escaped. Once the cooker reaches full pressure, the heat is lowered to maintain pressure; timing the recipe begins at this point.

It takes several minutes for the pressure cooker to reach the selected pressure level. It can take as long as 10 minutes depending on: the quantity of food, the temperature of the food (cold or frozen food delays pressurisation), the amount of liquid, the power of the heat source and the size of the pressure cooker. Using boiled water from a kettle quickens the heating process.

The newer generation pressure cookers, which have no weights, expel air from inside before reaching full pressure. A common mistake is for the user to start timing when a coloured pop-up indicator rises, which happens when there is the slightest increase in pressure, instead of waiting for the cooker to reach its selected pressure level.

The typical pop-up indicator only shows that the cooker has pressure inside, which does not reliably signal that the cooker has reached the selected pressure. This pop-up indicator often acts as an interlock, preventing the lid from being opened while there is internal pressure. Manufacturers may use their own terminology for it, such as calling it a *locking indicator*.

As the internal temperature rises, the pressure also rises until it reaches the design gauge pressure. With first generation designs, the pressure regulator weight begins levitating above its nozzle, allowing excess steam to escape. In second generation pressure cookers, either a relief valve subsequently opens, releasing steam to prevent the pressure from rising any further or a rod rises with markers to indicate the pressure level, without venting steam. At this stage, the heat source should be reduced because heat is only needed to maintain pressure. As a rough guide, medium heat is the highest setting required on any domestic stove to maintain the pressure level throughout cooking time.

Recipes for foods using raising agents (e.g., steamed puddings) call for gentle pre-steaming, without pressure, in order to activate the raising agents prior to cooking and achieve a light, fluffy texture.

## Food Containers

Small containers such as plastic pudding containers, can be used in a pressure cooker, provided that the containers (and any covering used) can withstand temperatures of 130 °C (266 °F) and are not placed directly on the interior base. The containers can be used for cooking foods that are prone to burning on the base of the pressure cooker. A lid for the container may be used, provided that the lid allows some steam to come into contact with the food and the lid is securely fitted (e.g., foil or greaseproof paper, pleated in the centre and tied securely with string).

Cracked containers are not suitable. Cooking time is longer when using covered containers because the food is not in direct contact with the steam. Since non-metal containers are poorerheat conductors, the type of container material stated in the recipe cannot be substituted without affecting the outcome.

For example, if the recipe time is calculated using a stainless steel container and a plastic container is used instead, the food at the bottom of the container may be under-cooked, unless the cooking time is increased. Containers with thicker sides, e.g., oven-proof glass or ceramic containers, which are slower to conduct heat, will add about 10 minutes to the cooking time. Liquid can be added inside the container when pressure cooking foods such as rice, which need to absorb liquid in order to cook properly.

## Pre-frying Ingredients

The flavour of some foods, such as meat and onions, can be improved by gently cooking with a little pre-heated cooking oil, butter or other fat in the open pressure cooker over medium heat (unless the manufacturer advises against this) before pressure cooking. It is important not to overheat the empty pressure cooker and never heat the empty cooker with the lid and gasket in place. Overheating can cause warping and other damage. The pressure cooker needs to cool briefly before adding liquid; otherwise some of the liquid will evaporate instantly, possibly leaving insufficient liquid for the entire pressure cooking time; if deglazing the pan, this has to be taken into account.

## PRESSURE RELEASE METHODS

After cooking, there are three ways of releasing the pressure, either quickly or slowly, before the lid can be opened. Recipes for pressure cookers state which release method is required at the end of the cooking time for proper results. Failure to follow the recommendation may result in food that is under-cooked or over-cooked. Only one of these release methods is used after timing, as recommended in the recipe.

To avoid opening the pressure cooker too often while cooking different vegetables with varying cooking times, the vegetables that take longer to cook can be cut into smaller pieces and vegetables that cook faster can be cut into thicker pieces.

### Cold Water Quick Release

This method is the fastest way of releasing pressure with portable pressure cookers; it is recommended to read the manufacturer's instruction book, as some may advise against the cold water release or require it to be performed differently.

The cold water release method involves using slow running cold tap water, over the edge of the pressure cooker lid, being careful to avoid the steam vent or any other valves or outlets and never immersing the pressure cooker under water. It is most suitable for foods with short cooking times. It takes about 20 seconds for the cooker to cool down enough to lower the pressure so that it can be safely opened. This method is not suitable for electric pressure cookers.

### Manual, Normal, Eegular, or Automatic Release

This method is sometimes called a *quick release,* not to be confused with the cold water release. It involves the quick release of vapor by lifting (or removing) the valve, pushing a button, or turning a dial. It is most suitable to interrupt cooking to add food that cooks faster than what is already in the cooker. For example, since meat takes longer to cook than vegetables, it is necessary to add vegetables to stew later so that it will cook only for the last few minutes. Unlike the cold water release method, this release method does not cool down the pressure cooker. The user must release the steam with caution to avoid scalding injury. This release method is not suitable for foods that foam and froth while cooking; the hot contents might spray outwards due to the pressure released from the steam vent. This release method takes about two minutes to release the pressure before the lid can be opened.

### Natural Release

The natural release method allows the pressure to drop slowly; this is achieved by removing the pressure cooker from the heat source and allowing the pressure to lower without action. It takes approximately 10 to 15 minutes (possibly longer) for the pressure to disappear before the lid can be opened. On many pressure cookers, a coloured indicator pin will drop when the pressure has gone.

This natural release method is recommended for foods that foam and froth during cooking, such as rice, legumes, or recipes with raising agents such as steamed puddings. The texture and tenderness of meat cooked in a pressure cooker can be improved by using the natural release method. The natural release method finishes cooking foods or recipes that have longer cooking times because the inside of the pressure cooker stays hot. This method is not recommended for foods that require very short cooking times, otherwise the food overcooks.

## ADVANTAGES

Foods cook much faster with pressure cooking than with other methods (except for small quantities in microwave ovens). Pressure cooking requires much less water than conventional boiling, so food can be ready sooner. Less energy is required than that of boiling, steaming, or oven cooking. Since less water or liquid has to be heated, the food reaches its cooking temperature faster. Using more liquid than necessary wastes energy because it takes longer to heat up; the liquid quantity is stated in the recipe. Pressure cookers can use much less liquid than the amount required for boiling or steaming in an ordinary saucepan. It is not necessary to immerse food in water. The minimum quantity of water or liquid used in the recipe to keep the pressure cooker filled with steam is sufficient. Because of this, vitamins and minerals are not leached (dissolved) away by water, as they would be if food were boiled in large amounts of water. Due to the shorter cooking time, vitamins are preserved relatively well during pressure cooking.

Several foods can be cooked together in the pressure cooker, either for the same amount of time or added later for different times. Manufacturers provide steamer baskets to allow more foods to be cooked together inside the pressure cooker.

Food is cooked at a temperature above the normal boiling point of water, killing most micro-organisms. A pressure cooker can be used as an effective sterilizer for jam pots, glass baby bottles, or for water while camping.

The pressure cooker speeds cooking considerably at high altitudes, where the lower atmospheric pressure reduces the boiling point of water. Lower water temperature reduces water's effectiveness for cooking or preparing hot drinks. The increased temperatures due to pressure cooking are also used to promote the Maillard reaction to develop more desirable flavor profiles that would not be obtainable using temperatures typical of boiling. The flavours are more concentrated in the higher temperature and sealed environment of the pressure cooker, so less seasoning is required.

## DISADVANTAGES

Pressure cookers are considerably more expensive than conventional saucepans of the same size. The additional gasket (sealing ring) requires special care when cleaning (e.g., not washed with kitchen knives), unlike a standard lid for a saucepan. Food debris must be cleaned from the gasket after every use.

The gasket/sealing ring needs replacing with a new one about once a year (or sooner if it's damaged e.g. a small split). A very dry gasket can make it difficult or impossible to close the lid. Smearing the gasket sparingly with vegetable oil alleviates this problem (using too much vegetable oil can make the gasket swell and prevent it sealing properly).

In order to inspect the food, the pressure cooker needs to be opened, which halts the cooking process. With a conventional saucepan, this can be done in a matter of seconds by visually inspecting the food. As a result, accurate timing is essential for the recipe e.g. with an audible timer.

The increased weight of conventional pressure cookers makes them unsuitable for applications in which saving weight is a priority, such as camping. However, small, lightweight pressure cookers are available for mountain climbers.

A minimum quantity of liquid is required to create and maintain pressure, as indicated in the manufacturer's instruction manual. More liquid is required for longer cooking times. This is not desirable for food requiring much less liquid, but recipes and books for pressure cookers take this into account.

## SAFETY FEATURES

Early pressure cookers equipped with only a primary safety valve risked explosion from food blocking the release valve. On modern pressure cookers, food residues blocking the steam vent or the liquid boiling dry will trigger additional safety devices. Modern pressure cookers sold from reputable manufacturers have sufficient safety features to prevent the pressure cooker itself from exploding. When excess pressure is released by a safety mechanism, debris of food being cooked may also be ejected with the steam — which is loud and forceful.

This can be avoided if the pressure cooker is regularly cleaned and maintained in accordance with the manufacturer's instructions and never overfilled with food and/or liquid: a pressure cooker should never be filled more two-thirds full with solid food, half full for liquids and foods that foam and froth (e.g., rice, pasta), and no more than one-third full forpulses (e.g., lentils). Adding a tablespoon of cooking oil minimises foaming.

Modern pressure cookers typically have two or three redundant safety valves and additional safety features, such as an interlock lid that prevents the user from opening the lid when the internal pressure exceeds atmospheric pressure, preventing accidents from a sudden release of hot liquid, steam and food. If safety mechanisms are not correctly in place, the cooker will not pressurize the contents. Pressure cookers should be operated only after reading the instruction manual, to ensure correct usage.

For first generation pressure cookers with a weighted valve or "jiggler", the primary safety valve or regulator is usually a weighted stopper, commonly called "the rocker" or "vent weight".

This weighted stopper is lifted by the steam pressure, allowing excess pressure to be released. There is a backup pressure release mechanism that releases pressure quickly if the primary pressure release mechanism fails (e.g., food jams the steam discharge path).

One such method is a hole in the lid that is blocked by a low melting point alloy plug and another is a rubber grommet with a metal insert at the center. At a sufficiently high pressure, the grommet will distort and the insert will blow out of its mounting hole to release pressure.

If the pressure continues to increase, the grommet itself will blow out to release pressure. These safety devices usually require replacement when activated by excess pressure. Newer pressure cookers may have a self-resettable spring device, fixed onto the lid, that releases excess pressure.

On second generation pressure cookers, a common safety feature is the gasket, which expands to release excess pressure downward between the lid and the pot. This release of excess pressure is forceful and sufficient to extinguish the flame of a gas stove.

Pressure cookers sold in the European Union (EU) must comply with the Pressure Equipment Directive.Pressure cookers sold in the European Union (EU) must comply with the Pressure Equipment Directive.

## USE AT HIGH ALTITUDES

A pressure cooker can be used to compensate for lower atmospheric pressure at high elevations. The boiling point of water drops by approximately 1 °C per every 294 metres of altitude (1 °F per every 540 feet (160 m) of altitude), causing the boiling point of water to be significantly below the 100 °C (212 °F) at standard pressure. Without the use of a pressure cooker, boiled foods may be undercooked, as described in Charles Darwin's *The Voyage of the Beagle*:

- Having crossed the Peuquenes [Piuquenes], we descended into a mountainous country, intermediate between the two main ranges, and then took up our quarters for the night. We were now in the republic of Mendoza. The elevation was probably not under 11,000 feet (3,400 m) [...]. At the place where we slept water necessarily boiled, from the diminished pressure of the atmosphere, at a lower temperature than it does in a less lofty country; the case being the converse of that of a Papin's digester. Hence the potatoes, after remaining for some hours in the boiling water, were nearly as hard as ever. The pot was left on the fire all night, and next morning it was boiled again, but yet the potatoes were not cooked.

At higher altitudes, the boiling point of liquid in the pressure cooker will be slightly lower than it would be at sea level. When pressure cooking at high altitudes, cooking times need to be increased by approximately 5% for every 980 feet (300 m) above 2,000 feet (610 m) elevation.

The absolute pressurein a pressure cooker will always be lower at higher altitudes, since the pressure cooker can only add the same amount of internal pressure over existing atmospheric pressure at any altitude. The lower atmospheric pressure at high altitudes results in less absolute pressure inside a pressure cooker, compared to higher atmospheric pressure at lower altitudes.

Lightweight pressure cookers as small as 1.5 litres (0.40 US gal) weighing 1.28 kilograms (2.8 lb) are available for mountain climbers. Sherpas often use pressure cookers in base camp.

## SCIENCE OF PRESSURE COOKING

The boiling temperature of water (and water-based liquids) is determined by the ambient atmospheric pressure. Pressure cookers always require liquid in order to cook food under pressure. At sea level, the boiling temperature of water is 100 °C (212 °F) and excess heat only increases the rate at which water evaporates into steam vapour; more heat does not increase the temperature of the water. At higher altitudes above sea level, the atmospheric pressure is lower and thus the boiling temperature of water is lower, because the lower atmospheric pressure pushing on the water makes it easier for the water molecules to escape to the surface compared to higher atmospheric pressure.

Inside a pressure cooker, once the water (liquid) is boiling and the steam is trapped, the pressure from the trapped steam increases and this pushes on the liquid, which increases its boiling temperature, because it becomes harder for the water molecules to escape from the surface as the pressure increases on it. The heat applied to the liquid by the heat source continues to create more steam pressure and the extra heat also raises the temperature of the liquid under this increased pressure.

Both the liquid and steam are at the same temperature. Once the selected pressure level is reached, the pressure regulator on the lid indicates this and now the heat source can be lowered to maintain that pressure level and save energy, since extra heat will not increase the temperature of the liquid if the pressure is not allowed to rise — excess pressure will only escape as fast-flowing steam from the lid.

Steam and liquids transfer heat more rapidly than dry air. As an example, the hot *air* inside an oven at, say 200 °C (392 °F), won't immediately burn your skin, but the wet steam from a boiling kettle at 100 °C (212 °F) will scald your skin almost instantly and 'feel' hotter, despite the steam (and water) in the kettle being at a lower temperature than the air inside a hot oven. Since steam and liquids heat substances faster, the pressure cooker can cook food quicker — under pressure—compared to ordinary cooking methods.

## USE IN FOOD DETOXIFICATION

Some food toxins can be reduced by pressure cooking. A Korean study of aflatoxins in rice (associated with *Aspergillus* fungus) showed that pressure cooking was capable of reducing aflatoxin concentrations to 12–22% of the amount in the uncooked rice. Pressure cookers are *not* guaranteed to destroy all harmful microorganisms in food, especially when used for short periods of time.

## FOODS UNSUITABLE FOR PRESSURE COOKING

Some foods are not recommended for pressure cooking. Foods such as macaroni, cranberries, cereals and oatmeal could expand too much, froth, and sputter, which can block the steam vent.

# RAMEKIN

**Fig.** Two styles of ramekin

**Fig.** Another ramekin, with a plain exterior

A ramekin /ræmjkjn/ or ramequin, also known as a bouillon bowl, is a small glazed ceramic or glass serving bowl used for the preparation and serving of various food dishes. The word is from America (as *ramequin*), and before that Middle Dutch and Middle Low German – see *ramekin* for details.

## DETAILS

With a typical volume of 50–250 ml (1.8–8.8 imp fl oz; 1.7–8.5 US fl oz), ramekins are commonly used for serving a variety of dishes such as *crème brûlée,* French onion soup, molten chocolate cake, *moin moin,* cheese or egg dishes, *poi,* potted shrimps, ice cream, *soufflé,* baked *cocottes,* crumbles, or scallops, or used to serve side garnishes and condiments alongside an entrée. They also can be used for appetizers such as mixed olives.

Traditionally circular with a fluted exterior, ramekins can also be found in novelty shapes, such as flowers, hearts or stars.

Ramekins are often built to withstand high temperatures, as they are frequently used in ovens, or in the case of *crème brûlée,* exposed to the flame of a cooking torch.

# ROASTING PAN

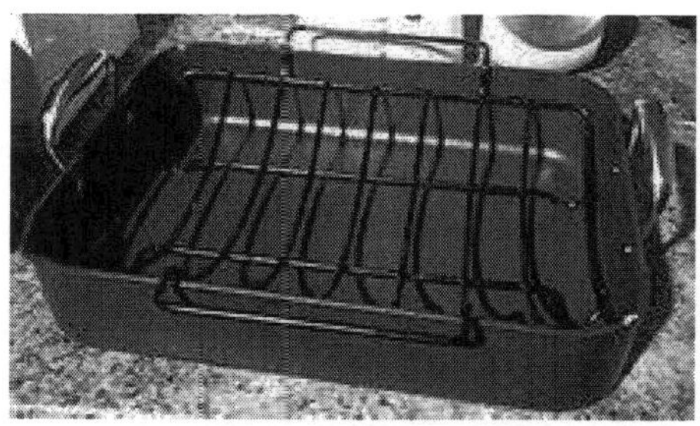

**Fig.** A large roasting pan with a removable rack and a non-stick surface coating.

A roasting pan is a piece of cookware used for roasting meat in an oven, either with or without vegetables or other ingredients. A roasting pan may be used with a rack that sits inside the pan and lets the meat sit above the fat and juice drippings.

A shallow roasting pan is normally used for roasting small cuts of meat, but large-size roasting pans are also used for cooking large poultry such as turkey or goose, or for larger cuts of meat. A deep roasting pan can hold vegetables and other ingredients that meat can sit on rather than a rack, letting the vegetables absorb the fat and juice from the meat while cooking. A deep roasting pan can also be used as a baking dish or basin, holding smaller baking dishes that must be surrounded by boiling water.

## ROASTING PAN MATERIALS

Roasting pans are made in several materials that offer their own unique benefits:

- Aluminum foil: inexpensive and disposable after one use
- Stainless steel: may have a non-stick coating
- Coated enamelware: has a non-stick surface

- Cast iron: cast-iron cookware conducts heat well and can be used to brown meat on the stovetop before placing into the oven for roasting
- Clay cooker: a covered clay pot can brown food if the temperature of the oven is raised toward the end of cooking

## COVERED OR UNCOVERED ROASTING PANS

Covering or uncovering a roasting pan will depend upon the type of meat being roasted, or the recipe being followed. Generally, meat that is high in fat content, such as duck, has no need of being covered during roasting. A lean cut of meat, however, will benefit from being covered during a long roasting time, to retain juices and soften the meat (for example, in using a tajine for roasting meat).

## ROASTING RACKS

A roasting rack may be an accessory part of the roasting pan. A rack may be horizontal and lay flat on the roasting pan, or it may be a standing rack that sits vertically in the pan. A standing rack is most commonly used for roasting poultry. A variation of the roasting pan standing rack is the beer can chickenrecipe.

## SPRINGFORM PAN

**Fig.** Close-up of spring

**Fig.** Base and wall belt

**Fig.** Pan with finished cheesecake

**Fig.** Springform pan used to make a Deep-dish pizza crust

A springform pan is a type of bakeware that features sides that can be removed from the base. Springform refers to the construction style of this pan. The base and the sides are separate pieces that are held together when the base is aligned with a groove that rings the bottom of the walls. The pan is then secured by a latch on the exterior of the wall. This tightens the 'belt' that becomes the walls of the pan and secures the base into the groove at the base of the walls.

## DESIGN

The springform pan has a long history. The most common springform pan is the nine-inch round. However, small circular pans are common along with squares, rectangles, and hearts. They come in a variety of materials including anodized aluminum, heavy-gauge steel, and glass. Optional features include a non-stick surface and a waterproof seal around the base.

This pan is used to bake dishes that cannot be easily inverted for removal from the pan. Some of the most common recipes to call for springform pans are cheesecakes and tortes. The easy removal of the sides from a springform pan lends itself to dishes with delicate bottom layers such as the graham cracker crumb crusts commonly constructed for cheesecakes. Springform pans, however, are also used in the preparation ofpizzas, quiches, and frozen desserts.

Although most cheesecakes are baked in a water bath, this does not mean that springform pans are waterproof around the base. Many may be waterproof initially. However, as the latch loosens and the coating wears off this waterproof feature will fade. For this reason many will wrap the pan in aluminum foil.

There are many types and finishes of springform pans. While the most common bottom is smooth, bottoms can also be waffled or glass.

## STOCK POT

**Fig.** A stainless steel stockpot.

Stock pot is a generic name for one of the most common types of cooking pot used worldwide. A stock pot is traditionally used to make stock (cooking) or broth, which can be the basis for cooking more complex recipes. It is a wide pot with a flat bottom, straight sides, a wide opening to the full diameter of the pot, two handles on the sides, and a lid with a handle on top.

French Chef Auguste Escoffier (1846-1935) published "A Guide to Modern Cookery" in 1907. On the first page, Escoffier writes, "stocks are the keynote of culinary structure" in French cuisine. A stock or broth is made by simmering water for several hours, to continuously cook added foods such as pieces of meat, meat bones, fish or vegetables. The slow simmering process transfers flavours, colours and nutrients to the water, where they blend, and a new ingredient is thus created, the broth or stock.

A broth made with meat or meat bones creates a base with concentrated flavours and aromas, even without the addition of salt or herbs or spices. This is what is referred to as soup base. Stock pots are also used for cooking stews, porridge, boiled foods, steamed shellfish, and a vast variety of recipes.

Stock pots have great versatility, and so they are used for many cooking purposes, and occasionally non-cooking purposes. Large stock pots may be used at home to boil clothing, wool or yarn for colour dying, for example. They do not come in standard sizes. The size of the pot is normally given on the manufacturer's label by volume, for example 12 litres.

The most common materials for manufacturing stock pots are stainless steel, aluminium, copper and enamel (Vitreous enamel) on metal. More expensive types of stock pots have bottoms that are made of layers of different metals, to enhance heat conductivity.

A recent innovation sculpts the pot sides to harness the boiling liquid into a self-stirring pot

## TAJINE

A tajine or tagine is a historically Berber dish from North Africa that is named after the type of earthenware pot in which it is cooked. A similar dish, known as tavvas, is found in the cuisine of Cyprus. The traditional method of cooking with a tagine is to place the tagine over coals.

### THE TAJINE POT

**Fig.** Ceramic tajines.

The traditional tajine pot is formed entirely of a naturalclay, which is sometimes painted or glazed. It consists of two parts: a base unit that is flat and circular with low sides and a large cone- or dome-shaped cover that sits on the base during cooking. The cover is designed to promote the return of all condensation to the bottom.

Tajines can also be cooked in a conventional oven or on a stove top. Tajine is traditionally cooked over hot charcoal leaving an adequate space between the coals and the tajine to avoid having the temperature rise too fast. Large bricks of charcoal are purchased specifically for their ability to stay hot for hours. Smaller pieces of charcoal are reserved for cooking brochettes (barbecue)and other grilled meats.

Other methods are to use a tajine in a slow oven or on a gas or electric stove top, on lowest heat necessary to keep the stew simmering gently. A diffuser – a circular piece of aluminum placed between the tagine and burner – is used to evenly distribute the stove's heat. European manufacturers have created tajines with heavy cast-iron bottoms that can be heated on a cooking stove to a high temperature. This permits the browning of meat and vegetables before cooking. Tajine cooking may be replicated by using a slow cooker or similar item; but the result will be slightly different. Many ceramic tajines are exquisite examples of show pieces as well as functional cooking vessels. Some tajines, however, are intended only to be used as decorative serving dishes.

**Fig.** Electrical tajine

## MOROCCAN TAJINES OR STEWS

Moroccan tajine dishes are slow-cooked savory stews, typically made with sliced meat, poultry, or fish together with vegetables or fruit. Spices, nuts, and dried fruits are also used. Common spices include ginger, cumin, turmeric, cinnamon, and saffron. Paprika and chili are used in vegetable tajine.

The sweet and sour combination is common in tajine dishes like lamb with dates and spices. Tajines are served with couscous or bread. Because the domed or cone-shaped lid of the tajine pot traps steam and returns the condensed liquid to the pot, a minimal amount of water is needed to cook meats and vegetables. This method of cooking is very practical in areas where water supplies are limited or where public water is not yet available.

**Fig.** Calf, prunes and almonds

**Fig.** Lamb with plum and eggs

**Fig.** Tajine with olives and vegetables

**Fig.** Tajine

**Fig.** Tajine with almonds

**Fig.** Tajine with carrots

**Fig.** Tajine with lamb and mango

**Fig.** Tajine with chicken

## TUNISIAN TAJINE

**Fig.** Tunisian tajine

What Tunisians refer to as a "tajine" is very different from the Moroccan dish. Tunisian tajine is more like an Italian frittata. First, a simple ragout is prepared, of meat cut into very small pieces, cooked with onions and spices, such as a blend of dried rosebuds and ground cinnamon known as *baharat* or a robust combination of ground coriander and caraway seeds; this is called tabil.

Then something starchy is added to thicken the juices. Common thickeners include cannellini beans, chickpeas,breadcrumbs or cubed potatoes. When the meat is tender, it is combined with whatever ingredient has been chosen to be the dominant flavoring. Examples include but are not limited to fresh parsley, driedmint, saffron, sun-dried tomatoes, cooked vegetables, or even stewed calves' brains. Next, the stew is enriched with cheese and eggs.

Finally, this egg and stew is baked in a deep pie dish, either on the stove or in the oven until top and bottom are crisply cooked and the eggs are just set. When the tajine is ready, it is turned out onto a plate and sliced into squares, accompanied by wedges of lemon. Tunisian tajines can be made with seafood or as a completely vegetarian dish.

In rural parts of Tunisia, home cooks place a shallow earthenware dish over glowing olive wood, fill it, cover it with a flat earthen pan, and then pile hot coals on top. The resulting tajine is crusty on top and bottom, moist within, and is infused with a subtle smoky fragrance.

## WOK

**Fig.** Stir frying with a wok

A wok (in Cantonese) is a versatile round-bottomed cooking vessel originating from Guangdong Province in China. It is one of the most common cooking utensils in China and also used in East and Southeast Asia, as well as becoming a popular niche cooking tool throughout much of the industrialized world.

Woks are often used in a range of different Chinese cooking techniques, including stir frying,steaming, pan frying, deep frying, poaching, boiling, braising, searing, stewing, making soup, smoking and roasting nuts. Wok cooking is done with a long handle called *chahn* (spatula) or *hoak* (ladle). The long handles of these utensils allow cooks to work with the food without burning their hands.

## REGIONAL VARIANTS OF THE WOK

Mandarin Chinese uses different words for wok, simplified Chinese: •; traditional Chinese: K"; literally "cooking pot" *guô* or simplified Chinese: 'pÜƒ•; traditional Chinese: 'pÜƒK" *chÎocàiguô*. In Indonesia the wok is known as a *penggorengan* or *wajan*. In Malaysia it is called a *kuali* (small wok) or *kawah*(big wok). In the Philippines it is known as a *kawali* and also called a "wadjang".

In Japan the wok is called a *chukanabe* (literally, "Chinese pot" or "-NïƒK""). In India, two varieties of the wok exist: a more traditional Chinese style wok with a wider diameter called the "cheena chatti" (literally, "Chinese pot" in Malayalam and Tamil), and a slightly deeper vessel with a narrower diameter and a similar shape, known as a karahi. Woks may have originated during Chinese military marches, when soldiers began to give their helmets a double role at camp.

## CHARACTERISTICS

**Fig.** A wok sits next to a karahi on aWestern-style stove. It is a cooking utensil (or vessel, if preferred). Note that the flatter-bottomed karahi (right) is sitting on an ordinary burner cover, while the round-bottomed wok is balanced on a wok-ring

The wok's most distinguishing feature is its shape. Classic woks have a rounded bottom. Hand-hammered woks are sometimes flipped inside out after being shaped, giving the wok a gentle flare to the edge that makes it easier to push food up onto the sides of the wok. Woks sold in western countries are sometimes found with flat bottoms—this makes them more similar to a deep frying pan. The flat bottom allows the wok to be used on an electric stove, where a rounded wok would not be able to fully contact the stove's heating element. A round bottom wok enables the traditional round spatula or ladle to pick all the food up at the bottom of the wok and toss it around easily; this is difficult with a flat bottom. With a gas hob, or traditional pit stove, the bottom of a round wok can get hotter than a flat wok and so is better for stir frying. Most woks range from 300 to 360 mm (12 to 14 in) or more in diameter.

Woks of 360 mm (14 in) (suitable for a family of 3 or 4) are the most common, but home woks can be found as small as 200 mm (8 in) and as large as 910 mm (36 in). Smaller woks are typically used for quick cooking techniques at high heat such asstir frying (Chinese: chÎo, 'p). Large woks over a meter wide are mainly used by restaurants or community kitchens for cooking rice or soup, or for boiling water.

## Materials

The most common materials used in making woks today are carbon steel and cast iron. Although the latter was the most common type used in the past, cooks tend to be divided on whether carbon steel or cast iron woks are superior.

## Carbon Steel

Currently, carbon steel is the most widely used material, being relatively inexpensive compared to those of other materials, relatively light in weight, providing quick heat conduction, and having reasonable durability. Their light weight makes them easier to lift and quicker to heat. However, carbon steel woks tend to be more difficult to season than those made of cast-iron ('seasoning', or carbonizing the cooking surface of a wok, is required to prevent foods from sticking, as well as removing metallic tastes and odors).

Carbon steel woks vary widely in price, style, and quality, which is based on ply andforming technique. The lowest quality steel woks tend to be stamped by machine from a single 'ply' or piece of stamped steel.

Less expensive woks have a higher tendency to deform and misshape. Cooking with lower quality woks is also more difficult and precarious since they often have a "hot spot". Higher quality, mass-produced woks are made of heavy gauge (14-gauge or thicker) steel, and are either machine-hammered or made of spun steel.The best quality woks are almost always hand-made, being pounded into shape by hand ("hand hammered") from two or more sheets of carbon steel which are shaped into final form by a ring-forming or hand-forging process.

## Cast-iron

Two types of cast-iron woks can be found in the market. Chinese-made cast-iron woks are very thin (3 mm (0.12 in)), weighing only a little more than a carbon steel wok of similar size, while cast-iron woks typically produced in the West tend to be much thicker (9 mm (0.35 in)), and very heavy. Because of the thickness of the cast-iron, Western-style cast-iron woks take much longer to bring up to cooking temperature, and its weight also makes stir-frying and *bao* techniques difficult.

Cast-iron woks form a more stable carbonized layer of seasoning which makes it less prone to food sticking on the pan. While cast-iron woks are superior to carbon steel woks in heat retention and uniform heat distribution, they respond slowly to heat adjustments and are slow to cool once taken off the fire. Because of this, food cooked in a cast-iron wok must be promptly removed from the wok as soon as it is done to prevent overcooking. Chinese-style cast-iron woks, although relatively light, are fragile and are prone to shattering if dropped or mishandled.

**Non-stick**

Steel woks coated with non-stick coatings such as PFA and Teflon, a development originated in Western countries, are now popular in Asia as well.These woks cannot be used with metal utensils, and foods cooked in non-stick woks tend to retain juices instead of browning in the pan. As they necessarily lack the carbonizing or seasoning of the classic steel or iron wok, non-stick woks do not impart the distinctive taste or sensation of "wok hei."The newest nonstick coatings will withstand temperatures of up to 260 °C (500 °F), sufficient for stir-frying.

Woks are also now being introduced withclad or five-layer construction, which sandwich a thick layer of aluminum or copper between two sheets of stainless steel. Clad woks can cost five to ten times the price of a traditional carbon steel or cast-iron wok, yet cook no better; for this reason they are not used in most professional restaurant kitchens. Clad woks are also slower to heat than traditional woks and not nearly as efficient for stir-frying.

**Aluminium**

Woks can also be made from aluminium. Although an excellent conductor of heat, it has somewhat inferior thermal capacity as cast iron or carbon steel, it loses heat to convection much faster than carbon steel, and it may be constructed much thinner than cast iron. Although anodized aluminium alloys can stand up to constant use, plain aluminium woks are too soft and damage easily. Aluminium is mostly used for wok lids.

**Handles**

The handles for woks come in two styles: loops and stick. Loop handles mounted on opposite sides of the wok are typical in southern China. The twin small loop handles are the most common handle type for woks of all types and materials, and are usually made of bare metal. Cooks needing to hold the wok to toss the food in cooking do so by holding a loop handle with a thick towel (though some woks have spool-shaped wooden or plastic covers over the metal of the handle). Cooking with the tossing action in loop-handled woks requires a large amount of hand, arm and wrist strength. Loop handles typically come in pairs on the wok and are riveted, welded or extended from the wok basin.

**Fig.** A stick-handled flat-bottomed peking pan. While the surface looks like Teflon, it is actually well-seasoned carbon steel

Stick handles are long, made of steel, and are usually welded or riveted to the wok basin, or are an actual direct extension of the metal of the basin. Stick handles are popular in northern China, where food in the wok is frequently turned with a tossing motion of the arm and wrist when stir-frying food.

The classic stick handle is made of hollow hammered steel, but other materials may be used, including wood or plastic-covered hand grips. Because of their popularity in northern China, stick-handled woks are often referred to as "pao woks" or "Peking pans" Stick handles are normally not found on cast iron woks since the wok is either too heavy for the handle or the metal is too thin to handle the tensile stress exerted by the handle. Larger-diameter woks with stick-type handles frequently incorporate a "helper" handle consisting of a loop on the opposite side of the wok, which aids in handling.

## COOKING

The wok can be used in a large number of cooking methods. Before the introduction of western cookware it was often used for all cooking techniques including:

- Boiling: For boiling water, soups, dumplings, or rice. In the latter case, guoba often forms.
- Braising: Braised dishes are commonly made using woks. Braising is useful when reducing sauces.
- Deep frying: This is usually accomplished with larger woks to reduce splashing, but for deep frying of less food or small food items, small woks are also used.
- Pan frying: Food that is fried using a small amount of oil in the bottom of a pan
- Roasting: Food may be cooked with dry heat in an enclosed pan with lid. Whole chestnuts are dry roasted by tossing them in a dry wok with several pounds of small stones.

- Searing: Food is browned on its outer surfaces through the application of high heat
- Smoking: Food can be hot smoked by putting the smoking material in the bottom of the wok while food is placed on a rack above.
- Steaming: Done using a dedicated wok for boiling water in combination with steaming baskets
- Stewing: Woks are sometimes used for stewing though it is more common in Chinese cuisine to use either stoneware or porcelain for such purposes, especially when longer stewing times are required. Small woks are for hot pot, particularly in Hainan cuisine. These are served at the table over asterno flame.
- Stir frying: Frying food quickly in a small amount of oil over high heat while stirring continuously.

**Wok Hei**

*Wok hei* is the flavour, tastes, and "essence" imparted by a hot wok on food during stir frying. It is particularly important for Chinese dishes requiring high heat for fragrance such as char kuay teow and beef chow fun. Out of the Eight Culinary Traditions of China, wok hei is encountered the most in Cantonese cuisine, whereas it may not even be an accepted underlying principal in some of the otherChinese cuisines.

To impart *wok hei* the traditional way, the food is cooked in a seasoned wok over a high flame while being stirred and tossed quickly. Constant contact with the heat source is crucial as the addition of new ingredients and each toss of the wok will inevitably cool the wok down, therefore cooking over flame is preferred.

Consequently, many chefs (especially those with less-than-ideal cookers) may cook in small batches to overcome this problem so that the wok is still as hot as it can be and to avoid "stewing" the food instead. When cooking over gas stoves or open flame, it additionally allows for the splattering of fine oil particles to catch the flame into the wok; this is easily achieved when experienced chefs toss the wok and can be a demonstration of experience. For these reasons it is preferable to cook over an open flame rather than other types of stove. It should also be noted that cooking with coated woks (e.g. non-stick) will not give the distinct taste of wok hei. The distinct taste of wok hei is partially imbued into the metal of the wok itself from former cooking sessions and brought out again when cooking over high heat. In practical terms, the flavour imparted by chemical compounds results from caramelization, Maillard reactions, and the partial combustion of oil that come from charring and searing of the food at very high heat in excess of 200 °C (392 °F).Aside from flavour, there is also the texture of the cooked items and smell involved that describes *wok hei*.

# WONDER POT

**Fig.** A Passover brownie cake baked in a Wonder Pot.

Wonder Pot (Hebrew: ñéø ôìà , *seer peh-leh*) is an Israeli invention for baking on top of a gas stove rather than in an oven. It consists of three parts: an aluminium pot shaped like a Bundt pan except smooth-sided rather than fluted, a hooded cover perforated with venting holes, and a thick, round, slightly domed metal disc with a center hole that is placed between the pot and the flame.

A Wonder Pot can be used to bake cakes, casseroles, rice, potatoes, apples, and even meat and chicken.

## HISTORY

**Fig.** A Wonder Pot (right) in use onPassover.

The Wonder Pot gained popularity during Israel's era of national austerity in the 1950s, when most citizens did not own an oven. The concept was based on models from Germany and Eastern Europe, and was first manufactured by the Palalum company (the company name was a contraction of the words *pele* (wonder) and*aluminium*). Later the Wonder Pot was manufactured by other companies in the Haredi sector, including the Matlum company, which continues to produce the item today.

The Wonder Pot retained its popularity through the 1970s, especially among new immigrants who did not have ovens. During its heyday, the Wonder Pot spawned its own bestselling cookbook. The introduction of themicrowave oven and a national desire to dissociate with the austerity mentality put an end to its widespread use. However, the Wonder Pot is still used by Israeli Haredi families for baking kugels, and it is also popular in this sector on the holiday of Passover for those who do not have a kosher-for-Passover oven.

Today the Wonder Pot is considered a nostalgic Israeli kitchen item. It is still sold in traditional housewaresstores, via marketing outlets, and in Haredi communities such as Bnei Brak and Jerusalem. In the late 2000s decade, a housewares store calling itself *Seer Peh-leh* ("Wonder Pot") opened in the Talpiotneighborhood of Jerusalem.

## HOW IT WORKS

**Fig.** Metal disc placed between the Wonder Pot and the flame

The Wonder Pot is effective at baking on top of the stove for three reasons: its aluminium material, its hole, and the metal disc separating it from the flame.

The aluminium material allows heat to spread uniformly. The center hole of the pot focuses the flame and creates heat dispersion around the inside of the cake. The metal disc lifts the pot off the fire, reducing and focusing the flame.

Baking in the Wonder Pot without the metal disc will produce a cake that is dry on the bottom and thick and wobbly in the center. The metal disc is sold in different thicknesses and diameters to accommodate different baking times and larger flames. The lid of the Wonder Pot is perforated with small holes to release steam. Baking time in a Wonder Pot varies from 40 to 50 minutes.

The Wonder Pot produces high and airy cakes. In addition to baking, the Wonder Pot is an effective medium for cooking vegetables, legumes, and rice in layers. It can also be used to cook kugels, casseroles, pasta dishes, meat, and chicken.

## CAULDRON

**Fig.** Hungarian goulash in a traditional *"bogrács"* (cauldron)

A cauldron (or caldron) is a large metal pot (kettle) for cooking and/or boiling over an open fire, with a large mouth and frequently with an arc-shaped hanger.

### ETYMOLOGY

The word cauldron is first recorded in Middle English as *caudroun* (13th century). It was borrowed from Old Northern French or Anglo-Norman *caudron* (Norman-Picard *caudron,* French *chaudron*). It represents the phonetical evolution of Vulgar Latin **caldario* for Classical Latin *caldârium* "hot bath", that derives from*cal(i)dus* "hot".

The Norman-French word replaces probably the initial Old English word *etel* (German *(Koch)Kessel*"cauldron", Dutch *(kook)ketel* "cauldron"), Middle English *chetel*. The word kettle comes from the Old Norse variant spelling *ketill* "cauldron".

### SYMBOLISM AND MYTHOLOGY

Cauldrons have largely fallen out of use in the developed world as cooking vessels. While still used for practical purposes, a more common association inWestern culture is the cauldron's use in witchcraft—a *cliché* popularized by various works of fiction, such as Shakespeare's play *Macbeth*. In fiction, witches often prepare their potions in a cauldron. Also, in Irish folklore, a cauldron is purported to be where leprechauns keep their gold and treasure.

In some forms of Wicca, incorporating aspects of Celtic mythology, the cauldron is associated with the goddess Cerridwen. Celtic legend also tells of cauldrons that were useful to warring armies: dead warriors could be put into a cauldron and then be returned to life, save that they lacked the power of speech. It was suspected that they lacked souls. These warriors could go back into battle until they were killed again. In Wicca and some other forms of neopagan or pagan belief systems the cauldron is still used in magical practices.

Most often a cauldron is made of cast iron and is used to burn loose incense on a charcoal disc, to make black salt (used in banishing rituals), for mixing herbs, or to burn petitions (paper with words of power or wishes written on them).

Cauldrons symbolize not only the Goddess but also represent the womb (due to the fact that it holds something) and on an altar it represents earth because it is a working tool. Cauldrons are often sold in New Age or "metaphysical" stores and may have various symbols of power inscribed on them.

**Fig.** A Bronze Age cauldron made from sheet bronze and a flesh-hook

The holy grail of Arthurian legend is sometimes referred to as a "cauldron", although traditionally the grail is thought of as a hand-held cup rather than the large pot that the word "cauldron" usually is used to mean. This may have resulted from the combination of the grail legend with earlier Celtic myths of magical cauldrons.

Archeologically intact actual cauldrons with apparent cultural symbolism include:

- The Gundestrup cauldron, made in the 2nd or 1st century BC, found at Gundestrup, Denmark
- A Bronze Age cauldron found at Hassle, Sweden
- The cauldron where the Olympic Flame burns for the duration of the Olympic Games

Cauldrons known only through myth and literature include:

- Dagda's Cauldron
- The Cauldron of Dyrnwch the Giant

# MICROWAVE

## MICROWAVE SOURCES

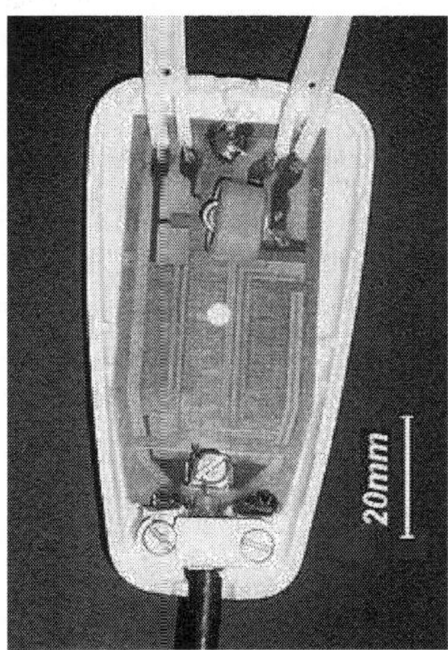


**Fig.** Stripline techniques become increasingly necessary at higher frequencies, as in this antenna splitter.

High-power microwave sources use specializedvacuum tubes to generate microwaves. These devices operate on different principles from low-frequency vacuum tubes, using the ballistic motion of electrons in a vacuum under the influence of controlling electric or magnetic fields, and include the magnetron (used in microwave ovens), klystron,traveling-wave tube (TWT), and gyrotron. These devices work in the density modulated mode, rather than thecurrent modulated mode. This means that they work on the basis of clumps of electrons flying ballistically through them, rather than using a continuous stream of electrons.

**Fig.** Cutaway view inside a cavity magnetron as used in a microwave oven

Low-power microwave sources use solid-state devices such as the field-effect transistor (at least at lower frequencies), tunnel diodes, Gunn diodes, and IMPATT diodes. Low-power sources are available as benchtop instruments, rackmount instruments, embeddable modules and in card-level formats. A maser is a solid state device which amplifies microwaves using similar principles to the laser, which amplifies higher frequency light waves.

All warm objects emit low level microwave black body radiation, depending on their temperature, so in meteorology and remote sensing microwave radiometers are used to measure the temperature of objects or terrain . The sun and other astronomical radio sources such as Cassiopeia A emit low level microwave radiation which carries information about their makeup, which is studied by radio astronomers using receivers called radio telescopes. The cosmic microwave background radiation (CMBR), for example, is a weak microwave noise filling empty space which is a major source of information on cosmology's Big Bangtheory of the origin of the Universe.

## USES

### Communication

Before the advent of fiber-optic transmission, most long-distance telephone calls were carried via networks ofmicrowave radio relay links run by carriers such as AT&T Long Lines. Starting in the early 1950s, frequency division multiplex was used to send up to 5,400 telephone channels on each microwave radio channel, with as many as ten radio channels combined into one antenna for the *hop* to the next site, up to 70 km away.

Wireless LAN protocols, such as Bluetooth and the IEEE 802.11 specifications, also use microwaves in the 2.4 GHz ISM band, although 802.11a uses ISM band and U-NII frequencies in the 5 GHz range. Licensed long-range (up to about 25 km) Wireless Internet Access services have been used for almost a decade in many countries in the 3.5–4.0 GHz range.

The FCC recently carved out spectrum for carriers that wish to offer services in this range in the U.S. — with emphasis on 3.65 GHz. Dozens of service providers across the country are securing or have already received licenses from the FCC to operate in this band. The WIMAX service offerings that can be carried on the 3.65 GHz band will give business customers another option for connectivity.

Metropolitan area network (MAN) protocols, such as WiMAX (Worldwide Interoperability for Microwave Access) are based on standards such as IEEE 802.16, designed to operate between 2 to 11 GHz. Commercial implementations are in the 2.3 GHz, 2.5 GHz, 3.5 GHz and 5.8 GHz ranges.

Mobile Broadband Wireless Access (MBWA) protocols based on standards specifications such as IEEE 802.20 or ATIS/ANSI HC-SDMA (such asiBurst) operate between 1.6 and 2.3 GHz to give mobility and in-building penetration characteristics similar to mobile phones but with vastly greater spectral efficiency.

Some mobile phone networks, like GSM, use the low-microwave/high-UHF frequencies around 1.8 and 1.9 GHz in the Americas and elsewhere, respectively. DVB-SH and S-DMB use 1.452 to 1.492 GHz, while proprietary/incompatible satellite radio in the U.S. uses around 2.3 GHz for DARS.

Microwave radio is used in broadcasting and telecommunication transmissions because, due to their short wavelength, highly directional antennas are smaller and therefore more practical than they would be at longer wavelengths (lower frequencies).

There is also more bandwidth in the microwave spectrum than in the rest of the radio spectrum; the usable bandwidth below 300 MHz is less than 300 MHz while many GHz can be used above 300 MHz. Typically, microwaves are used in television news to transmit a signal from a remote location to a television station from a specially equipped van. Seebroadcast auxiliary service (BAS), remote pickup unit (RPU), and studio/transmitter link (STL).

Most satellite communications systems operate in the C, X, $K_a$, or $K_u$ bands of the microwave spectrum. These frequencies allow large bandwidth while avoiding the crowded UHF frequencies and staying below the atmospheric absorption of EHF frequencies. Satellite TV either operates in the C band for the traditional large dish fixed satellite service or $K_u$ band for direct-broadcast satellite. Military communications run primarily over X or $K_u$-band links, with $K_a$ band being used for Milstar.

## Radar

Radar uses microwave radiation to detect the range, speed, and other characteristics of remote objects. Development of radar was accelerated during World War II due to its great military utility. Now radar is widely used for applications such as air traffic control, weather forecasting, navigation of ships, and speed limit enforcement.

A Gunn diode oscillator and waveguide are used as a motion detector for automatic door openers.

## Radio Astronomy

Most radio astronomy uses microwaves. Usually the naturally-occurring microwave radiation is observed, but active radar experiments have also been done with objects in the solar system, such as determining the distance to the Moon or mapping the invisible surface of Venus through cloud cover.

## Navigation

Global Navigation Satellite Systems (GNSS) including the Chinese Beidou, the American Global Positioning System(GPS) and the Russian GLONASS broadcast navigational signals in various bands between about 1.2 GHz and 1.6 GHz.

### Heating and Power Application

A microwave oven passes (non-ionizing) microwave radiation (at a frequency near 2.45 GHz) through food, causing dielectric heating primarily by absorption of the energy in water. Microwave ovens became common kitchen appliances in Western countries in the late 1970s, following development of inexpensive cavity magnetrons. Water in the liquid state possesses many molecular interactions that broaden the absorption peak. In the vapor phase, isolated water molecules absorb at around 22 GHz, almost ten times the frequency of the microwave oven.

Microwave heating is used in industrial processes for drying and curing products.

Many semiconductor processing techniques use microwaves to generate plasma for such purposes asreactive ion etching and plasma-enhanced chemical vapor deposition (PECVD).

Microwave frequencies typically ranging from 110 – 140 GHz are used in stellarators and more notably intokamak experimental fusion reactors to help heat the fuel into a plasma state. The upcoming ITERThermonuclear Reactor is expected to range from 110–170 GHz and will employ Electron Cyclotron Resonance Heating (ECRH).

Microwaves can be used to transmit power over long distances, and post-World War II research was done to examine possibilities. NASA worked in the 1970s and early 1980s to research the possibilities of using solar power satellite (SPS) systems with largesolar arrays that would beam power down to the Earth's surface via microwaves.

Less-than-lethal weaponry exists that uses millimeter waves to heat a thin layer of human skin to an intolerable temperature so as to make the targeted person move away. A two-second burst of the 95 GHz focused beam heats the skin to a temperature of 130 °F (54 °C) at a depth of 1/64th of an inch (0.4 mm). The United States Air Force and Marines are currently using this type of active denial system.

## MICROWAVE OVEN

A microwave oven, or a microwave, is a kitchen appliance that cooks or heats food by dielectric heating. This is accomplished by using microwave radiation to heat water and other polarized molecules within the food. This excitation is fairly uniform, leading to food being more evenly heated throughout (except in thick objects) than generally occurs in other cooking techniques.

Basic microwave ovens heat food quickly and efficiently, but do not brown or bake food in the way conventional ovens do. This makes them unsuitable for cooking certain foods, or to achieve certain culinary effects. Additional kinds of heat sources can be added to microwave packaging, or into combination microwave ovens, to add these additional effects.

The use of high-frequency electric fields for heating dielectric materials had been proposed in the 1930s, for example US patent 2,147,689 states"This invention relates to heating systems for dielectric materials and the object of the invention is to heat such materials uniformly and substantially simultaneously throughout their mass. ... It has been proposed therefore to heat such materials simultaneously throughout their mass by means of the dielectric loss produced in them when they are subjected to a high voltage, high frequency field."

The heating effect of microwaves was discovered accidentally in 1945. Percy Spencer, an American self-taught engineer from Howland, Maine, was building magnetrons for radar sets with the American company Raytheon. He was working on an active radar set when he noticed that a peanut chocolate bar he had in his pocket started to melt. The radar had melted his chocolate bar with microwaves.

The first food to be deliberately cooked with Spencer's microwave was popcorn, and the second was an egg, which exploded in the face of one of the experimenters. To verify his finding, Spencer created a high density electromagnetic field by feeding microwave power into a metal box from which it had no way to escape. When food was placed in the box with the microwave energy, the temperature of the food rose rapidly.

On October 8, 1945 Raytheon filed a U.S. patent for Spencer's microwave cooking process and an oven that heated food using microwave energy was placed in a Boston restaurant for testing. In 1947, the company built the Radarange, the first microwave oven in the world. It was almost 1.8 metres (5.9 ft) tall, weighed 340 kilograms (750 lb) and cost about US$5000 each. It consumed 3 kilowatts, about three times as much as today's microwave ovens, and was water-cooled. An early commercial model introduced in 1954 consumed 1.6 kilowatts and sold for US$2000 to US$3000. Raytheon licensed its technology to the Tappan Stove company in 1952. They tried to market a large, 220 volt, wall unit as a home microwave oven in 1955 for a price of US$1295, but it did not sell well. In 1965 Raytheon acquired Amana. In 1967 they introduced the first popular home model, the countertop Radarange, at a price of US$495.

In the 1960s, Litton bought Studebaker's Franklin Manufacturing assets, which had been manufacturing magnetrons and building and selling microwave ovens similar to the Radarange. Litton then developed a new configuration of the microwave, the short, wide shape that is now common. The magnetron feed was also unique. This resulted in an oven that could survive a no-load condition indefinitely. The new oven was shown at a trade show in Chicago, and helped begin a rapid growth of the market for home microwave ovens. Sales volume of 40,000 units for the US industry in 1970 grew to one million by 1975. Market penetration in Japan, which had learned to build less expensive units by re-engineering a cheaper magnetron, was faster.

Several other companies joined in the market, and for a time most systems were built by Defence contractors, who were most familiar with the magnetron. Litton was particularly well known in the restaurant business. By the late 1970s the technology had improved to the point where prices were falling rapidly.

Often called"electronic ovens" in the 1960s, the name"microwave ovens" later became standardized, often now referred to informally as simply"microwaves." Formerly found only in large industrial applications, microwave ovens were increasingly becoming a standard fixture of most kitchens. The rapidly falling price of microprocessors also helped by adding electronic controls to make the ovens easier to use. By 1986, roughly 25% of households in the U.S. owned a microwave oven, up from only about 1% in 1971 . Current estimates hold that over 90% of American households own a microwave oven.

## PRINCIPLES

A microwave oven works by passing non-ionizing microwave radiation, usually at a frequency of 2.45 gigahertz (GHz)-a wavelength of 122 millimetres (4.80 in)-through the food. Microwave radiation is between common radio and infrared frequencies. Water, fat, and other substances in the food absorb energy from the microwaves in a process called dielectric heating. Many molecules (such as those of water) are electric dipoles, meaning that they have a positive charge at one end and a negative charge at the other, and therefore rotate as they try to align themselves with the alternating electric field of the microwaves. This molecular movement represents heat which is then dispersed as the rotating molecules hit other molecules and put them into motion.

Microwave heating is more efficient on liquid water than on fats and sugars (which have a smaller molecular dipole moment), and also more efficient than on frozen water (where the molecules are not free to rotate). Microwave heating is sometimes explained as a resonance of water molecules, but this is incorrect:

Such resonance only occurs in water Vapour at much higher frequencies, at about 20 GHz. Moreover, large industrial/commercial microwave ovens operating at the common large industrial-oven microwave heating frequency of 915 MHz—wavelength 328 millimetres (12.9 in)—also heat water and food perfectly well.

A common misconception is that microwave ovens cook food "from the inside out". In reality, microwaves are absorbed in the outer layers of food in a manner somewhat similar to heat from other methods. The misconception arises because microwaves penetrate dry non-conductive substances at the surfaces of many common foods, and thus often induce initial heat more deeply than other methods. Depending on water content, the depth of initial heat deposition may be several centimetres or more with microwave ovens, in contrast to broiling (infrared) or convection heating, which deposit heat thinly at the food surface. Penetration depth of microwaves is dependent on food composition and the frequency, with lower microwave frequencies (longer wavelengths) penetrating better.

## DESIGN

*A microwave oven consists of:*

- A high voltage power source, commonly a simple transformer or an electronic power converter, which passes energy to the magnetron
- A cavity magnetron, which converts high-voltage electric energy to microwave radiation
- A magnetron control circuit (usually with a microcontroller)
- A waveguide (to control the direction of the microwaves)
- A cooking chamber

The frequencies used in microwave ovens were chosen based on two constraints. The first is that they should be in one of the industrial, scientific, and medical (ISM) frequency bands set aside for non-communication purposes. Three additional ISM bands exist in the microwave frequencies, but are not used for microwave cooking. Two of them are Centreed on 5.8 GHz and 24.125 GHz, but are not used for microwave cooking because of the very high cost of power generation at these frequencies.

The third, Centreed on 433.92 MHz, is a narrow band that would require expensive equipment to generate sufficient power without creating interference outside the band, and is only available in some countries. For household purposes, 2.45 GHz has the advantage over 915 MHz in that 915 MHz is only an ISM band in the ITU Region 2 while 2.45 GHz is available worldwide.

Most microwave ovens allow users to choose between several power levels. In most ovens, however, there is no change in the intensity of the microwave radiation; instead, the magnetron is turned on and off in duty cycles of several seconds at a time.

This can actually be heard (a change in the humming sound from the oven), or observed when microwaving airy foods which may inflate during heating phases and deflate when the magnetron is turned off. For such an oven, the magnetron is driven by a linear transformer which can only feasibly be switched completely on or off.

Newer models have inverter power supplies which use pulse width modulation to provide effectively-continuous heating at reduced power so that foods are heated more evenly at a given power level and can be heated more quickly without being damaged by uneven heating.

The cooking chamber itself is a Faraday cage which prevents the microwaves from escaping. The oven door usually has a window for easy viewing, but the window has a layer of conductive mesh some distance from the outer panel to maintain the shielding. Because the size of the perforations in the mesh are much less than the microwaves' wavelength, most of the microwave radiation cannot pass through the door, while visible light (with a much shorter wavelength) can.

**Variants and Accessories**

A variant of the conventional microwave is the convection microwave. A convection microwave oven is a combination of a standard microwave and a convection oven. It allows food to be cooked quickly, yet come out browned or crisped, as from a convection oven.

Convection microwaves are more expensive than conventional microwave ovens. Some convection microwaves—those with exposed heating elements—can produce smoke and burning odors as food spatter from previous microwave-only use is burned off the heating elements.

More recently, some manufacturers have added high power quartz halogen bulbs to their convection microwave models, marketing them under names such as "Speedcook", "Advantium" and "Optimawave" to emphasize their ability to cook food rapidly and with good browning. The bulbs heat the food's surface with infrared (IR) radiation, browning surfaces as in a conventional oven. The food browns while also being heated by the microwave radiation and heated through conduction through contact with heated air.

The IR energy which is delivered to the outer surface of food by the lamps is sufficient to initiate browning caramelization in foods primarily made up of carbohydrates and Maillard reactions in foods primarily made up of protein. These reactions in food produce a texture and taste similar to that typically expected of conventional oven cooking rather than the bland boiled and steamed taste that microwave-only cooking tends to create.

In order to aid browning, sometimes an accessory browning tray is used, usually composed of glass or porcelain. It makes food crisp by oxidising the top layer until it turns brown. Ordinary plastic cookware is unsuitable for this purpose because it could melt.

Frozen dinners, pies, and microwave popcorn bags often contain a thin susceptor made from aluminium film in the packaging or included on a small paper tray. The metal film absorbs microwave energy efficiently and consequently becomes extremely hot and radiates in the infrared, concentrating the heating of oil for popcorn or even browning surfaces of frozen foods. Heating packages or trays containing susceptors are designed for single use and are discarded as waste.

**Sizes**

*Portable or Desktop*: This is the smallest size of microwave oven in the market.

The common models measure around 28 centimetres (11 in) tall, 38 centimetres (15 in) wide and 25 centimetres (9.8 in) deep. Some of the experimental models on trial are as small as 19 centimetres (7.5 in) tall, 6 centimetres (2.4 in) wide and 15 centimetres (5.9 in) deep. Some of these use 12 V DC power supplies.

- *Compact*: A compact microwave oven, also called small, is the smallest type typically available. Compacts are the most popular size of microwave oven, dominating the market. A typical model is no more than 50 centimetres (20 in) wide, 35 centimetres (14 in) deep and 30 centimetres (12 in) tall. These ovens are rated between 500 and 1000 watts and have less than 28 litres (0.99 cu ft) in capacity. These ovens are primarily used for reheating food and making microwave meals and popcorn. The largest models can accommodate 2 litres (1.8 imp qt) round casserole dishes and are suitable for light cooking. These ovens are not made to cook large amounts of food. Typically these models cost less than USD$100 (around £50).
- *Medium-capacity*: These models' heights and depths are only marginally larger than compacts, but they are typically more than 50 centimetres (20 in) wide. Their interiors are typically between 30 and 45 litres (1.1 and 1.6 cu ft), and power ratings are 1000-1500 W. These are the common"family sized" microwave ovens. They tend to have a few more"auto-cook" features, and some incorporate grills or even conventional-oven heating elements.
- *Large-capacity*: These are designed for cooking large meals. Large-capacity ovens can handle 25 by 35 centimetres (9.8 by 14 in) casserole dishes and cook tall items like roasts or turkey breasts, with a large number of"auto-cook" and precise temperature control measures. Large-capacity ovens normally use over 2000 W and have over 60 litres (2.1 cu ft) of capacity. These ovens are normally well over 50 centimetres (20 in) wide, as much as 50 centimetres (20 in) deep, and at least 30 centimetres (12 in) high.
- *Built-in*: These are built into cabinetry and are typically more expensive than similar sized countertop models. Some models include exhaust fans to allow installation above cooktops.

## USES

Microwave ovens are generally used for time efficiency in both industrial applications such as restaurants and at home, rather than for cooking quality, although some modern recipes using microwave ovens rival recipes using traditional ovens and stoves.

Professional chefs generally find microwave ovens to be of limited usefulness because browning, caramelization, and other flavour-enhancing reactions cannot occur due to the temperature range. On the other hand, people who want fast cooking times can use microwave ovens to prepare food or to reheat stored food (including commercially available pre-cooked frozen dishes) in only a few minutes. Microwave Ovens can also be used to defrost items that will later be cooked by traditional methods, cutting the time it takes to defrost foods naturally. Microwave ovens are also useful for the ease in which they can perform some traditionally cumbersome kitchen tasks, such as softening butter or melting chocolate. Popcorn is an item popular with microwave oven users.

## EFFICIENCY

A microwave oven converts only part of its electrical input into microwave energy. A typical consumer microwave oven consumes 1100 W of electricity in producing 700 W of microwave power, an efficiency of 64%. The other 400 W are dissipated as heat, mostly in the magnetron tube. Additional power is used to operate the lamps, AC power transformer, magnetron cooling fan, food turntable motor and the control circuits. Such wasted heat, along with heat from the product being microwaved, is exhausted as warm air through cooling vents.

A consideration for rating the efficiency of a microwave oven is to assess how much energy is wasted by using other forms of cooking.

For example, when heating water, a microwave oven heats just the mugful of water itself. When using a kettle, a heating element heats the kettle itself plus the water plus any extra water which is then left unused in the kettle, although electric kettles automatically shut off as soon as the water is boiled. Depending upon the size of the kettle and the amount of excess water, the efficiency of microwave ovens can be comparable, though if only the required amount of water is used electric kettles are generally more efficient.

Cooking in conventional ovens entails heating the internal structure of the oven and the air it contains to cooking temperature and, additionally, it involves maintaining that temperature against convective and radiative losses of heat for a longer time than is usual with a microwave oven. The efficiencies of conventional cooking methods can be difficult to quantify but tend to be lower.

## BENEFITS AND SAFETY FEATURES

Commercial microwave ovens all use a timer in their standard operating mode; when the timer runs out, the oven turns itself off.

Microwave ovens heat food without getting hot themselves. Taking a pot off a stove, with the exception of an induction cooktop, leaves a potentially dangerous heating element or trivet that will stay hot for some time. Likewise, when taking a casserole out of a conventional oven, one's arms are exposed to the very hot walls of the oven. A microwave oven does not pose this problem.

Food and cookware taken out of a microwave oven are rarely much hotter than 100 °C (212 °F). Cookware used in a microwave oven is often much cooler than the food because the cookware is transparent to microwaves; the microwaves heat the food directly and the cookware is indirectly heated by the food. Food and cookware from a conventional oven, on the other hand, are the same temperature as the rest of the oven; a typical cooking temperature is 180 °C (356 °F). That means that conventional stoves and ovens can cause more serious burns.

The lower temperature of cooking (the boiling point of water) is a significant safety benefit compared to baking in the oven or frying, because it eliminates the formation of tars and char, which are carcinogenic. Microwave radiation also penetrates deeper than direct heat, so that the food is heated by its own internal water content. In contrast, direct heat can fry the surface while the inside is still cold. Pre-heating the food in a microwave oven before putting it into the grill or pan reduces the time needed to heat up the food and reduces the formation of carcinogenic char. Unlike frying and baking, microwaving does not produce acrylamide in potatoes, however unlike deep-frying, it is of only limited effectiveness in reducing glycoalkaloid (i.e. Solanine) levels. Acrylamide has been found in other microwaved products like popcorn.

## Heating Characteristics

In a microwave oven, food may be heated for so short a time that it is cooked unevenly, because heat requires time to diffuse through food, and microwaves only penetrate to a limited depth. Microwave ovens are frequently used for reheating previously cooked food, and bacterial contamination may not be killed if the safe temperature is not reached, resulting in foodborne illness, as with all inadequate reheating methods.

Uneven heating in microwaved food can be partly due to the uneven distribution of microwave energy inside the oven, and partly due to the different rates of energy absorption in different parts of the food. The first problem is reduced by a stirrer, a type of fan that reflects microwave energy to different parts of the oven as it rotates, or by a turntable or carousel that turns the food; turntables, however, may still leave spots, such as the Centre of the oven, which receive uneven energy distribution.

The location of dead spots and hot spots in a microwave can be mapped out by placing a damp piece of thermal paper in the oven. When the water saturated paper is subjected to the microwave radiation it becomes hot enough to cause the dye to be released which will provide a visual representation of the microwaves.

If multiple layers of paper are constructed in the oven with a sufficient distance between them a three dimensional map can be created. Many store receipts are printed on thermal paper which allows this to be easily done at home.

The second problem is due to food composition and geometry, and must be addressed by the cook by arranging the food so that it absorbs energy evenly, and periodically testing and shielding any parts of the food that overheat.

In some materials with low thermal conductivity, where dielectric constant increases with temperature, microwave heating can cause localized thermal runaway. Under certain conditions, glass can exhibit thermal runaway in a microwave to the point of melting.

Due to this phenomenon, microwave ovens set at too-high power levels may even start to cook the edges of the frozen food, while the inside of the food remains frozen. Another case of uneven heating can be observed in baked goods containing berries. In these items, the berries absorb more energy than the drier surrounding bread and also cannot dissipate the heat due to the low thermal conductivity of the bread.

The result is frequently the overheating of the berries relative to the rest of the food. The low power levels which mark the "defrost" oven setting are designed to allow time for heat to be conducted from areas which absorb heat more readily to those which heat more slowly. More even heating will take place by placing food off-centre on the turntable tray instead of exactly in the centre.

Microwave heating can be deliberately uneven by design. Some microwavable packages (notably pies) may contain ceramic or aluminum-flake containing materials which are designed to absorb microwaves and heat up (thereby converting microwaves to less penetrating infrared) which aids in baking or crust preparation by depositing more energy shallowly in these areas. Such ceramic patches affixed to cardboard are positioned next to the food, and are typically smokey blue or gray in colour, usually making them easily identifiable. Microwavable cardboard packaging may also contain overhead ceramic patches which function in the same way. The technical term for such a microwave-absorbing patch is a susceptor.

## EFFECTS ON FOOD AND NUTRIENTS

Any form of cooking will destroy some nutrients in food, but the key variables are how much water is used in the cooking, how long the food is cooked, and at what temperature. Microwave ovens do convert vitamin B12 from the active to inactive form, making approximately 30-40% of the B12 contained in foods unusable by mammals.

Spinach retains nearly all its folate when cooked in a microwave; in comparison, it loses about 77 Per cent when cooked on a stove, because food on a stove is typically boiled, leaching out nutrients. Steamed vegetables tend to maintain more nutrients when cooked on a stovetop than in a microwave. Bacon cooked by microwave has significantly lower levels of carcinogenic nitrosamines than conventionally cooked bacon.

## HAZARDS

Liquids can superheat when heated in a microwave oven in a container with a smooth surface. That is, the liquid reaches a temperature slightly above its normal boiling point without bubbles of vapour forming inside the liquid. The boiling process can start explosively when the liquid is disturbed, such as when the user takes hold of the container to remove it from the oven or while adding solid ingredients such as powdered creamer or sugar. This can result in spontaneous boiling (nucleation) which may be violent enough to eject the boiling liquid from the container and produce severe scalding. It is commonly, but wrongly, thought that only distilled water exhibits this behaviour.

Closed containers and eggs can explode when heated in a microwave oven due to the increasing pressure of steam. Products that are heated too long can catch fire. Though this is inherent to any form of cooking, the rapid cooking and unattended nature of microwave oven use results in additional hazard. Microwave oven manuals frequently warn of such hazards. Because the microwave oven's cavity is enclosed and metal, fires are generally well contained.

Simply switching off the oven and allowing the fire to consume the available oxygen with the door closed will typically contain and quickly extinguish the fire, thus limiting any damage to the oven itself.

Any metal or conductive object placed into the microwave will act as an antenna to some degree, resulting in an electric current. This causes the object to act as a heating element. This effect varies with the object's shape and composition, and is sometimes utilized for cooking.

Any object containing pointed metal can create an electric arc (sparks) when microwaved. This includes cutlery, aluminum foil, ceramics decorated with metal, twist-ties containing metal wire, the metal wire carry-handles in paper Chinese take-out food containers, or almost any metal formed into a poorly conductive foil or thin wire; or into a pointed shape. Forks are a good example: This is because the tines of the fork resonate with the microwave radiation and produce high voltage at the tips. This has the effect of exceeding the dielectric breakdown of air, about 3 megavolts per metre (3×106 V/m). The air forms a conductive plasma, which is visible as a spark. The plasma and the tines may then form a conductive loop, which may be a more effective antenna, resulting in a longer lived spark. When dielectric breakdown occurs in air, some ozone and nitrogen oxides are formed, both of which are unhealthy in large quantities.

It is possible for metal objects to be microwave-oven compatible, although experimentation by users is not encouraged. Microwaving an individual smooth metal object without pointed ends, for example, a spoon or shallow metal pan, usually does not produce sparking. Thick metal wire racks can be part of the interior design in microwave ovens . In a similar way, the interior wall plates with perforating holes which allow light and air into the oven, and allow interior-viewing through the oven door, are all made of conductive metal formed in a safe shape.

The effect of microwaving thin metal films can be seen clearly on a Compact Disc or DVD (particularly the factory pressed type). The microwaves induce electric currents in the metal film, which heats up, melting the plastic in the disc and leaving a visible pattern of concentric and radial scars. It can also be illustrated by placing a radiometre inside the cooking chamber, creating plasma inside the vacuum chamber.

Another hazard is the resonance of the magnetron tube itself. If the microwave is run without an object to absorb the radiation, a standing wave will form. The energy is reflected back and forth between the tube and the cooking chamber. This may cause the tube to'cook' itself and burn out. Thus dehydrated food, or food wrapped in metal which does not arc, is problematic without being an obvious fire hazard.

Some magnetrons have ceramic insulators with a piece of beryllium oxide (beryllia) added-these ceramics often appear somewhat pink or purple-coloured. The beryllium in such oxides is a serious chemical hazard if crushed and ingested, e.g., inhaling dust. In addition, beryllia is listed as a confirmed human carcinogen by the IARC; therefore, broken ceramic insulators or magnetrons should not be handled. This is obviously only a danger if the microwave oven becomes physically damaged, i.e., cracked ceramics, or upon opening and handling the magnetron directly, and as such should not occur during normal usage.

Certain foods, such as grapes, if carefully arranged, can also produce arcing. A naked flame, being made of conductive plasma, will do the same, so burning candles, matches, paper, etc should not be put in a microwave oven.

## Microwave Radiation

The microwaves emitted by the source in a microwave oven are confined in the oven by the material out of which microwave oven is constructed.

Tests have shown confinement of the microwaves in commercially available ovens to be so nearly universal as to make routine testing unnecessary. United States Food and Drug Administration's Centre for Devices and Radiological Health, a U.S. Federal Standard limits the amount of microwaves that can leak from an oven throughout its lifetime to 5 milliwatts of microwave radiation per square centimetre at approximately 2 inches from the surface of the oven. This is far below the exposure level currently considered to be harmful to human health. The radiation produced by a microwave oven is non-ionizing. It therefore does not have the cancer risks associated with ionizing radiation such as X-rays, ultraviolet light, and high-energy particles.

Long-term rodent studies to assess cancer risk have so far failed to identify any carcinogenicity from 2.45 GHz microwave radiation even with chronic exposure levels, *i.e.*, large fraction of one's life span, far larger than humans are likely to encounter from any leaking ovens.

However, with the oven door open, the radiation may cause damage by heating; as with any cooking device. Every microwave oven sold has a protective interlock so that it cannot be run when the door is open or improperly latched.

## VACUUM FILLER

**Fig.** Vacuum filler

A vacuum filler is a machine used for filling pasty products. The pasty products are moved with the aid of a vane cell feed system under a vacuum.

### OBJECTIVE

**Fig.** AL-System demonstration

Levelling the weight of pre-packaged goods in the food sector, especially those involving viscous or pasty products, places extremely high demands on thereproducible accuracy of filling and portioning systems. In order to achieve this, technical and technological issues as well as product-specific characteristics have to be taken into account. In addition to the aforementioned factors, the requirements on the quality of an end product is a key issue when selecting or implementing a technical process solution. The development of vacuum filling machines has made it possible to fulfill both the technical and the quality-related requirements.

In the food sector, moving or transporting fluids is achieved with the aid of pump technology. Colloquially, this is known as filling or portioning. Various different types of pumps are used, depending on the type of filling products to be moved.

Vacuum fillers with vane cell feed systems and vacuum feeding are commonly used for viscous products. The products are transported with the aid of a hopper with a feeding device, a vane cell feed system under a vacuum and appropriate volume expulsion in the pump housing. This is basically a volumetric feed principle, which means that a certain weight is defined via a volume.

In addition to the vane cell feed systems,also known as rotary vane pumps, there are also screw feed systems with feed augers, toothed wheel feed systems and evacuated lifting cylinders. With all these systems, transportation is achieved via volume expulsion under a vacuum. Vacuum fillers are traditionally used in the meat processing industry as well as in other food sectors. They can also be found in some non-food sectors. Generally speaking, vacuum fillers can be used for filling pasty and compressible products.

## HISTORY

The first vacuum filler was developed in the early 1960s. The technology has been refined since then.

## REQUIREMENTS/EFFECTS

The pumpability of viscous or pasty products has a key effect on the reliable function of a vacuum filler. Filling products in the food sector can be characterised with the aid of various different properties related to their pumpability ("fillability"). They are either physical characteristics that can be measured directly or they are sensory attributes.

### Gas Content/density

The gas content is also called the "air content". The air content of a fluid is the percentage share of air that enters the fluid during grinding/mixing processes. This can be measured using special apparatus and has a direct relationship to the density of a fluid.

### Compressibility

The compressibility depends on the air content of a fluid. A high level of compressibility is linked to a high gas content in the fluid.

### Viscosity

Viscosity is a measure of the consistency of a fluid. The higher the viscosity, the higher the consistency of the fluid is (it is less fluid); the lower the viscosity, the lower the consistency of it is (more fluid). Highly-viscous filling products in the food processing industry are primarily found in the meat, bakery products and convenience food sectors. These highly-viscous substances are commonly referred to as being "pasty". The fluidity is the basic requirement for the pumpability of a fluid. The viscosity can also be determined using suitable rheological measuring apparatus. In the food sector, the viscosity is primarily dependent on the fluid content of the filling product.

### Temperature

The temperature is a key factor for pumpability as it has a direct effect on the viscosity as well as on the product quality.

### Texture, Fibrousness, Dimensions of the Inserts

Specific sensory characteristics of a filling product have a significant effect on the assessment of the fillability and compliance with the precise weight.

### Weight Accuracy

With the help of modern filling technology in the food sector, accurate portioning with a difference of up to 1% in relation to the required volume of a portion can be achieved.

## MODE OF OPERATION

**Fig.** Conveyor

The key element of a vacuum filler is the vacuum filling principle. The filling product is fed into the feed system mechanically via a hopper with actively driven feeding auger, as well as via vertical "vacuum suction". Pre-evacuated cells of a vane cell feed system move underneath the hopper. The pressure difference relative to the ambient pressure (underpressure) caused by the evacuation ensures that the cells are filled with product. The feed system moves continuously, thus generating a continuous filling flow. The product is portioned by means of cyclic movements of the feed system. Each cell of the feed system has a particular volume.

The portion is defined by the rotation distance of the rotor. The portioning volume is therefore set in the control system by multiplying the rotor's rotation distance by the number of the feed system cells within it. The portion weight must be determined in the control system via the portion volume parameter with the aid of scales.

## Structure and Technical Requirements

Vacuum fillers are primarily used in the food trade and in the food industry. Special criteria apply to the design of machines in the food sector due to specific hygiene standards and hygiene regulations. This includes, for example, ensuring that they are easy to dismantle, have level surfaces and seals that can be rinsed from the rear, no dead spaces, ergonomic shapes, a small range of parts and detectable materials/materials suitable for food use.

Relatively aggressive ambient conditions, such as reactive detergents, reactive or abrasive filling media, intensive high-pressure cleaning and extreme ambient temperatures, are also faced. Vacuum fillers are therefore made of a high proportion of stainless steel with a very robust design. Moving parts can be easily dismantled and can be cleaned individually. In addition to the mechanical or design-related issues, complex electronic components in a vacuum filler also have to be taken into account.

## Vane Cell feed System with Hopper

The vane cell feed system mainly consists of a rigid pump housing with attached side plate that is fixed to the pivoting hopper, and a removable rotor with pump vanes and cam. Depending on the machine size there are various different sizes of vane cell feed systems with parts with appropriate dimensions.

The hopper can be swivelled to clean and dismantle surfaces and parts that come into contact with filling product. The driven rotor with an appropriate number of slots is located in the pump housing, in which pump vanes form cells with defined volumes when the machine is closed, supported by the cam. Induced by the rotor movement when the machine is started, the cells move in the direction of the vane cell feed system outlet and therefore ensure that a defined product flow is achieved. The weight accuracy of a feed system is partially dependent upon the production precision of the parts and their degree of wear.

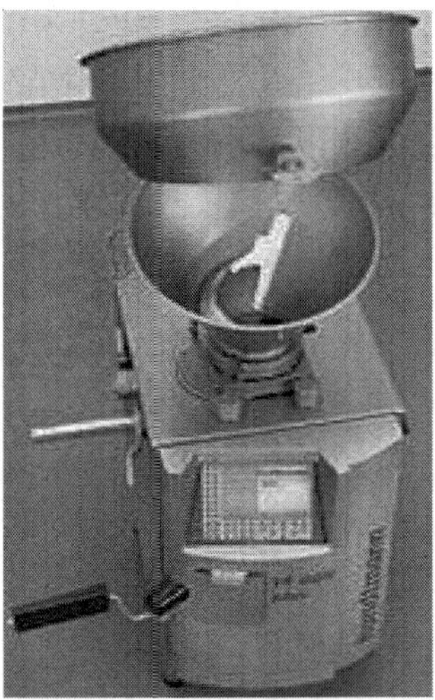

**Fig.** hopper with mechanical feeding auger

## Vacuum System

The cells are filled by evacuating the vane cell feed system. By applying a vacuum via a vacuum pump, the filling products are gently drawn out of the hopper into the feed system as soon as an evacuated cell moves underneath the hopper. The vacuum pump is protected by an integrated water separator. The level of vacuum can be set according to the filling product. In addition to the feed effect, the filling product is simultaneously evacuated to a certain extent (approx. 2–4 %). This means that the air content of the filling product decreases and the filling product becomes denser.

## Feeding

**Fig.** Feeding

The term feeding in the context of vacuum fillers refers to actively moving the filling media in the direction of the lower part of the hopper to support the vacuum approach within the hopper. Feeding is achieved by using moveable feeding augers with scrapers/rigid counter arms. The feeding auger is driven in synchronisation with the rotation of the rotors.

Due to the special geometry of both augers and the parallel rotation movement, the filling product is moved vertically in the direction of the vane cell feed system.

The required feed intensity depends on the viscosity of the media to be filled. Less active feed is needed with low-viscosity media than with high-viscosity product. There are therefore a variety of combinations or versions of the parts involved in the feeding process.

**Machine Base**

The machine base acts as the stand for a vacuum filler. For hygiene reasons, bases are made completely of stainless steel. The compact machine base is designed to ensure that it can be moved easily using lifting equipment.

**Lifting Device**

Lifting devices allow the hopper to be loaded using standard trolleys. They can either be fixed onto the vacuum filler or a mast type lifting device can be positioned separately next to the vacuum filler. Lifting devices can be driven hydraulically or electrically.

**Control and Drive Systems**

**Fig.** vacuum filler monitor touch control

A computer-aided control system is required for operating the various functions associated with a vacuum filler. Usually, several drives are integrated into the vacuum fillers for the various different applications. With the most modern generations of vacuum fillers, the drives are implemented by means of servo motors and appropriatebus systems.

**Sealing Devices**

To produce individual portions from homogenous product via a feed system, a "sealing device" is always required at the feed system outlet. This device separates portions and is controlled in synchronisation with the portion output. These devices could be linking devices for sausages, clippers for portionable sausages, dosing valves for tubs and cans, cutting devices for dough as well as forming equipment for dumplings.

### Other Feed System Principles

Generally speaking, vacuum fillers can be equipped with various different feed systems. However in principle, the basic machine structure, with a hopper, vacuum system, feeding device, machine base, lifting device, control system and sealing device, is very similar. Depending on the application, each type of feed system has advantages and disadvantages.

### Screw Feed System with Feed Augers

With a screw feed system, two counter-rotating screws form cells within a housing; they are moved in the direction of the pump when the screws are rotated. The filling product is again moved into the screw feed system with the aid of a vacuum and mechanical feeding devices.

### Toothed wheel Deed System

An outer toothed ring is driven, rotating an inner toothed wheel with it. The toothed wheels form cell segments as they move against each other. The cell content is transported through the toothing and it is then voided and ejected in the outlet area.

### Feeding Via Lifting Cylinders

Feeding via alternately moving lifting cylinders is the simplest feed system principle. The volume is defined by the geometry of the cylinders, and the portion size is determined by the number of strokes.

### Hopper Vacuum Systems

The additional creation of a hopper vacuum is a variation of the vacuum filler concept. The vacuum system is enhanced with an additional vacuum pump, specially designed for the hopper. The hopper is closed and is connected to an upstream reservoir. The vacuum present in the hopper allows filling product to be drawn into the filling machine from the reservoir. The filling product is also intensively evacuated.

# 5

# Kitchen Operation

## INTRODUCTION

Every topic that is operating a kitchen should either elect or appoint a kitchen steward. The proper supervision of the kitchen is sufficiently demanding in time that it justifies having a member responsible for its management. The steward should sign all bills and/or receipts when turning them over to the Treasurer for payment or record keeping purposes. The Treasurer then has the authority to make the necessary disbursements. The responsibility of the steward is strategic when considering that he is the one person who will either make the income for the kitchen 'cover' expenses or have the kitchen Realise a deficit. The Treasurer must formulate and discuss the kitchen budget with the steward. It must be determined exactly what amount may be spent for food on a weekly basis.

The Treasurer must, from time to time, check up on the status of kitchen costs with the steward to make sure he is remaining within his allotted budget. Only by using measures designed to impose strict controls on the operation of the kitchen can the unit be kept from incurring a large deficit.

## MENUS

The most frequent source of complaint in houses is the food. The reason for this is usually not in its preparation, but rather in the choice of menus. A good steward will plan well balanced, varied menus, and will garnish his main meals with relishes, appetizers, soups and salads; all of which are inexpensive and have often proved to be excellent investments in good will and nutrition. Avoid a set menu for each day of the week. Nothing hurts morale more than "Thursday is macaroni and cheese day."

### HOW TO LOSE MONEY IN THE KITCHEN?

There are several well established ways in which a kitchen operation can lose money. The first is by the patronage of dishonest vendors who will bill you for a certain weight or quantity of merchandise, and then won't deliver the correct amount. The steward should arrange delivery times with the vendors so that he may personally inspect each delivery. If the delivery is insufficient according to the delivery slip, the slip should be changed before the steward signs it, acknowledging receipt of the merchandise. When buying in less than full case quantities, a count should be made carefully at the time of delivery to ascertain that the amount or quantity is as stated on the delivery receipt or invoice.

A second area of loss is when the kitchen 'help' frequently takes home considerable quantities of food when they leave the house at the end of the day. It is taken for granted that kitchen 'help' eat their meals while on the premises. It is, however, known that some people who work in kitchens take home enough food to supply their entire families. This can constitute a considerable drain on finances.

To prevent a third area of loss, arrangements should be made to keep the kitchen and food storage area locked at all times when the cook is not on duty. It is a sad fact, but true, that disappearance of food and supplies costs every unit of money out of their kitchen budget.

A fourth loss is the practice of permitting members to eat at odd hours or between meals. Definite serving hours must be established for each meal and the kitchen declared "off limits" at all other times.

## GUEST MEALS

Each topic should define and regulate guest meals in their bylaws. Such meals are equally the evening or Sunday meal, which normally constitute 60 Per cent of the daily meal cost per "boarder", and any charge for such meals should be based on that percentage, as a minimum. Any member who abuses a guest privilege is costing each 'boarder'; thus, he is being unfair to the its members.

There are cases where a member not living in the house wishes to eat certain meals on a regular basis at the house. Such rates may be established by using the daily meal cost per boarder, and using 60 Per cent of that amount to be charged for evening or Sunday meals, 25 Per cent of that amount for the noon meal and 15 Per cent of that amount for breakfast. Even then, a member is not paying his full share and it is reasonable to add 10 Per cent to these rates.

The practice of refunding for missed meals can become very involved and should not be done unless there is an unusual situation or it is for an extended period of time.

Since most Treasurers have had little or no training in food management, consideration of the following six topics would be helpful in obtaining a more efficient and less costly dining facility in your kitchen.

- *Labour*:
  - Hire reliable cooks, follow up on job application references.
  - Pay liveable wages.

- Work out acceptable working hours (no more than 48 hours a week).
- Laws are very strict with regard to payment of overtime. Know the laws!
- Don't make unusual demands.
- Have some incentive plans.
- Give pay raises, when appropriate.
- Provide good physical working conditions.
- Listen to employee's problems—don't ignore their suggestions.
- Place yourself in their position.
- Set ground rules and be sure both sides understand them.
- Let employees know about vacations, wages, days off, etc.
- Let employees know to whom they are to report (chain of command).
- Compliment them when they have done a good job.
- Cost of Labour should never exceed 30 Per cent of your total board income.

• *Purchasing*:
  - Don't buy from everyone—be selective.
  - Know what you are getting.
  - Designate one person to do the buying.
  - Get price lists from vendors.
  - It is not always necessary to buy Premium, Prime, Grade A, etc., in food items.
  - Don't buy more than needed.
  - Take advantage of good buys.
  - Know delivery times.
  - Don't accept poor merchandise.
  - Try to set up food purchasing on competitive bids—shop around.
  - Food cost should not exceed 50 Per cent of your board income.
  - Utilize or create a food purchasing cooperative.

• *Equipment*:
  - Take care of equipment.
  - Do 'preventable' maintenance when possible.
  - Replace worn out equipment as soon as possible.
  - Follow company instructions on equipment as to cleaning, safety, etc.
  - Watch for warranty on equipment.
  - Purchase Labour saving devices.

  - Purchase commercial grade equipment, not home grade equipment.
- *Sanitation*:
  - Don't ever let this aspect of the kitchen operation deteriorate.
  - Be strict in this area (you'll never be sorry).
  - Give the cook assistance in this area.
  - If bothered by rats, mice or insects, call in a qualified exterminator.
  - Discard or replace equipment that is unsanitary.
  - Have plenty of hot water.
  - *Charges and Collections:*
  - Collect from all who are not paying for 'board' but eating occasional meals.
  - For extra functions, the kitchen account should be reimbursed by the account sponsoring the event (i.e., social, rush, homecoming).
  - Don't put anyone on a free meal basis.
- *Administration*:
  - Take a monthly inventory of kitchen supplies and food.
  - Are you having excessive leftovers?
  - Strictly enforce rules on notifying cook when people won't be eating a particular meal.
  - Your total board cost per man should not exceed that charged by the dormitories.
  - Set up kitchen policy similar to dormitories.
  - Consider increasing board prices following increases in food and prices or cut down on meals, quantity or service.
  - Have your cook sign a year long contract.

*Caution*: In many college towns, unscrupulous fraternity cooks, to whom the inefficient steward leaves the buying, receive personal rebates, either in money or merchandise. Too much emphasis cannot be put on the importance of checking up regularly on the kitchen ?help?, of switching dealers occasionally and of checking regularly on deliveries as they come in.

## KITCHEN EMPLOYEES

The employment of a knowledgeable, reliable and likeable cook should not be a hasty, poorly planned process. Your topic is entering into a strictly business relationship and you should approach the hiring of your cook in that manner.

*The following are tips when hiring kitchen employees*:

- Have the applicant fill out a simple job application. The job application serves as a source of information, both during the interview and following employment (if that should happen).
- Check out job and personal references listed on the application. Don't take anything for granted. Find out what kind of employee your applicant was, job attendance record and general attitude.
- The applicant should be personally interviewed by the President and Treasurer. If they are in agreement that the applicant is qualified, the advisor should personally interview the applicant.
- If all are in agreement that hiring the applicant is in the best interest, employ the applicant.
- Before employing an applicant, make sure there is agreement on wages, time off (including vacations), insurance, working hours, job expectations and sick days.
- In attempting to establish a fair wage, check with the other fraternities and sororities on campus, and the dormitory food service, to determine what they are paying their employees—that will be the fair wage.
- The dormitory food service is a good source of potential employees. Don't be afraid to advertise in the local newspaper.
- Refer to Internal Revenue Service guidelines in order to comply with federal and state employment laws.

## EMPLOYMENT CONTRACT

There are 'pros' and 'cons' to using an employment contract that should be obvious.

*'Pros' to utilizing a contract when employing kitchen personnel*:

- The employee has a legal responsibility to fulfill commitments stated in the contract.
- The contract specifies job expectations and wages so as to avoid future disputes.
- It lets the employee know you mean 'business'.

*'Cons' to utilizing a contract when employing kitchen personnel*:

- The topic has a legal responsibility to employ the person in accordance with the conditions of the contract and limits the 'grounds for discharging' an employee.
- Regardless of the status of the kitchen account, the topic must pay the employee in accordance with the conditions of the contract.

## FOOD PURCHASING COOPERATIVES

Many campuses and/or Greek Systems operate a food purchasing 'coop'. These coops are mostly referred to as a Fraternity Management Association *(which may offer additional services)* or simply, the Fraternity Coop, and can save thousands of dollars every year by buying in quantity.

Because of the wide array of these coops, both in operation and quality, it is recommended that you investigate it, if it exists on your campus. If one doesn't exist, have you thought about starting one? The operation of a kitchen facility is no small task. However, if done properly. Additionally, it can produce substantial profits for the properly managed. Most certainly, it provides an opportunity for members to develop their management, decision making and leadership skills.

## ESSENTIAL DUTIES/RESPONSIBILITIES

- Gathers all dirty dishware from tubs brought to the dishroom, rinses and stacks in dishracks, always clearing dishes of leftovers and trash in order to prepare for automated washing.
- Loads full dishracks on belt and ensures correct placement in accordance to the instructions for the operation of the machine. Operates automatic dish washing machine by using controls as instructed.
- Loads dishwashing solutions into automatic dispensers and regulates the output of detergents and chemicals to the dishwashing machine by monitoring and adjusting controls.
- Unloads clean dishes from racks after being processed through dish machine, inspects for cleanliness and carefully stacks in specified carts and shelves for the easy use by restaurant and kitchen staff.
- Manually scrubs pots, pans and other kitchen equipment that cannot be washed automatically, using detergents, scourers, and special solutions as required. Inspects for cleanliness, manually dries with hand towels, and puts away in correct places.
- Manually polishes all silver, stainless steel and pewter used in food service, using standard polishing cloth and products, in order to present clean and attractive equipment to diners.
- Maintains the automatic dishwashing equipment in good condition and working order in accordance with manufacturers' instructions in order to prolong the life of the equipment, prevent breakdowns and to meet mandated health compliance regulations.
- Keeps the dishroom in clean and orderly condition at all times by sweeping, mopping, emptying trash, wiping counters and equipment

and organizing shelves in order to maintain a sanitary work station and to meet mandated health compliance requirements.

- Mops kitchen floors as requested and at end of each shift, cleans all kitchen work surfaces as regularly scheduled by manager including walls, ceilings, hoods, vents and ovens.
- Gathers all trash cans from kitchen work areas at end of each shift and empties into outside trash compactor.
- Sweeps loading dock and kitchen entrance areas, clearing litter and debris to trash bins, for the safety of employees and purveyors.
- Performs other duties as assigned, requested or deemed necessary by management.

**OTHER DUTIES/RESPONSIBILITIES**

- Contacts purveyors and contractors, in writing or by phone, when in need of product or service.
- Unloads deliveries as they arrive, and accounts for ordered items by comparing packing lists to actual items received. Transports deliveries to stock room by carrying boxes or using a dolly. Assists the stock room personnel with sorting and storing of delivered goods.
- Maintains clean employee breakroom and restrooms by sweeping, mopping, cleaning counters and refilling supplies on a daily basis.
- Provides assistance to other employees and departments to contribute to the best overall performance of the department and hotel.

# 6

# Kitchen Chemistry

## INTRODUCTION

### HOW CAN WE CHANGE SUBSTANCES?

This unit uses the context of food preparation and cooking for students to explore examples of changes in their everyday life. Students learn to classify materials as solids, liquids or gases according to their observable properties. They also learn to identify reversible or non-reversible changes in substances. They use appropriate scientific vocabulary to describe and explain their observations.

Students select and use simple measuring equipment in the preparation of food and come to an understanding of the differences between mixing, dissolving, melting, boiling and evaporating during preparation and cooking. Students use a range of appropriate methods to record observations and describe safety requirements associated with their experiments.

When planning this unit, it may be useful to incorporate ideas and strategies from *the Science Continuum P-10* critical teaching ideas A gas is matter and Melting and dissolving

## CONCEPTS

- The purpose of classification is to identify objects with common or similar properties.
- Substances such as household materials exist as a solid, liquid or gas and can usually be distinguished from each other by their properties.
- Heating and cooling substances may cause materials to change their state; changes of state are described as reversible.
- The change of state from solid to liquid is called 'melting'; from liquid to gas is 'evaporation'; from gas to liquid, 'condensation' and from liquid to solid, 'freezing' or 'solidification'.

- When one material is mixed in another and its particles seem to disappear the substance is described as being soluble. A soluble solid dissolves to form a mixture called a solution, an insoluble substance does not.
- Preparation and cooking of food involves reversible changes and changes that are more difficult to reverse.

Explore the relationships between ideas about matter in *The Science Continuum P-10* Concept Development Maps (Chemical Reactions, Conservation of Matter and States of Matter).

## MOTIVATION ACTIVITIES

### How can we Sort what's in the Kitchen?

Students sort household products such as items found in kitchen cupboards, the fridge and the pantry into groups. They devise their own basis for sorting the various objects and discuss reasons for their decisions. They develop a shared understanding of the term 'classification'.

### Are they Solid, Liquid or Gas or Something in between?

Prepare a selection of materials in separate screw top jars. Appropriate materials include: coloured water, oil, liquid soap, air, talcum powder, thick paste or slime, honey, soft dough, blocks of wood, paper pieces, polystyrene balls, seeds and erasers.

Students examine them without opening the jars and say whether they think the contents are solids, liquids or gases.

Students indicate materials that they find difficult to classify. Responses could be tallied and block graphs drawn. Under supervision they open the jars and examine the contents using their sense of touch. As a class, students discuss the properties or characteristics that can be used to distinguish between solids, liquids and gases.

## EXPLORATION ACTIVITIES

Where relevant, students identify the observable properties of solids, liquids and gases such as appearance, smell (if any) and texture or feel. Discuss safety aspects with them.

Make available hand lenses or magnifying glasses and other equipment such as balances. Students could make hand or electronic drawings, tables and images to record their observations.

### What kind of Change?

Students heat ice blocks and observe any changes which take place. They hold a cold plate above the container. Students describe the changes they observe in terms of change of state such as:

- From solid to liquid (melting)
- From liquid to water vapour (evaporating)
- From vapour to liquid (condensing).

They draw a simple diagram and use appropriate terminology to explain what has taken place.

Students can conduct an experiment at home. They could fill a plastic bottle with water and place it upright in the freezer overnight without its stopper. Students then note and report their observations on the following day. In class discussion, they can seek to explain their observations. They should be supported to infer that the volume of the ice is greater than that of the water. Note that this is atypical as solids generally decrease in volume when changing from liquid to solid.

**The Big Melt: Investigating Melting**

Students plan and carry out a simple investigation into changes that take place when heating everyday cooking ingredients such as: copha, butter, cheese, chocolate, and sugar (sugar cube).

They pose questions such as 'Which material will melt the fastest?'

With assistance, students identify variables and explain how to make the investigation a fair test. The sugar cube could be selected as a suitable volume of comparison for all materials.

Students predict changes they think would occur in the substances as they cool and compare their predictions with what actually happens.

Students construct databases and draw diagrams to record the results of their investigations and use terms such as 'melting' and 'solidifying' correctly. They identify changes which were reversible and those that are more difficult to reverse. Students look for patterns in their data, suggest generalizations and design experiments to test their ideas.

**Do all kinds of Sugar Dissolve at the Same Rate?**

With assistance, students design a fair test to find out which kind of sugar will dissolve in water most quickly. Kinds of sugar to investigate include brown sugar, cane sugar, icing sugar and lump sugar. They construct spreadsheets to record results of experimental work and with help, create bar graphs to illustrate their results.

Students write a scientific report and make inferences based on their data using the expressions 'dissolve' and 'making a solution' correctly. They begin to distinguish between the processes of dissolving and melting. They explain in what way their test was 'fair'.

Students pour each of the sugar solutions produced in the activity into shallow saucers and leave them in a sunny place. Based on their experience they predict the outcome of the experiment and observe any changes daily.

They discuss their findings and are assisted to describe the processes which took place in terms of evaporation of water from the solution to leave the sugar crystals remaining. Students discuss whether the changes observed are easy or difficult to reverse.

### Exploring Oobleck

Oobleck is made by mixing cornflour and water together (2 parts cornflour to 1 part water) and green food colouring can also be added.

Students mix, pour, beat and strike the Oobleck mixture and discuss how it behaves in each case. As a class, they discuss whether the mixture behaves as a solid or liquid, or whether it seems to have the properties of both. Their answers can be left open.

### Which Mixes with which?

Predict-Observe-Explain is a useful approach to investigating changes which take place when different substances are mixed with different liquids.

Small amounts of the following materials: salt, butter, flour, and orange cordial are each mixed separately in three different liquids: water, cooking oil and methylated spirits.

Students identify variables and suggest ways of controlling them and draw up a table to record their observations. They look for patterns in their findings identifying which materials dissolve in which liquids and which do not. They should find that a substance behaves differently; it can be soluble in one liquid but insoluble in another.

Students could extend their investigation by discussing whether the processes are reversible or not and suggest possible methods of separating the various mixtures obtained.

## APPLICATION ACTIVITIES

### Making Chocolate Crackles and Muffins or Popping Corn

Different small teams make chocolate crackles, popcorn or muffins and investigate the processes involved.

They transfer their understandings and classify each of their ingredients as a solid, liquid or gas. They describe or create a flow chart that demonstrates the procedure to follow and identify stages in the process when mixing, dissolving, melting, boiling or evaporating is evident.

They describe the effects of the addition or removal of heat on the processes that they observe. They compare the properties of the ingredients they started with to those of the final products.

Students should be encouraged to present their findings in a variety of forms.

## CLEANING CHEMICALS AND EQUIPMENT

### Chemicals

Bleach: used for sanitizing. Available from the non-perishables catalog. Used to sanitize food preparation surfaces. One tablespoon per gallon of water achieves the accepted standard for food prep surface sanitation of 200 ppm. You can also keep a bottle in the bathrooms for sanitizing door handles and other areas that are touched a lot, or for tough mildew stains in the showers.

Blue concentrate: a concentrated multi-purpose cleaning liquid. The bottle has a measuring device built right in! To measure, take off the small lid and squeeze the bottle until the right amount is measured. Dumping the bottle over will only empty the measure amount. On the back of the bottle is a concentration chart. Blue concentrate is used to clean (not sanitize) counters and mop floors.

Comet: ordered from Costco, this powder bleach cleanser can be used in both kitchen and bathroom to clean and sanitize. It is usually used on toilets and showers but can also be used on counters and floors too.

Dish Soap comes from Costco and is usually Dawn. Since all dishes must be hand washed, this is very important to have.

Dishmachine detergent: a white solid brick that goes in the dispenser on the wall. The solid is not harmful to your hands, but is necessary for cleaning your dishes properly. It's fairly expensive, but you won't go through it that often unless you're a bigger house. Contains chlorine-based chemicals but used alone, is not acceptable for sanitizing.

Food service hand soap: a *clear* liquid soap that comes in a small box for easy mounting into hand soap dispensers It's more expensive, less pleasant-smelling, and tougher on your hands than its pink counterpart, but you have to have it in your kitchen and the bathroom closest to your kitchen.

Lotion Hand Soap: similar to food service hand soap, but it is *pink* and has added lotion to be less harsh on your hands, and is cheaper. Members usually prefer it but Health Inspectors don't.

Mineral oil: used to seal wooden cutting boards and butcher blocks. Prevents wood from cracking, rotting, retaining smells and stains, etc. Indispensable for houses with such wooden items.

Powdered soap: Boraxo-brand powdered soap. Not very commonly used for hand-washing due to its abrasive quality. Very useful in making home-made cleaning solutions.

Reel-a-Peel: an orange-scented degreaser that is used only for metal surfaces. It's a little expensive but it works really well on grease. You have to order the case so if you try to order one or two bottles, it won't come. Reel a Peel is not food safe, so make sure to sanitize any food preparation surfaces after using.

Rinse Aid is a green brick that turns into liquid and will make your dishes shiny. It's expensive and not necessary. Most houses don't use it.

Sanitizing fluids: for the sanitizers used in the kitchens of all houses. There are two kinds, red and yellow. CZ is the only house that currently uses the red, which is a quaternary ammonium chloride (quat) sanitizer. The other houses use a yellowish liquid which is basically a stronger version of household bleach. If you get something delivered to your house that isn't yellowish (red at CZ) or doesn't say sanitizer, don't use it and return back to CK.

Score: orange solid that can be used with the dispensers currently installed in most houses. In solution, Score is a degreaser. Not for use on wood. The dispensers malfunction frequently so make sure that the concentration is right once dispensed. Useful at low concentrations (a teaspoon or so per gallon) to mop floors if oil or grease has been spilled on them. Gloves should be worn.

Shamrock: green solid also used in dispensers but for dish-washing using the 3-compartment method. Does not sanitize; must be followed by a sanitizing treatment.

Vegetable oil: Can also be used to clean the griddle. Much more pleasant then vinegar. Canola oil can also be used, but its more expensive. Do not use olive or corn oil as their smoke points are too low. Scrape any debris from griddle. Cover with oil and turn all burners on high. Make sure oil doesn't all run off. Once any grime starts to darken noticeably (but before it starts to smoke) turn off the burners. Allow hot oil to cool. (5-10 minutes) Scrub griddle briefly with griddle brick to introduce the abrasive material onto the griddle (optional). Using the griddle handle-pad-screen combo and a little elbow grease, scrub til shiny!

White Vinegar: can be used to clean griddle top. If you warm the griddle and use white vinegar to clean, the grease and food comes off very easily. (Our griddle is actually silver) Make sure not to heat the griddle up too much or the vinegar will evaporate too quickly and its fumes are hard on the nose. Also can be used with large-grain salt to scrub rust off of abused woks. Not advisable for cast iron skillets (some warm water and a potato are gentler).

Windex is an ammonia-based glass cleaner. Great for mirrors and windows. *Caution: do not mix with bleach! Mixing these two products releases a toxic gas.*

Wood oil soap is used specifically for wood floors. Not as abrasive as many other cleaning chemicals. Mix the soap according to the label and use on wood for a lemony scent.

**Equipment**

Aprons: are really useful for cleaning dishes so dish washers don't get wet while doing dishes. Available in various materials including cloth, vinyl and rubber. Workshifters are more likely to wash dishes faster and complain less when you provide these for them. Also good for keeping sauces or oil from splashing onto clothing. An absolute must for naked cooking.

Bottle brush: You guessed it, used for cleaning bottles or other long skinny containers.

Brooms: used to sweep. Make sure you have enough so workshifters don't use it as an excuse not to do workshifts.

Dish gloves: yellow gloves purchased at Costco. They're latex, so some people might have allergies.

Dish mop: often a small sponge or soft-bristled brush attached to a handle or small pole, similar to a bottle brush but usually softer and more versatile.

Dust pans: used in conjunction with brooms to remove dust and dirt from the floor. They seem to disappear very often.

Floor/deck brush: can be used to sweep large, fairly smooth areas as well as for more intensive floor scrubbing. Wrapping an old rag or t-shirt around a deck brush is a great alternative to old, stinky string mops.

Floor mats: large thick rubber mats with holes and small bumps to decrease dangerous floor situations. Must be removed and cleaned every time floors are mopped, not to be replaced until floors are dry.

Gong brush: medium-sized bristly brush, useful for washing dishes that don't require heavy scrubbing

Griddle Brick is a black abrasive brick that is really good for cleaning your griddle. They get smaller with each use, so you'll have to keep ordering them.

We have tried a white one made from recycled plastic but most houses found them to be less effective. Best used in conjunction with the handle-pad-screen kit described below

Griddle handle-pad-screen set: another tool for cleaning the griddle. Consists of a handle (usually blue) attached to a metal plate with bumps on it. An absorbent fiber pad is placed against the metal plate, followed by a mesh metal screen. The pad and screen rely on pressure and friction to stay attached so use caution to keep from plunging your hand into scorching hot oil!

Griddle scraper: a blade on a long handle that allows for more weight to be used when scraping the grill. This should be used to scrape off food right after it's made and not to actually clean the griddle. It's really expensive, but worth it if your griddle gets used a lot.

Griddle scraper blade: metal blade that attaches to the long handle to make the griddle scraper. Cannot be used independently of handle.

Heavy-duty dish gloves: blue and yellow heavy-duty gloves from East Bay Restaurant Supplies.

Mop handles: Often in stock at CK, used with string mop refills.

Nitrile gloves are used as an alternative to latex gloves for general cleaning needs. They are medical grade so not many people will have allergies to them. You can get them from Costco.

Nylon scrubber: not as abrasive as steel scrubber, but still very useful for washing dishes, especially plastic or ceramic.

Plunger: Used for unclogging toilets or sinks. Just don't use the same on both. Encouraging members to plunge their own messes will keep your maintenance manager happy.

Potwash gloves: Extra-thick black rubber gloves with cloth lining inside. Perfect for hours of scrubbing pots and pans with steel scrubbers. Watch out for fruit fly accumulation if not properly washed off and hung to dry. It has been purported you can stick your hand in a pot of boiling water and not feel a thing with these gloves. I wouldn't suggest trying it.

Spray Bottles: used to mix and apply cleaning chemicals or other solutions. Make sure that all spray bottles are clearly marked. Also, it's a good idea to put chemical mixing directions on the bottles to avoid members refilling a bottle incorrectly.

Sponges are very useful for cleaning basically everything. Costco offers two types:blue and yellow, other options are available from the NP catalog. The blue Costco sponge is not effective for heavy-duty scrubbing and is therefore better suited for bathrooms. The yellow version's green scratchy side is much more abrasive and suitable for pots and pans.

Squeegee: long thin rubber strip mounted on a short or long pole; used to remove excess water from surfaces. Ideal for windows and stainless steel dish pits.

Steel scrubber/wool: strong metal fibers bunched together to provide a highly abrasive scrubbing surface. Great for pots and pans, stainless steel counters, and other scratch-resistant surfaces. Not for use on any soft or porous surface.

String mops: come in two weights, 16 oz and 24 oz. This weight refers to the mop's weight when dry. Please note that they become significantly heavier once wet. Thus, the 16 oz is more popular (and cheaper).

Toilet brushes: As the name suggests, a brush (usually hard plastic bristles) used to clean toilets.

Trash Bags: three kinds available from Costco; black, clear, and white. The largest is the black, for 45 G trash cans. The clear are not as durable and are for 33 G trash cans. The white are the smallest for 13 G cans, with a red drawstring for cinching closed.

Vacuum Bags can be ordered for the ghostbuster-style vacuum. There should be two parts to the inside of your vacuum; a gray cloth filter and the paper bag. The gray cloth filter can be washed in case one your members uses the vacuum without the bag. Bags are disposable.

## AVOID KITCHEN HAZARDS

### Check Kitchen Exhaust Ventilation

Check to be sure kitchen range hoods are being used during cooking and that the vent duct is NOT venting into attics or living spaces, otherwise mold growth may become more likely in those areas. Exhaust venting is particularly important for gas stoves because of the danger of Carbon Monoxide Poisoning.

### Practice Covered Cooking

Cover pots and pans while cooking food in order to help reduce steam escaping into your home (less humidity helps reduce mold, mildew, and dust mites). Covered cooking also means faster cooking, so often this will save energy too.

### Stop Moisture-loving Mold at the First Drip

Look for and correct wet conditions that may cause mold. Inspect frequently for any signs of water leaks or condensation under and around water pipes, drain pipes, sinks, faucets, garbage disposals, dishwasher, vent ducts, windows, and refrigerators and freezers (lines, drip pans, door seals).

### Worse-Case Water Damage Scenarios

Just before leaving for vacation consider shutting off water valves to kitchen or laundry appliance supply lines to prevent possible rupture while you are away. I usually close off the valves to the washing machine at least, but would probably do the same for the refrigerator if I were able to get to it more easily.

I know of someone who had a water line to his washing machine break while he was away for weeks. It caused thousands of dollars in water damage and a severe mold problem in several levels of the home. Not good at all. His misfortune made me a lot more aware of how important it is to avoid water damage and possible mold growth. Even small water leaks, given enough time, can do a lot of damage and contribute to indoor allergies.

### Cooking Up Inhalation Hazards

Burning and Frying greasy foods can produce persistent indoor air pollution and produce a sticky residue on objects throughout the home. Be sure to ventilate the house if smoke and odor becomes a problem while cooking. More than just being unpleasant, such air pollutants as Polycyclic Aromatic Hydrocarbons may be released and create very poor indoor air quality for an extended period in air-tight homes. These tiny combustion particles and gases may also increase the risk of diseases such as cancer and lung disease. Reduced life-expectancy due to indoor cooking fire pollution is a major air quality problem in poorer areas of some third world countries, such as in India, where the cultural norm is kitchens with improperly ventilated open fires fueled by wood or dung.

**Teflon Flu and Canaries in the Kitchen**

Be aware that there is growing evidence that Non-stick Teflon pots and pans may produce very toxic particles and fumes while being pre-heated or during cooking. Inhalation of these Teflon fumes have been correlated to possible flu-like symptoms (referred to as "Teflon Flu"), and this Teflon poison has also killed many pet birds, such as African Grey parrots.

**Colorless...Odorless...Deadly Gas**

Potentially deadly Carbon Monoxide Gas is a particular danger in kitchens with gas stoves. Be sure combustion equipment is properly installed, used, and maintained. Gas appliances should be regularly inspected by a professional who has the equipment to find gas leaks or to detect improper combustion which can lead to Carbon Monoxide hazards in the home. Exhaust from gas stoves and other fuel powered equipment should be vented to the outside of the home. Also, be sure your home has properly installed functional Carbon Monoxide detectors in the proper locations.

**Cockroach Allergy?**

Avoid exposure to Cockroach allergens, which results from Roach feces and degraded body parts. This can become a serious indoor air problem, especially for children with Asthma or people with respiratory conditions. Cockroach allergies are particularly prevalent in low income urban housing developments and unsanitary living environments where garbage and food wastes sustain significant Roach infestations.

**Starve Them Out of House and Home**

Avoid Cockroach infestations by cleaning up all food spills immdediately. Remove and discard garbage bags regularly and keep temporary garbage storage areas free of trash and bits of food waste. Never leave dirty dishes/pots/pans out overnight. Keep food in air-tight containers. Clean the kitchen and other areas regularly. Basically don't make it easy for Roaches to find food in or around your home. If you do have to hire an exterminator, ask what chemicals will be used and do thorough research to understand the possible hazards of the pesticides used.

## I Have Banned Pesticides from My Property

It is best to avoid all pesticide use. I stopped using most household chemicals, pesticides in particular, decades ago. However, if you do use pesticides, be very aware of the potential for food and beverages to become contaminated by airborne droplets, vapors, or surface residues in or around your kitchen during or after treatment. Remove any objects or small appliances that may become contaminated with any amount of the pesticide and then later come into direct contact with food, such as food storage containers, toasters, or dishes.

Remove all food and drink items before pesticides are applied, and be aware that these chemicals can persist for a long time inside and may also cause irritation of the eyes, nose, and throat; plus increased cancer risk, or neurological / organ damage, especially in the very young. Below is a section with more information about what is in Roach Killer.

Keep pesticides and other chemical products out of reach of children and follow the use, storage, and disposal instructions very closely. Opt for eco-friendly exterminators that specialize in chemical-free pest control (or chemical-free "Integrated Pest Management"), or who use more "inert" chemicals proven to be less toxic to humans and pets. Almost all exterminators will claim their products are "non-toxic" to humans, but many are lying or are unaware of the true hazards of what they use. You really have to do your research to know who you are dealing with. More on that coming soon.

## Volatile Organic Compounds in Your Air

Many kitchen household chemical products, such as those covered in the chemical product section below, tend to emit dangerous gases known as Volatile Organic Compounds or VOCs - which are a major cause of indoor air pollution and Sick Building Syndrome. This toxic gas release, or "off-gasing", is usually highest during and immediately after use, but the gases may still slowly escape from areas of application, or from the containers even while in storage. Eliminate as many of the below toxic kitchen household chemicals as possible, and replace those remaining with low or no-VOC alternatives. Either way, try to remove all chemicals from living spaces, especially the kitchen, if possible.

There are other sources of VOC in your home that can not feasibly be removed because they are part of the building's structure. Examples are presswood products, oriented strand board (OSB), plywood, laminates, adhesives in building materials, and some types of flooring such as carpeting or foam pads. See the last tip about having your home air tested for these most common and very health damaging of indoor air toxins.

## Deadly Chemical Gases of Your Own Making: Chloramine

NEVER mix household chemicals because dangerous chemical reactions may result or toxic gases may be relesed into the air. Examples are potentially deadly Chloramine and Chlorine gas which may be release when Chlorine Bleach is combined with acidic products such as Drain Cleaners, vinegar, or ammonia.

**Don't Be An Illegal Dumper of Household Chemicals**

NEVER pour chemicals down the drains to dispose of them! This is often illegal, regardless of whether your wastewater goes into a residential septic system or a city sewer system. Not only can this destroy the natural microbial activity needed for healthy septic tank waste decomposition, but it is dangerous and irresponsible due to the above described potential for chemical reactions, toxin releases, and environmental damage such as groundwater pollution.

**Hot Topic: Smoke Detectors and Extinguishers**

Be sure the rooms and hallways of your home, especially near the kitchen area, has Smoke Detectors in good working order. But do be aware that some Smoke Detectors contain a small amount of a radioactive element known as Americium.

A properly classed kitchen fire-extinguisher (one that will work on grease fires) is also a must-have. Be sure to check the extinguisher gauge periodically to be sure it is still fully charged and ready for use, and make sure all occupants know where to find and how to use the extinguisher. Mount or place extinguishers where they can be easily seen and accessed.

**Got GFI Outlets to Reduce Electrocution Hazards?**

To reduce the risk of electrocution where electrical outlets are located next to water sources in the kitchen or other rooms of your home, check to be sure Ground Fault Interrupt (GFI) outlets have been installed. These are special circuits that will trip to immediately cut of the power to the outlet upon being shorted out, such as in the event of exposure to water. Sockets are required to be GFI outlets if they happen to be located within a certain distance of water sources such as faucets or in outside areas like a porch where rain and other water sources could be an issue.

GFI outlets are a legal requirement to comply with building codes in most areas. In case you are wondering which of your outlets may already be GFI - look for those which may have a test button near the sockets. In my home this indicates they are GFI, but in your home they may appear differently. If in doubt, consult with an electrician to see if your dwelling meets electrical building code standards of safety.

**Dark Side of the Platics Generation**

There is growing concern over health damaging toxins leaching into foods and beverages from plastic packaging and storage containers. Bisphenol-A is one such plastic-derived toxin that is now being detected in most everyone's bloodstream and which has some serious health implications such as increased risk of cancer. Learn what my family is doing to avoidBisphenol-A and why maybe you should also start to eliminate plastics from your kitchen too. You can also learn more about the types of plastics in the section below.

**Remove the Guess Work: Test Your Home Air for Chemicals and Hidden Mold**

If you would like to know how many indoor chemicals you may be breathing and where they are coming from - or if you would like to find out if your kitchen or other rooms may harbor hidden mold colonies, for example - behind walls, under / inside appliances, in ceilings, or in sub-flooring - I recommend you test your indoor air for hidden mold + over 400 chemicalssimultaneously. An accurate home air test is the best way to quantify and find the sources of indoor air pollution in your kitchen or any other rooms in or around your home.

## KITCHEN CHEMICALS

A kitchen is just like a science laboratory, don't think the only chemicals in your kitchen are those under the sink. All the ingredients you cook with are themselves made up of chemical compounds—some complex and some quite simple.

### ACIDS

Acids are found in several household cleaning compounds, pool chemicals, solvents, wet cell batteries, and radiator flushers and cleaners. Acids, which have a pH range of 0 to 6.9, may be corrosive and produce severe burns on contact. Vinegar, which contains four to six Per cent acetic acid, is generally considered nontoxic.

Skin contact with acid may produce severe pain and risk of secondary infection and scarring. Chronic skin exposure to acids may cause mild irritation, dermatitis, or roughened skin. Inhalation of fumes may produce nose and throat irritation, coughing, chest pain, and even pulmonary edema. The onset of symptoms following inhalation of vapours may be delayed for several hours.

When working with household products containing acids, wear protective gloves. Make sure the ventilation is adequate. Refer to the specific product for disposal recommendations.

### AEROSOLS

Aerosol sprays contain an active ingredient and a liquid or gaseous propellant that is packed under at least 40 pounds of pressure per square inch. These pressurized aerosol containers are explosive and may be flammable.

The actual product propelled by the aerosol, such as some oven cleaners, can be corrosive or poisonous, therefore requiring great care.

Aerosol sprays should be used with care. The fine particles emitted from aerosol sprays are easily breathed deeply into the lungs and quickly absorbed into the bloodstream. Thus, a chemical that is harmless to your skin may become extremely dangerous if inhaled as a mist.

Acute symptoms include headache, nausea, dizziness, shortness of breath, eye and throat irritation, skin rash, burns, lung inflammation, and liver damage. If spray is misdirected, chemical burns and eye injury can also occur. Intentionally inhaling aerosol gases for kicks, sometimes called "sniffing" or "huffing," has resulted in the death of several young Americans. An aerosol container should never be heated significantly above room temperature because it can explode. Storage of cans in direct sunlight, car trunks, and near furnaces, stoves, and ovens can result in explosion. When heated, aerosol gases can turn into toxic gases including fluorine, chlorine, chloride or hydrogen fluoride, or phosgene. Breathing these vapours can be very harmful to you.

Significant environmental impact from aerosol sprays led to alterations in their design. Several of the Chloro-fluorocarbons (CFCs) that have been used in aerosol sprays in the past reacted with and reduced the ozone layer in the upper atmosphere.

Reduction in the ozone layer and the resulting rise in ultraviolet radiation reaching the earth can result in increased rates of skin cancer, skin aging, eye damage, and Vitamin D poisoning. Before buying or using aerosol sprays, weigh their convenience against their potential health and environmental hazards.

- *Use*: Consider alternatives to aerosol sprays, including alternative methods of application. If you are using an aerosol spray, try not to breathe the released particles; stand out of the way of the mist and make certain the mist is being blown away from you.
- *Storage*: Do not store near heat or flames. Keep away from children.
- *Disposal*: If the aerosol can is empty, dispose of it in the trash bound for the landfill. Aerosol cans burned in trash barrels can explode, scattering propellant and product. If ingredients are left in the can the best thing to do is to use the product up as intended. If you must dispose of an aerosol can that isn't empty, discharge the contents of the container into a deep cardboard box outdoors, and allow it to dry. When the can is empty, it and the cardboard box can be thrown in the trash. If you discharge the contents be very careful: Do not spray near children, animals, or areas of human contact such as playgrounds or gardens. Avoid inhaling the vapours.
- *Alternatives*: For the most part, aerosol sprays are no more effective than pouring, wiping, brushing, or dusting. Try to purchase products

in pump spray, roll-on, liquid, or non-aerosol spray. Spray guns may be desirable in a case where you want to cover a large surface evenly.

## AIR FRESHENERS

Air fresheners work in one of the following four ways: by interfering with your ability to smell by way of a nerve-deadening agent; by coating your nasal passages with an undetectable oil film; by covering up one smell with another; and (rarely) by breaking down the offensive odor. Despite their name, air fresheners do little to freshen the air.

Aerosol fresheners can be harmful to lungs if inhaled in high concentrations or for prolonged periods of time. Solid fresheners may be poisonous if eaten by children or pets.

- *Use*: If freshener is in aerosol form, do not breathe fumes. Avoid skin contact. Use only in well-ventilated areas.
- *Storage*: Keep out of the reach of children and pets. Store away from heat or flame.
- *Disposal*: It is best to use up air freshener as it was intended. For unwanted portions of solid air freshener, allow to evaporate by exposing it to the air.
- *Alternatives*: There are several nontoxic ways to freshen the air in your home.

*Hazardous constituents and possible effects*:

- *Formaldehyde*: A suspected carcinogen and a strong irritant to the eyes, throat, skin and lungs
- *Petroleum distillates*: Irritates skin, eyes, respiratory tract; may cause fatal pulmonary edema; flammable
- *P-dichlorobenzene*: Vapour irritating to skin, eyes and throat, causes liver damage in animal studies
- *Aerosol propellants*: Either associated with brain damage or highly flammable

## ALKALIES AND ALKALINES

Alkalies are commonly found in bleach, Ammonia automatic dishwashing detergent, low phosphate detergents, drain cleaners, oven cleaners, lime, colour wave hair preparations, depilatories, alkaline disk batteries, Clinitest tablets for home glucose testing, and wet cement. Alkalies, also called bases, all have a pH range of 7.1 to 14.0.

The corrosive effects of alkaline chemicals usually occur rapidly, sometimes with exposures as short as one second. Severe skin irritation and burns can occur from skin contact. Inhalation of fumes from alkalies may cause watering of the eyes, sneezing, coughing, choking, shortness of breath, and inflammation and irritation from the nose to lungs. When working with household products that are alkaline or contain alkalies, wear gloves to protect your skin. Make sure ventilation is adequate.

## ALL PURPOSE CLEANERS

The ingredients in all-purpose cleaners are a combination of detergents, grease cutting agents, and possibly solvents and disinfectants. These products may contain one or more of the following hazardous ingredients: Ammonia, ethylene glycol monobutyl acetate, sodium hypochlorite, and trisodium phosphate. Depending upon the ingredients contained in the particular cleaner, they can be mildly to extremely irritating to the skin, eyes, nose, and throat, and corrosive if swallowed. Chronic irritation may occur from repeated use.

Do not mix ammonia-based cleaners with bleach-based cleaners. Hazardous fumes will result! Cleaners that contain phosphates present a water pollution hazard.

*Use*: Wear gloves. Make sure that the ventilation is adequate. Do not mix different cleaners together as toxic fumes may result.

*Hazardous constituents and Possible Effects*:

- Ammonia: Fumes irritate eyes and lungs; can cause burns or rashes on skin; can produce deadly chloramine gas if mixed with chlorine containing products
- Ethylene glycol monobutyl acetate: Poisons animals, who are attracted to sweet smell; can cause damage to internal organs through skin absorption; inhalation can cause dizziness
- Sodium hypochlorite: Corrosive to skin and mucous membranes; fumes irritating.

## STAY AWAY FROM HYDROFLUORIC ACID FOLKS!!! IT'S A KILLER!!!

- *Use*: Do not use products with hydrofluoric acid. If the aluminum cleaner ingredients are not on the label, you cannot assume hydrofluoric acid is not in the product. If you are using a product which contains this ingredient, protect all exposed skin in addition to wearing protective gloves, safety goggles, and a respirator with an acid gas cartridge.
- *Storage*: Store away from children.
- *Disposal*: If aluminum cleaner is in liquid form take it to a household hazardous waste collection. If collection is not available, then flush down the drain with plenty of water. If you are on a septic tank or lagoon, dispose of small quantities over a number of days. If cleaner

is in solid paste form and has completely hardened, it may then be thrown in the trash destined for the landfill.

## AMMONIA

Ammonia, a colourless gas or liquid with a sharp irritating odor, can be found in household cleaners, wax removers, glass and window cleaners, and oven cleaners. In strong concentrations, such as may be found in commercial products, ammonia vapours and liquids can be corrosive causing severe burns and irritation to the skin, eyes, and lungs.

Household ammonia contains 5-10% ammonia and is considered to be an irritant rather than a corrosive hazard. Vapours, even in low concentrations, can cause severe eye, lung, and skin irritation. Chronic irritation may occur if ammonia is used over long periods of time. Do not mix ammonia with chlorine bleach or bleach products!

When ammonia and bleach are mixed, a chloramine gas results which can cause coughing, loss of voice, feeling of burning and suffocation, and even death.

Ammonia inhalers are sometimes mistaken by children for candy. These inhalers or smelling salts will cause burns to the lips and mouth if chewed.

- *Use*: Wear protective gloves, safety goggles, and a respirator with an ammonia cartridge. Use ammonia only in well-ventilated areas where there is plenty of fresh air.
- *Storage*: Store away from children.
- *Disposal*: Empty containers can be thrown in the trash. It is best to use up the product as intended, but if you must dispose of an unused portion, flush down the drain with plenty of water. If you are on a septic tank or lagoon, dispose of small quantities over a number of days.
- *Alternatives*: Vinegar, like ammonia, will cut through grease and grime but without the irritation produced by ammonia and ammonia vapours.

## ANTI-BACTERIAL CLEANER

*Cleaners are used to remove dirt*: Antibacterial cleaners remove dirt and kill bacteria. Bacteria are organisms too small to see with just your eyes. Some bacteria cause diseases or make you sick. Others do not.

Antibacterial cleaners come in a spray can or pump bottle container. They are commonly used in the kitchen to clean things that come in contact with food, like cutting boards and counter tops. Keeping these areas clean will help prevent harmful bacteria from contaminating your food. It is especially important to clean areas that come in contact with raw meats. Raw meats can also carry bacteria. Use an antibacterial kitchen cleaner or wash the area with hot soapy water.

If cleaning the kitchen you may be using antibacterial cleaners to do the job. If so, you need to be sure to always read the label first to know how to properly use these products and for safety information.

Antibacterial cleaners usually contain water, a fragrance, a surfactant, and a pesticide. The surfactant breaks up the dirt, the pesticide kills the bacteria, the fragrance makes it smell good and the water holds the cleaner together. In antibacterial cleaners the pesticides are commonly quaternary ammonium or phenolic chemicals. They are known as antimicrobial pesticides.

Antibacterial cleaners are very irritating to your eyes and skin and will burn your throat. It's a good idea to wear latex dishwashing gloves to help protect your skin when using these cleaners. If you get some on the cleaner on your skin or in your eyes, wash it off immediately.

## ANTIFREEZE

Antifreeze contains ethylene glycol which is poisonous when ingested. Ingestion may result in depression followed by respiratory and cardiac failure, kidney damage and brain damage. Manufacturers of antifreeze are required to clearly post dangers on the label and provide a childproof cap, which minimizes the danger of accidental ingestion by children. However, antifreeze when improperly disposed of can endanger the health of pets.

Each year, thousands of dogs and cats are poisoned by discarded or leaking antifreeze. The sweet taste of antifreeze attracts pets who lap up puddles of antifreeze they find. To prevent this danger, wash down or absorb puddles of antifreeze with an absorbent material such as kitty litter and dispose of the absorbent in the trash.

- *Use*: Follow label directions. Never heat antifreeze. This would release toxic fumes.
- *Storage*: Store away from heat and in a well-ventilated area. Keep away from children and pets.
- *Disposal*: The major components of antifreeze can be broken down by organisms in a sewage treatment plant. If your home is connected to a sanitary or municipal sewer system, household quantities of antifreeze can be flushed down the drain with plenty of water.
- The solution is not so easy for those homes with a septic tank because antifreeze can overwhelm the organisms in your septic system, causing damage to the system. If your wastewater goes into a septic tank, very small amounts over a period of time can be flushed with plenty of water. Better yet, ask a friend, relative, or Neighbour who is hooked up to the sanitary sewer system to use their drain to dispose of your household quantity of used antifreeze. Do not pour antifreeze into storm sewer openings, sinkholes, or abandoned wells where they will directly pollute the water.

*Hazardous constituent and Possible Effects*:

- *Ethylene Glycol*: Poisons animals, who are attracted to the sweet smell; can cause damage to internal organs through skin absorption; inhalation can cause dizziness.
- There is a new type of antifreeze available that contains Propylene Glycol. Propylene glycol is much less toxic than ethylene glycol. An animal would have to consume a lot more of this type of antifreeze, a quantity that is unlikely to be available, to get sick or to die. The bottle's label should tell you what is type of antifreeze it is.
- Some people who have vacation homes that they"close up" for the winter will pour antifreeze into toilets so the water doesn't freeze. In this case, these people should always use the less toxic antifreeze (the ones with propylene glycol in it) because pets can drink out of toilets and can become poisoned.

## ARSENIC

Arsenic is a highly toxic, naturally occurring grayish- white element used as a poison in pesticides and herbicides. Arsenic is also found as an ingredient in pigments and wood preservatives. Arsenic contained in wolmanized lumber will not release toxic compounds unless burned. Some treated lumber contains Arsenic in the form of Copper Chromated Arsenate.

Arsenic can be harmful through inhalation, absorption through skin and mucous membranes, skin contact, and ingestion.

Accidental poisoning can occur through breathing fumes, licking paintbrushes to a point when using pigments containing arsenic, or from wearing inadequate clothing when applying arsenic-based products.

Effects of mild poisoning from inhalation include loss of appetite, nausea, and diarrhea. Effects of more severe chronic or acute exposure include skin lesions, skin rash, chronic headaches, apathy, garlic odor on breath, a metallic taste in the mouth, a bronzing pigment of the skin resembling" raindrops on a dusty road," and possible damage to the liver. Arsenic and arsenic compounds are known cancer-causing agents and have been implicated in lung and skin cancer and associated with birth defects.

## ASPHALT/ ROOFING TAR

In the paving and roofing trades, a tar or asphalt is applied in a hot liquid form that cools into a semi-solid covering. Asphalt is a residue of petroleum refining.

Tar is produced by distillation of coal, oil, lignite, peat, or wood. Inhalation of hot asphalt fumes can cause eye and respiratory tract irritation, headaches, nausea, and nervousness. Skin exposure to hot tar can cause serious burns. Wear protective gloves.

## AUTOMATIC TRANSMISSION FLUID

Automatic transmission fluid, used to pull the clutch and lubricate automobile transmissions, is mainly composed of mineral oil. Automatic transmission fluid is flammable at high temperatures and relatively nontoxic unless swallowed and aspirated.

Used automatic transmission oil contains environmentally toxic heavy metals including Lead. The heavy metal in used fluid can cause severe nervous system damage to wildlife and other animals if disposed of improperly.

- *Use*: When draining fluid wear gloves and avoid skin contact.
- *Storage*: Store used transmission fluid in a plastic container with a tight-fitting lid. Clearly mark what is in the container and store on a high shelf out of the reach of children and pets.
- *Disposal*: If not contaminated with other products, used and unused automatic transmission fluid may be accepted for recycling at local service stations that also accept used motor oil or at the highway transportation department. Ask first before dumping the used fluid into an oil collection tank because some Centres may not accept it. Carry the transmission fluid in a plastic container with a tight-fitting lid or, if the fluid is unused, in its original container.

## BATTERIES—WET CELL

Automobile, boats, and tractor batteries are wet cell batteries which contain Lead and a solution of sulfuric acid. When activated, the electrolyte solution in the battery produces explosive gases which are easily ignited. Manufacturers of batteries containing sulfuric acid must use labels which warn consumers of the dangers from battery acid and accumulated gases. Sulfuric acid is extremely caustic. Fumes are strongly irritating, and contact can cause burning and charring of the skin; it is exceedingly dangerous to eyes. Lead is poisonous in all forms and accumulates in our bodies and in the environment.

- *Use*: Wear protective gloves. Do not get battery acid on you or your clothing. If you do, wash your hands or body immediately and put baking soda on your clothes where the battery acid splashed. Do not attempt to neutralize acids on the skin or when swallowed. Flushing with or drinking sodium bicarbonate creates thermal heat from the acid base reaction, causing further injury. Do not stand by an uncapped battery while the motor is running; it can splash on you. After touching a battery, wash hands thoroughly before touching eyes or mouth. Keep all sources of flames, including cigarettes, away from batteries.
- *Storage*: Store away from children, especially curious children who might want to break open the battery to see what is inside. Keep

away from all sources of sparks, including flames. Store under a tarp or in a covered area.

- *Disposal*: Recycle used batteries! Improper disposal of batteries presents an environmental hazard. It is important and easy to dispose of batteries by recycling them and it is usually possible to trade in old batteries where you purchase new ones. To locate the recycler nearest to you, look up "Batteries" in the Yellow Pages of the phone book. Depending upon the market place, you may get a small amount of money for your recycled battery, but the fact that you do not have to pay to dispose of this highly hazardous waste makes it a bargain to recycle batteries.

## CAMPHOR

Camphor is a colourless or a white crystal granule or cake product obtained from the wood of the camphor tree. It may also be synthetically derived. Some products such as lotions, astringents, and moth repellents still contain camphor as an active ingredient. In 1980, the Food and Drug Administration set a limit of 11% allowable camphor in consumer products and totally banned products labeled as camphorated oil, camphor oil, camphor liniment, and camphorated liniment.

Camphor, readily absorbed through the skin, produces the sensation of warmth and slight local anesthesia. Camphor poisoning produces seizures and may be preceded by mental confusion, irritability, neuromuscular hyperactivity, and jerky movements of the extremities. Camphor poisoning from household products may occur following oral ingestion. Symptoms occur five to ninety minutes following ingestion.

## CARBON MONOXIDE

Carbon monoxide is a colourless gas which is practically odorless, tasteless, and non-irritating. Carbon monoxide is always formed when a fuel containing carbon is inadequately burned with poor ventilation. Kerosene, charcoal, coal, wood stoves, and automobile exhaust fumes are common sources of carbon monoxide poisoning. Natural gas in the United States does not contain carbon monoxide, but it may form if the gas is burned without adequate air supplies.

Carbon monoxide starves the body and brain of oxygen. Carbon monoxide poisoning produces symptoms ranging from headache, dizziness, flushed skin, disorientation, troubled thinking, abnormal reflexes, shortness of breath, fainting, and convulsions, to coma and even death. Heart problems are also aggravated by the presence of carbon monoxide because the heart must pump harder.

Children, persons with respiratory illness or anemia, and the aged may be particularly sensitive. Chronic exposure to low carbon monoxide levels impairs judgement and increases the time required to make decisions. If you have an attached garage, always make sure the door to the house is closed and the garage door is open when the car is running. If you think that you have a problem with carbon monoxide fumes, contact your local or state Department of Health for assistance.

## CARBON TETRACHLORIDE

Because of its excellent solvent properties and non flammability, carbon tetrachloride has been in use for many decades in commercial products such as dry cleaning solvents, grease solvents, and fire extinguishing agents. Today it is used only in industry and as a fumigant. In 1970, the Food and Drug Administration banned carbon tetrachloride and any mixture containing it for use in the home. The FDA classified carbon tetrachloride as a substance so hazardous that no warning label could be devised that would adequately protect the householder.

Carbon tetrachloride is a cellular toxin that produces cellular destruction throughout the body, especially in the liver, kidney, and central nervous system. It is toxic by all routes of exposure: inhalation, absorption, skin contact, and oral ingestion. Although uniquely potent, carbon tetrachloride is in many respects representative of a large class of related chlorinated hydrocarbon solvents.

Disposal: If you find a product containing carbon tetrachloride, secure and hold for professional household hazardous waste collection or give it to a licensed hazardous waste handler.

## CARBURETOR CLEANER

*Hazardous constituents and Possible Effects*:

- *Cresol*: Corrosive to tissue, damages liver, kidneys, lungs, pancreas and spleen
- *Methylene Chloride*: A suspected carcinogen; vapours cause carbon monoxide accumulation in blood
- *Sodium Chromate*: Causes contact dermatitis

## CARPET CLEANER

*Hazardous constituents and Possible Effects*:

- *Perchloroethylene*: Fumes are carcinogenic and acutely toxic, cause dizziness, sleepiness, nausea, loss of appetite and disorientation
- *Naphthalene*: Damages liver; prolonged Vapour exposure has led to cataract formation

These ingredients are most commonly found in commercial"spot removers", rather than water-based detergent products or rub-in cleansing powders.

## CRESOL

Cresol, a highly caustic, colourless solid or liquid with a sweet tarry odor, is used mainly as a disinfectant. Cresol is very corrosive to all tissues. When it comes in contact with the skin it may not produce any burning sensation immediately. Prickling and intense burning will occur followed by loss of feeling. If cresol contacts the eyes it may cause extensive damage. Cresol vapours and liquids are absorbed through inhalation and eye and skin contact. Repeated or prolonged exposure to low concentrations of cresol can produce chronic systemic poisoning. Symptoms of poisoning include vomiting, difficulty in swallowing, diarrhea, loss of appetite, headache, fainting, dizziness, mental disturbance and skin rash. Cresol attacks the central nervous system, respiratory system, liver, kidneys, skin and eyes.

## DETERGENT

The word"detergent" refers to household cleaning products which are based on non-soap, synthetic surfactants and which are primarily used for laundering and dishwashing. There are several types of detergents including automatic dishwashing, hand dishwashing, enzyme, and low-phosphate detergents.

All detergents contain"cationic,""anionic," or"non- ionic" detergents. Cationic detergents are the most toxic when taken internally. Symptoms from ingestion include nausea, vomiting, shock, convulsions, and coma as quickly as one to four hours after ingestion, due to rapid absorption. By themselves, anionic detergents have low toxicity causing mild, local irritation of skin and eyes. But the addition of"builders" to anionic detergents is common and makes anionic detergents alkaline and caustic.

Non ionic detergents have low toxicity. At most, mild irritation of the skin and mucous membranes occurs. Ingestion causes no hazardous effects. Some typical nonionic detergents are alkyl aryl polyether sulfates, alcohol sulfonates, alkyl phenol polyglycol ethers, and polyethylene glycol alkyl aryl ethers.

Detergents are responsible for many household poisonings. Part of the problem is that detergent boxes are brightly coloured and attractive and commonly stored in low, accessible places.

There is a common misconception that low-phosphate detergents are "safe." While low phosphate detergents are safer to the environment, they are 100 to 1000 times more caustic than phosphate detergents. This means that low-phosphate detergents can cause serious burns if even a small amount is ingested. Since powdered granules are more difficult to accidentally swallow, powdered rather than liquid detergents may be a safer choice if you have small children in the home. All detergents should be carefully stored well away from the reach of children.

## AUTOMATIC DISHWASHING DETERGENT

Most automatic dishwashing detergents are alkaline with pH values of 10.5 to 12.0. These products may be classified as irritants or corrosives depending upon their composition, concentration, and physical form. Skin irritation or burns may occur following exposure to dissolved detergents. Toxicity may range from mild tissue causes severe burns. The fact that automatic dishwashing detergents contain phosphate causes environmental concerns. You might consider buying a powdered automatic detergent over a liquid variety, because powdered detergents are more difficult to mistakenly swallow Automatic dishwashing detergents may also contain sodium carbonate.

## HAND DISHWASHING DETERGENT

These products are intended for the handwashing of dishes. Hand dishwashing detergents are much less toxic than automatic dishwashing detergents. Hand dishwashing detergents are combinations of anionic and non-ionic detergents, glycols, alcohols, and salts. Exposure to the membranes of the mouth, throat, and gastro - intestinal tract may be irritating but not caustic. Anionic and non-ionic detergents are not well absorbed, and no toxic dose has been established. Hand dishwashing detergents are generally considered low in toxicity.

## ENZYME DETERGENT

Enzymes are found in various laundry detergents and pre-soaks to loosen soil and remove stains. The enzymes are obtained from selected strains of bacteria. Products which contain enzymes have irritating and sensitizing properties. Asthma and dermatitis may occur from industrial exposure to these enzyme products but would be unlikely from routine household use. Granulated detergents, which encapsulate the enzyme, are less toxic than powdered formulations to people who have become sensitized to these enzyme detergents.

## HAZING OF GLASSWARE, PROHIBITION ON DISHWASHING LEAD CRYSTAL

Glassware washed by dishwashing machines can develop a white haze on the surface over time. This may becaused by any or all of the processes, only one of which is reversible:

### Limescale Deposit

If the dishwasher has run out of the salt that recharges the ion exchange resin that softens the water, and the water supply is "hard", limescale deposits can appear on all items, but are especially visible on glassware. It can be removed by cleaning with vinegar or lemon juice, or a proprietary limescale removal agent. The dishwasher should either be recharged with salt, adjusted appropriately for the hardness of the supply water—or possibly this is a symptom of failure of the ion exchange resin in the water softener (which is one of the more expensive components). The resin may have stopped working because it has been poisoned by iron or manganese salts in the supply water.

## ITEMS THAT SHOULD NOT BE PUT IN A DISHWASHER

Some items can be damaged if washed in a dishwasher because of the effects of the chemicals and hot water. Lead crystal will be irreversibly damaged if put in a dishwasher, while aluminium items will discolour. Saucepan manufacturers often recommend handwashing due to the harsh effects of the chemicals on the pan coatings.

Valuable items—such as antiques—should be washed by hand as they may be dulled or damaged, and detergents will gradually fade the glazing and print. Sterling silver and pewter will oxidize and discolour from the heat. Furthermore, pewter has a low melting point and may warp in some dishwashers. Cast iron is likely to rust in a dishwasher.

Items soiled by wax, cigarette ash or anything which might contaminate the rest of the wash load (such as poisons or mineral oils) should not be put in a dishwasher. Objects contaminated by solvents may explode in a dishwasher.

Glued items, such as some cutlery handles or wooden cutting boards, may be melted or softened if dishwashed, especially on a hot wash cycle when temperatures can reach 75 °C; these high temperatures can also damage plastic items which are labelled as not being dishwasher safe, however some plastic items can be distorted or melted if placed in the bottom rack too close to an exposed heating element, hence many dishwasher-safe plastic items advise placing in the top rack only (many newer dishwashers have a concealed heating element away from the bottom rack entirely). Squeezing plastic items into small spaces may cause the plastic to distort in shape.

Dishwashers should only be used to wash normal household items, like plates, cutlery, cups, mugs, kitchenware etc. Items such as paintbrushes, tools, furnace filters etc. should not be put into a dishwasher as this will cause the subsequent washes to become contaminated and may cause damage to the appliance.

## DRYING

The heat inside the dishwasher dries the contents after the final hot rinse. Plastic and non-stick items may not dry properly compared to china and glass, which hold the heat better. Some dishwashers incorporate a fan to improve drying. Older dishwashers with a visible heating element may use the heating element to improve drying, however this uses more energy.

Governmental agencies often recommend air-drying dishes by either disabling or stopping the drying cycle to save energy.

## LEVEL OF SANITIZING

Dishwashers do not sterilize the utensils, as proper sterilization requires autoclaving at 121 °C with pressurized wet steam for at least 15 minutes. Commercial dishwashers can use one of two types of sanitizing methods: hot water sanitizing (using final rinse water at a temperature of at least 83 °C (180 °F)), or chemical sanitizing (by injecting chlorine in the final rinse water). Not all dishwashers are capable of reaching the high temperature required for hot water sanitizing. Medical grade dishwashers and sanitizers are starting to use ultrasonic cleaners, which use a liquid bath treated with sonics to remove particles and sterilize instruments.

Most consumer dishwashers use a 75°C thermostat in the sanitizing process. During the final rinse cycle, the heating element and wash pump are turned on, and the cycle timer (electronic or electromechanical) is stopped until the thermostat is tripped. At this point, the cycle timer resumes and will generally trigger a drain cycle within a few timer increments.

Most consumer dishwashers use 75°C rather than 83°C for reasons of burn risk, energy consumption, total cycle time, and possible damage to plastic items placed inside the dishwasher. With new advances in detergents, lower water temperatures (50–55°C) are needed to prevent premature decay of the enzymes used to eat the grease and other build-ups on the dishes. This also saves energy and can allow the washer to be hooked directly to the hot water supply for the house.

In the US, residential dishwashers can be certified to a NSF International testing protocol which verifies the cleaning and sanitation performance of the unit.

## SALT

Salt is the original food additive. Essential for life, salt (Sodium Chloride) controls many body functions. Salt is one of the five taste sensations we can detect with the sensors (or taste buds) on our tongues.

In the kitchen we use salt as a preservative, to help strengthen doughs, etc. and to emphasise flavours. Salt preserves food by taking out moisture and thus preventing bacterial growth.

The charge on the sodium and chloride ions in salt in doughs and meringues can help bind charged protein molecules and thus make them "stronger". Our tongues are particularly attuned to the taste of salt - presumably since we cannot make salt and need to get all our needs from our diet. Although salt was once one of the most precious of commodities, today salt is common place and added to nearly all processed foods both as a flavour enhancer and as a preservative.

## SUGARS

Sugars are made of molecules that consist of 6 carbon atoms joined together in a ring with associated hydrogen and oxygen atoms. The common sugar we buy from the supermarket is sucrose and consists of two such sugar rings joined together. Sugar provides energy. Sweet foods have always been important in our diet. In prehistoric times man had to get energy to chase the wildebeest to feed the family, so we developed a real sweet tooth. When refined sugar became available it was a very expensive commodity, but now that sugar is cheap and readily available we often eat too much - which is not good for us. In the kitchen sugar has many uses. Apart from simply making food taste sweet we use sugar in many dishes. Sugar molecules can link proteins together - making it much easier to beat egg whites into a meringue or helping the egg proteins thicken a custard.

## OILS AND FATS

Fats and oils give foods a rich, creamy, feel in the mouth so they are used in "comfort" food products such as chocolates and ice creams. In the kitchen we also use fats to fry - the high boiling points allows us to cook foods (e.g. chips and meats) at temperatures above 100°C where chemical reactions occur that develop interesting "browned" flavours. As with sugars our liking for fatty foods probably developed in pre-historic times. Fats are an excellent means of storing food energy - people who could lay down fat deposits when food was plentiful could then store the food energy for later lean times. Thus evolution would have favoured those of our ancestors who could put on weight easier. These days, with food readily available, it is a disadvantage to be able so easily to convert fats in food to fat on the body.

To a scientist oils and fats are members of the same group of molecules; they consist of three chains of carbon atoms with two hydrogen atoms attached to most carbons. The longer the chains the higher the melting point - so short chains give us the liquid oils and long chains the solid fats.

In saturated fats all the carbon atoms are joined by single and form straight chains. In mono-unsaturated two of the carbons and are joined to each by a double bond. This double bond introduces a kink in the chains and makes it difficult to pack the fat molecules in a crystal - so they have lower melting points than saturated fats. Poly-unsaturated fats have several such kinks in them giving them even lower melting points. It is the high melting point of saturated fats that makes them particularly dangerous to us - if solid fat deposits form in blood vessels they can stop the flow of blood leading to heart disease, etc.

## PROTEINS

Proteins are long molecules made by joining small building blocks (amino acids) together. Most of the biochemistry of our bodies is controlled by proteins - the sequence of amino acids determines the shape of the protein and its shape helps the protein perform its own function. For example, haemoglobin has a special shape that allows it to carry oxygen molecules around in the blood stream . When a muscle needs some oxygen it sends a chemical signal and the haemoglobin changes shape so the oxygen pops out.

We need a good deal of protein in our diets - our bodies break down the proteins we eat into their constituent amino acids which we then recycle to make the proteins our own bodies need. Proteins are amongst the most important molecules we use in the kitchen as they change their properties when heated or beaten and react together chemically at high temperatures. Eggs are mostly proteins dissolved in water. If we whisk eggs the proteins change shape (denature) and can form stable foams. If we cook eggs the proteins react to form a solid network - as in a hard-boiled egg. We use these changes when we make cakes and other baked goods - they are held together by the "glue" formed by the reacting proteins.

### STARCHES

The other main food group is made up from starches. Starches are large molecules made by joining many sugar rings together. Scientists often classify starches and sugars together - starches don't taste sweet since the long molecules are too large to reach the sensitive parts of the taste buds on our tongues. There are two main types of starch molecule; amylose in which the sugar rings are joined to make long strings and amylopectin in which the sugar rings are joined in a branched structure like a Christmas tree.

In the kitchen the major sources of starch are from root vegetables such as potatoes and from cereals - usually in the form of flour. We use starches to provide bulk and texture in baked goods - imagine a cake with no flour - it would just be a soufflé with no substance. Starch is formed by many plants in small granules - a typical granule may be a few thousandths of a millimetre across.

Of course, the granules are not purely amylopectin and amylose, the plants also incorporate some proteins as they make the granules. Starch granules with a high protein content will absorb a lot of moisture at room temperature, while those with low protein contents absorb but little water. Starch granules can absorb astonishing amounts of water (potato starch granules can easily absorb 100 times their own volume of water) so they make excellent thickeners.

## DIESEL FUEL AND KEROSENE

Both kerosene and diesel fuel are flammable and are petroleum distillate products. Kerosene is used in lamps, domestic heaters or furnaces, jet engine fuel, and as a solvent for greases and pesticides. Diesel fuel has a higher boiling point than kerosene and is used to power diesel engines.

Kerosene and diesel fuel can damage your health through inhalation, ingestion, and skin contact and absorption. The first symptoms of poisoning include confusion, restlessness, and tremors. Overexposure can lead to central nervous depression with symptoms of inebriation. This may be followed by nausea and headache and may eventually lead to coma and death. Aspiration of fluid into the lungs can occur during ingestion and vomiting. This may result in chemical pneumonia and lung lesions. Ingestion of kerosene is a special problem since it is frequently improperly stored in food containers and then swallowed by children.

*Use*: Never smoke around kerosene or diesel fuel. Keep the lid on when not in use. Do not use kerosene or diesel fuel to clean paint or grease from your body (use detergent and water instead or massage with a few drops of baby oil, butter or margarine, wipe dry, and wash with soap and water). Always wear protective gloves and wash your hands and exposed body parts before eating or smoking. Avoid breathing fumes.

If using a kerosene heater, provide adequate ventilation to remove combustion pollutants, such as carbon monoxide and sulfur dioxide. Use only low sulfur 1-K grade fuel in kerosene space heaters. Never use home heating oil or other fuels.

- *Storage*: Keep out of the reach of children and pets. Store in an approved safety container in a garage or outbuilding with good ventilation. If you have a water heater, furnace, or other sources of ignition in your garage, it may not be a safe place to store kerosene or diesel fuel. Keep away from heat, flame, and sources of ignition. Do not completely fill the container; kerosene and diesel fuel need room to expand.
- *Disposal*: There is usually little need to dispose of kerosene or diesel fuel since it can normally be used. However, kerosene or diesel fuel that has been contaminated or dirtied cannot be used and must be saved for disposal by a licensed hazardous waste collector or through a professional household hazardous waste collection Programme.

## DISINFECTANTS

Disinfectants are considered pesticides. They reduce some germs and are a temporary measure at best for making your home "germ free." Skin contact and vapours can be irritating and corrosive to the respiratory system and skin. Disinfectants are especially hazardous when dispersed from aerosol cans because the disinfectant can be easily ingested through the nose and mouth.

Disinfectants may contain one or more of the following hazardous substances: Ammonia, cationic detergents, cresol, lye, phenol, pine oil.

- *Use*: Avoid aerosol dispensers. Handle disinfectant with gloves to avoid corrosive effects and absorption through skin and wear safety goggles. Make sure ventilation is adequate with plenty of fresh air present. Do not use disinfectants around food, animals, or children.
- *Storage*: Keep away from children. Store in a well ventilated area.

- *Disposal*: Use up as intended. To dispose of unused or unwanted portions take the product to a hazardous household waste collection Centre. If collection is not available, then flush the product down the drain with plenty of water. If on a septic tank or lagoon, dispose of small quantities over a number of days.

*Hazardous constituents and Possible Effects*:

- *Ammonia*: Fumes irritate eyes and lungs; can cause burns or rashes on skin; can produce deadly chloramine gas if mixed with chlorine containing products.
- *Detergents*: Toxic and poisonous to ingest, causing nausea and in extreme cases - coma.
- *Cresol*: Corrosive to tissue, damages liver, kidneys, lungs, pancreas and spleen.
- *Lye*: Caustic product that burns skin, can cause blindness.
- *Phenol*: Central nervous system depression; severely affect circulatory system; corrosive to skin; suspected carcinogen.
- *Pine Oil*: Irritates eyes and mucous membranes.

## DRAIN CLEANERS

Chemical drain cleaners are extremely corrosive and dangerous to use. Common ingredients in drain cleaners include lye or sulfuric acid. These chemicals work by eating away materials, including your skin if it should come in contact. Likewise, vapours are harmful. If you are on a septic system, you should know that drain cleaners are hard on your system as they kill the microbial bacteria which are necessary to the workings of your septic tank.

The use of chemical drain cleaners as a "preventative" measure is not a good idea. Boiling water or a handful of baking soda and half cup of vinegar poured down the drain weekly is at least as effective as a chemical drain cleaner and much, much safer for you and the environment. Also effective, particularly in preventing clogs, are many brands of enzymatic cleaners.

If you have used a chemical drain cleaner and the clog still exists, Do not try to clear the drain with a plunger or pressurized drain opener. This would only invite splashback. Also, do not add other cleaners to the drain following the use of a commercial drain cleaner.

The combination of chemicals can produce toxic gas or become reactive and blow out of the sink and on to you. If a chemical drain cleaner has done nothing to help your clog and you still have standing water, then there is no reasonable choice except to call a professional to fix the clogged and now contaminated drain. Be sure to tell them what product was used in the drain so that they may adequately protect themselves.

If a drain cleaner claims to be "noncaustic" or "noncorrosive," it should state its ingredients. The product may still be poisonous if inhaled in heavy concentrations or swallowed.

- *Use*: Wear protective gloves and safety goggles. Avoid fumes.
- *Storage*: Store away from children.
- *Disposal*: Use up as intended. Take unused product to a hazardous household waste collection Centre. If collection is not available and if you are connected to a sanitary sewer or municipal sewer treatment, you may dispose of unwanted portions of drain cleaner by flushing down the drain with plenty of water. If you are on a septic tank or lagoon, small amounts of drain cleaner may be flushed with plenty of water over a number of days. It would be best, however, to ask a friend, relative, or Neighbour who is on a sanitary or municipal system to allow you to use their drain to dispose of your household quantity of drain cleaner.

*Hazardous constituents and Possible Effects*:

- *LYE*: Caustic causing burns to skin and in severe cases, blindness.
- *SULFURIC ACID*: Corrosive, causes severe skin burns, and can cause blindness.

## DRY CLEANING

Carbon tetrachloride, now banned from household products, was the Favourite solvent cleaner used in these products. A leading substitute, perchloroethylene or PERC, is a volatile, nonflammable solvent, that is fatal in large doses. There is concern over the chronic inhalation of perchloroethylene.

The primary effect from acute and chronic inhalation of vapours is depression of the central nervous system. Other toxic chemicals often found in spot removing products include trichloroethane, ethylene dichloride, naphtha, Benzene, and Toluene. All of these solvents present an inhalation and ingestion hazard. Some also present a hazard through skin absorption.

- *Use*: Wear nitrile gloves and arrange your work so that the fumes are blowing away from you. Do not allow children or pets into the room where you are working. Keep the lid on the fluid product as much as possible to avoid the solvent from volatilizing and being breathed. If you spill spot remover or dry-cleaning fluid on your skin, wash it off immediately with soap and water. If the solvent spills and puddles, absorb it with kitty litter and throw the wet absorbent material in a trash can outdoors. Never use dry-cleaning fluid or spot remover in a washing machine or put substances that are damp with solvent in a dryer. When you bring clothes home that have been dry-cleaned, take the plastic bag off and allow the clothes to air out well before wearing. When using a dry cleaning machine, to reduce vapours allow the door to remain ajar for a few minutes after the operation is complete. The solvent will evaporate quickly. Remove garments from the machine and allow to cool before handling.

- *Storage*: Store away from heat and flames in a box lined with plastic bags.
- *Disposal*: Currently available means offer no good way to dispose of leftover dry-cleaning fluid or spot remover. These solvents should be disposed of by a licensed hazardous waste handler or saved for a professional household hazardous waste collection. The best way to eliminate a waste problem is to carefully use up these products as they were intended.

*Hazardous constituents and Possible Effects*:

- *Carbon Tetrachloride*: Destructive to liver, kidney, and central nervous system by inhalation, absorption, skin contact, or ingestion.
- *Perchloroethylene*: Fumes are carcinogenic and acutely toxic, causing dizziness, sleepiness, nausea, loss of appetite and disorientation.
- *Trichloroethane*: Irritating to eyes and nose, can result in central nervous system depression and kidney damage.
- *Naphthas*: Inhalation causes drowsiness, headache, coma and cardiac arrest; irritate eyes, throat and skin.
- *Benzene*: Destroys ability to produce blood cells, can cause leukemia; flammable; carcinogen.
- *Toluene*: Produces headache, nausea, narcosis, central nervous system depression.

## FERTILIZER

Fertilizers are plant food supplements which commonly contain nitrogen, phosphorus, and potassium. The numbers on the fertilizer bag refer to the percentages by weight of nitrogen, phosphorus, and potassium, respectively. In general, liquid and granular fertilizers used for house plants and in the garden have a low degree of toxicity unless ingested in large quantities. Single ingredient fertilizers such as ammonium nitrate or lime are more likely to be toxic or corrosive.

Environmentally, overuse of fertilizers has resulted in contamination of surface water and groundwater. Excess nitrogen in drinking water can lead to methemoglobinemia, especially in children under the age of one, elderly persons, and sensitive farm animals such as hogs. Excess phosphorus in the water will result in algae blooms, increased biological oxygen demand, and fish kills.

Use: Carefully read the label before purchase and use. Follow all label directions, applying only the recommended amount. Twice as much fertilizer does not work twice as well and only increases the chance of runoff into surrounding water supplies. Wear gloves when handling fertilizer.

Storage: Store in a tightly sealed plastic bag away from children and pets. Clearly label the bag with the contents and store away from moisture.

Disposal: The best way to eliminate fertilizer waste is to use it up as intended. If you no longer want your fertilizer, check with a relative, Neighbour, or friend.

Fertilizers are usually in demand in the spring and summer months. If you are unable to find a way to use up your excess fertilizer and it does not contain pesticides, it may be placed in the trash destined for the landfill. If it contains pesticides, follow the procedures under Pesticides.

Alternatives: Animal manure, green manure, and compost are time-honoured alternatives to synthetic plant fertilizers.

## FORMALDEHYDE

Formaldehyde, also known as formalin, formal, and methyl aldehyde, is a colourless liquid or gas with a pungent odor. It is generally known as a disinfectant, germicide, fungicide, defoamer, and preservative. Formaldehyde is found in adhesives, cosmetics, deodorants, detergents, dyes, explosives, fertilizer, fibre board, garden hardware, germicide, fungicide, foam insulation, synthetic lubricants, paint, plastic, rubber, textile, urethane resins, and water softening chemicals.

Here is our Complete Guide to Formaldehyde which includes extensive health and MSDS information about the Brands, diseases, symptoms of exposure, sources, and jobs involving Formaldehyde hazards.

Inhalation of vapours produces irritation to the eyes, nose, and throat and frequently results in upper respiratory tract irritation, coughing, and bronchitis. Asthma may occur in sensitive individuals.

Severe exposure to fumes may lead to chemical pneumonia. Skin reactions after exposure to formaldehyde are very common because the chemical can be both irritating and allergy-causing. In addition, formaldehyde is involved in DNA damage and inhibits its repair.

Formaldehyde is a suspected human carcinogen and has been shown to produce mutations and abnormal organisms in bacterial studies. Formaldehyde fumes are liberated from plywood, particleboard, and chipboard, as well as urea formaldehyde foam insulation. Symptoms associated with exposure to formaldehyde fumes include mucous membrane irritation, upper respiratory tract irritation, eye irritation, skin rashes, itching, nausea, stuffy nose, headaches, dizziness, and general fatigue.

Toxicity is primarily related to the presence of formaldehyde gas. Toxicity may be relatively inconspicuous and nonspecific in nature. Patients suffering from formaldehyde toxicity have been misdiagnosed as having asthma, bronchitis, anxiety, depression, or hypochondria.

Severe prolonged vomiting and diarrhea in infants may be related to chronic exposure to formaldehyde fumes. An individual may become sensitized to formaldehyde following repeated exposure to these fumes.

If you have any questions or concerns about formaldehyde levels in your home, contact the office of air pollution control, your local or state Department of Health, or the American Lung Association office nearest you.

## FURNITURE CLEANER

Hazardous constituents and Possible Effects:

- *Petroleum distillates*: Irritate skin, eyes, respiratory tract; may cause fatal pulmonary edema; flammable.
- *Oil of cedar*: Central Nervous system depressant; may induce spontaneous abortion.

## FURNITURE POLISH

There are three general types of commercial furniture polish: solvents, emulsions, and aerosol sprays. Each type contains specific chemicals which aid in the application of the wax or oil to the furniture surface. Solvent polishes use a chemical solvent to dissolve the oil or wax into a liquid form. Emulsion polishes suspend the oil or wax in a liquid, usually water. Aerosol sprays are solvents or emulsion types packed under pressure.

Most polishes are flammable. Furniture polish may contain one or more of the following substances: Ammonia, naphtha, nitrobenzene, petroleum distillates, and phenol.

The health dangers most often associated with furniture polish are inhalation of fumes or vapours and poisoning from ingestion. Polishes that look drinkable, like strawberry soda or milk, are especially tempting to children.

- *Use*: When using furniture polish you should wear gloves, avoid skin contact with the polish, and provide adequate ventilation. Avoid polishes or stains with nitrobenzene.
- *Storage*: Store away from children and sources of flame.
- *Disposal*: Unused or unwanted portions of furniture polish which contain petroleum distillates or nitrobenzene should be held for a hazardous waste collection rather than disposing of them in the trash. The best way to avoid a disposal dilemma is to fully and carefully use the product up.

## GASOLINE

Gasoline, a petroleum distillate product combined with various additives, is flammable and highly toxic. Leaded gasoline contains tetraethyl Lead, a highly toxic metal compound. Unleaded gasoline contains high octane components such as Benzene (a known human carcinogen), ethylene dichloride (a known animal carcinogen), and methanol (a highly toxic compound).

Gasoline can be harmful to your health through skin contact, skin absorption, inhalation, or ingestion. The first symptoms of poisoning include flushing, slurred speech, staggering, and confusion. Overexposure may result in coma and death. Antioxidants added to keep gasoline from decomposing and forming resins can cause burns to skin and eyes.

*Use*: Never smoke around gasoline. Keep the lid on the can when not in use. Never siphon gasoline using the mouth because chemical pneumonia may result.

*Do not*:

- Use leaded gasoline for camp fuel.
- Use gasoline to start brush fires or wood stoves.
- Use any type of gasoline to clean paint or grease from your body (use soap or detergent and water or massage with a few drops of baby oil, butter or margarine, wipe dry, and wash with soap and water).

When handling gasoline wear NBR rubber, nitrile, or polyvinyl chloride gloves and thoroughly wash your hands before eating or smoking. Avoid breathing vapours.

- *Storage*: Keep out of the reach of children and pets. Store in an approved safety container in a garage or outbuilding with good ventilation. If you have a water heater, furnace, or other source of ignition in your garage, it may not be a safe place to store your gasoline. Keep away from heat, flame, and sources of ignition. Do not completely fill the container - gasoline needs room to expand. While it is a good idea to carry an emply gasoline can in the car, do not keep the can filled with gasoline; the gasoline could explode upon impact.
- *Disposal*: Generally, disposal of gasoline is no problem because it will be used up in an engine. However, dirty or contaminated gasoline cannot be burned in engines and must be saved for disposal by a licensed hazardous waste contractor or through a professional household hazardous waste collection Programme. For this reason, and health reasons, do not use gasoline as a cleaner or solvent. Never mix gasoline with waste oil. This would produce a highly flammable mixture.

*Hazardous constituents and Possible Effects*:

- *Tetraethyl lead*: Nerve toxin, small amounts are fatal

## GLASS AND WINDOW CLEANERS

Window and glass cleaner commonly contains isopropyl alcohol or Ammonia, water, and colouring. It may be mildly irritating to the eyes, skin, nose, and throat.

- *Use*: Always use window and glass cleaners in a well-ventilated area.
- *Storage*: Keep out of reach of children.
- *Disposal*: Unused or unwanted portions of window or glass cleaner should be flushed down the drain with plenty of water.

*Hazardous constituents and Possible Effects*:

- *Ammonia*: Fumes irritate eyes, lungs; can cause burns or rashes on skin
- *Isopropanol*: Irritates mucous membranes; ingestion results in drowsiness, unconsciousness and death

## HYDROFLUORIC ACID

Hydrofluoric acid is a highly toxic, highly corrosive, colour less, fuming liquid found in many aluminum cleaners. It's one of the few acids that is fatal with only a small area of skin exposure. It's such a powerful acid that it will even etch highly stable glass, alumina, and titanium materials.

Hydrofluoric acid acts differently from all other acids. The onset of injury proceeds inconspicuously but with grave effects. Hydrofluoric acid is highly corrosive to the skin and can produce first-degree burns. The pain from burns may be delayed for several hours, during which time the acid will burn deep into the skin. Burns may not become apparent for one to twenty-four hours and may appear as reddened, pasty white, blistered, or charred spots. Hydrofluoric acid can damage muscles, ligaments, and bone in its progression after skin exposure.

One can attest to the extreme dangers of Hydrofluoric Acid because we use it on a daily basis in our Inorganic labs. Hydrofluoric Acid and Fluoboric or Fluoroboric Acid are some of the few acids which will dissolve the silica and alumina based chemical catalysts we analyse. We take special precuations when using Hydrofluoric Acid because unlike the other acids we use, if enough Hydrofluoric Acid contacts the skin it can be deadly! Many have died from relatively small skin surface area exposure to Hydrofluoric Acid. It's an extremely painful way to die!

Throughout our labs we have easily accessible vials of Calcium Gluconate which is a cream to be immediately applied upon any skin contact with Hydrofluoric Acid. Calcium Gluconate quenches the reaction of Hydrofluoric

Acid with the body's calcium. It's an essential item to have around when using Hydrofluoric Acid because if exposure to Hydrofluoric Acid occurs a pernicious chain reaction ensues which affects tissue and blood eventually resulting in severe damage and likely death.

Because our labs use this deadly acid on a daily basis we have notified the authorities so they can be prepared in the event of an emergency due to Hydrofluoric Acid exposure. The local emergency responce teams, our own first responder emergency management teams, and the local hospitals have all been equipped with special injectable antidotes and the Calcium Gluconate cream which counteract the effects of Hydrofluoric Acid exposure.

**STAY AWAY FROM HYDROFLUORIC ACID FOLKS!!! IT'S A KILLER!!!**

*Use*: Do not use products with hydrofluoric acid. If the aluminum cleaner ingredients are not on the label, you cannot assume hydrofluoric acid is not in the product. If you are using a product which contains this ingredient, protect all exposed skin in addition to wearing protective gloves, safety goggles, and a respirator with an acid gas cartridge.

## HYDROGEN PEROXIDE

Hydrogen peroxide is a clear, colourless liquid. Common household hydrogen peroxide contains a 3-5% concentration. It is used as a disinfectant and deodorizer. However, the benefit is of short duration. In general, ingestion or skin exposure of small amounts of household hydrogen peroxide will cause no serious problems. It is mildly irritating to the skin and mucous membranes and causes a whitish discolouration. Industrial strength hydrogen peroxide used as a wood or hair bleaching agents (10% concentration H2O2) may result in severe burns to the skin, throat, and gastrointestinal tract.

*Disposal*: Unused or unwanted portions of household hydrogen peroxide should taken to a hazardous household waste collection Centre. If a collection Centre is not available, 3-5% peroxide solutions can be flushed down the drain. If you use a septic tank or lagoon, dispose of small quantities over several days. For information about disposing of 10% peroxide solutions, contact your local fire department or wastewater treatment plant.

## INSECT BATES FOR ANTS,COCKROACHES, AND CRICKETS

Insect baits are used to kill ants, cockroaches, and crickets inside your home. Baits work by attracting the insect to eat a food that contains an insecticide. An insecticide is a pesticide that kills insects.

For insect baits to work, areas where food is stored, prepared or eaten need to be kept clean. Because, if there are other foods around that the insect likes better, or finds first, it will probably not eat the bait at all.

So do baits kill just one insect at a time? No. Baits work by "tricking" the insect into eating something poisonous and spreading the poison to others. How do they spread the poison? Both ants and cockroaches leave a scent trail for others to follow to find the bait. Also, ants may carry some of the bait back to their colony to share with other ants. In a short time the insecticide kills the insects who have eaten the bait. But how fast a bait works depends on several things. It depends on the kind of pesticide in the bait, whether the insect likes the taste of the bait and whether there is other food around for the insect to eat instead.

You may have seen insect bait containers on counter tops, in cabinets, hidden behind stoves or refrigerators or on the floor near cracks or crevices where insects go in and out. They are usually square or round with a flat top, and about half an inch high. They may also be sort of dome shaped like an igloo.

The containers are about two (2) inches across in size and may be plastic or metal. The bait inside the container is usually a solid or a gel. Some baits aren't in a container at all. They can be tablets or gels that are put out for insects like cockroaches to eat. Always "Read the Label First" to know how to properly use these products and for safety information.

The insecticides commonly found in insect baits include abarmectin, propoxur, trichlorfon, sulfluramid, chlorpyrifos and boric acid.

What health and safety things do you need to think about with insect baits? Since the majority of insect baits are enclosed in containers it is not likely you will be exposed to the pesticides inside them. But if you find them, leave them alone. Do not move them or open them. Keep your pets away from them too. If you should touch one, wash your hands with plenty of soap and water to be sure that none of the pesticides that insects might have carried out of the container, got on your skin.

## INSECT SPRAY

Insect sprays are used to get rid of ants, bees, flies, roaches, spiders, wasps and many other insects - even lice. Insect sprays are pesticides known as insecticides. There are many different kinds of insecticides. The kind to use depends on the type of insect and where you want to use it. Read the product label to find out. Not all insecticides can be used in your house. Some can only be used outside. Some can be used on your dog, cat or parakeet - even your pet goat if you have one. Others can only be used on things like bedding, rugs, lawns or plants.

Insecticides used around your home usually come in the form of liquids, sprays or powders. Sometimes they are mixed with other products that are used around your house. Sometimes they are mixed with other pesticides. For example a fertilizer for your grass may have an insecticide in it. It could even have both an insecticide and a herbicide (weed killer) in it.

Examples of pesticide chemicals commonly found in insecticides are permethrin, diazinon, propoxur, and chlorpyrifos.

What health and safety things do you need to think about with insecticides? When you use an insecticide, especially indoors, make sure it doesn't get on food or things that come in contact with food like dish towels, dishes, silverware or counter tops. Insecticides can come in a spray can, bottle or container. Some insecticides that you buy from the store have to be mixed with water first before they can be used. Be sure that you always read the label first to know how to properly use these products and for safety information.

Insecticides can hurt your eyes. They can make you really sick if you breathe their fumes, get some in your mouth or on your skin and you don't wash it off right away. They can also be fatal. How you are effected depends on the route of exposure.

**LYE**

Lye, also known as caustic soda, sodium hydroxide, potassium hydroxide, and caustic potash, is commonly used in drain cleaner, oven cleaner, and in some nonphosphate detergents. Lye is extremely caustic. Its chemical action eats away materials (including skin tissue). Contact with skin or mucous membranes causes burns and frequently deep ulcerations with scarring. Mists, vapours, and dust can cause small burns. Eye contact causes severe damage, including blindness.

*Use*: Caustic products containing lye should be properly labeled with the words "Danger" and "Poison" to indicate their dangerous nature. Lye-based liquids usually contain a warning to avoid squeezing the container, but carelessness could lead to a disfiguring splash on the skin or a blinding squirt in the eye.

Products that contain lye in a pellet form sometimes require you to measure a spoonful out of an opening which is too small for a spoon to fit. This situation is very hazardous because lye-based pellets are easily spilled as one pours the product from the container onto the spoon. Be extremely careful when using lye-based products. Wear gloves and goggles in addition to protecting exposed skin. Avoid fumes by using only under conditions where adequate ventilation exists. Immediately wipe up spilled lye and wash off with plenty of water.

*Storage*: Keep products containing lye away from children and pets.

**METHANOL**

Methanol is made from the distillation of wood. Synonyms are methyl alcohol, wood alcohol, wood spirits, or curbinol. Methanol is used primarily in antifreeze compounds, paints, cements, inks, varnishes, shellacs, wood strippers, windshield wiper solvents, gasoline antifreeze and as a solvent in dyes. It is also used as a fuel in Sterno (4% methanol), home heating oil extenders, and may be added to Gasoline in place of ethanol to make gasohol.

Methanol is highly toxic and readily absorbed from a routes of exposure. Symptoms include malaise, headache, dizziness, confusion, abdominal cramps with excruciating pain and tenderness, stupor, weakness, and acidosis. When methanol is swallowed, Formaldehyde is metabolically generated. This formaldehyde is more toxic than the methanol itself. Blindness and death may occur following ingestion.

When using any product which contains methanol, be certain to wear gloves. Provide adequate ventilation, making sure that vapours are blowing away from you. To dispose of products that contain methanol, save for a household hazardous waste collection rather than flushing them down the drain or throwing them in the trash.

## METHYLENE CHLORIDE

Methylene chloride, known also as methylene dichloride and dichloromethane, is a colourless, volatile liquid with an ether-like odor. It is commonly found in septic tank cleaners, paint and varnish removers, degreasers, pesticides, aerosols, and Christmas bubble lights.

Methylene chloride irritates skin that comes in contact. When inhaled, it mimics carbon monoxide toxicity. Memory loss and liver and kidney damage are reported with chronic exposure.

Methylene chloride is a known animal carcinogen and a suspected human carcinogen. When heated, methylene chloride emits a highly toxic phosgene gas (nerve gas). The use of products containing methylene chloride by people with heart conditions has resulted in fatal heart attacks.

## MOTHBALLS

Mothballs are a distinctive smelling, volatile solid used to repel moths. Mothballs, which are classified as a pesticide, may look like candy to a child. They are poisonous when eaten and seizures can develop in less than one hour. Mothballs contain 100% of either naphthalene or paradichlorobenzene. Both of these ingredients can produce harmful effects when they enter your system through inhalation. Irritation to nose, throat, and lungs, headache, confusion, excitement or depression, and liver and kidney damage can result from exposure to mothball vapours over a long period of time.

Mothballs containing naphthalene are of special concern because naphthalene can promote a breakdown of red blood cells resulting in hemolytic anemia. Hemolytic anemia in mild form may cause only fatigue. In more severe cases, it can cause acute kidney failure. Young children are at particular risk. Poisonings have been reported following dressing infants in clothing that was stored with naphthalene mothballs, suggesting that absorption of naphthalene may occur through the skin.

The warning label on mothball products reads "avoid prolonged breathing of vapours." This label is at odds with the normal use of mothballs. By the very nature of their ingredients, mothballs give off strong odors (vapours which you can smell). These vapours tend to fill the entire home, making it nearly impossible to avoid prolonged breathing of vapours unless you live outdoors. The situation is complicated further when mothballs are placed in closets or rooms with poor ventilation, where the vapours build to high concentrations. Vapours are absorbed by clothes, blankets, and sheets resulting in direct exposure when you are around these items.

- *Use*: Avoid these products. If you do use mothballs, use them sparingly. Mothballs which contain paradichlorobenzene may be safer, if only because they do not promote hemolytic anemia.
- *Storage*: Store away from children and pets in a well ventilated area. Mothballs, if stored indoors, should be tightly wrapped in two plastic bags.
- *Disposal*: Mothballs should be taken to a licensed hazardous waste handler or saved for a professional household hazardous waste collection Programme.

## OVEN CLEANER

The majority of oven cleaners contain lye (sodium hydroxide or potassium hydroxide), which is an extremely corrosive ingredient. Whether the cleaners are contained in aerosol spray form, liquid, paste or powder, lye can attack skin, eyes, or internal organs. Lye in aerosol form is especially hazardous because small droplets containing lye can drift and land on skin, eyes, and sensitive lung surfaces. Labels on most oven cleaners warn that the product can burn skin and eyes and that fumes and vapours should be avoided.

- *Use*: Avoid aerosol oven cleaners. Wear an apron, protective gloves, safety goggles, and a respirator with an organic Vapour cartridge. Make sure there is plenty of fresh air and adequate ventilation present.
- *Storage*: Keep out of the reach of children.
- *Disposal*: Use up as intended. Take unused portions to a hazardous household waste collection Centre. If a collection Centre is unavailable, wrap in several layers of newspaper and dispose of in the trash.

Alternatives: Use a non-toxic oven cleaner.
*Hazardous constituents and Possible Effects*:

- Sodium hydroxide: Extremely corrosive, burns skin and eyes; usually fatal if swallowed; aerosols disperse chemicals, increasing inhalation dangers

- Potassium hydroxide: Extremely corrosive, burns skin and eyes; usually fatal if swallowed; aerosols disperse chemicals, increasing inhalation dangers

## SODIUM CARBONATE

Sodium carbonate, also known as soda ash, washing soda, or sal soda, is white odorless crystals used in the manufacture of soaps, shampoos, bath salts, and some mouthwashes. Sodium carbonate is strongly alkaline and as a dust, it is irritating to the eyes, nose, and upper respiratory tract.

Ingestion may produce corrosion of the gastrointestinal tract, vomiting, diarrhea, circulatory collapse, and death. When used in cosmetics it may cause scalp, forehead, and hand rashes.

## SULFURIC ACID

Sulfuric acid, also known as oil of vitriol, hydrogen sulfate, or spirit of sulfur, is available in powder form and as a colourless, odorless, oily liquid. Beware - it is a highly corrosive liquid! Sulfuric acid is used as an electrolyte in wet cell batteries and as an ingredient in toilet bowl cleaners (sodium bisulfate). Direct contact can cause burning and charring of the skin and causes rapid injury to the mucous membranes. It is exceedingly dangerous to the eyes. Exposure to sulfuric acid mist and subsequent inhalation causes irritation of the respiratory tract and mucous membranes including the eyes. The mist also causes etching of tooth enamel. Ingestion results in serious burns to the mouth, esophagus, and stomach. Even dilute sulfuric acid can irritate the skin and mucous membranes and cause scarring of the face and eyelids and irreparable damage to the cornea, resulting in blindness.

# CLEANING AND CLEANING MATERIALS

We know that any establishment has to be clean, well maintained and presentable at any given moment of time. But how to ensure well maintained premises? Cleaning is the most important and primary aspect of housekeeping. It is a process of removing dirt, dust and grime by using methods such as dusting, shaking, sweeping, mopping, washing or polishing. There are certain areas you may clean daily, whereas you may clean other areas occasionally or once/twice in a year. Since there are different types of surfaces like wall, counter tops, marble floors, ceramic tiles, wooden chairs, etc, special cleaning agents are used to clean these specific surfaces. As suggested, discuss these various aspects of cleaning as well as the materials and equipments used for cleaning.

## MEANING AND IMPORTANCE OF CLEANING

Cleaning involves sweeping floors, dusting furniture and other surfaces, mopping or washing floors, polishing surfaces, objects and accessories, scrubbing tiles, sinks, toilets, disinfecting drains, rearranging cleaned areas and putting things in their specific place. We can say that cleaning is a process of removing dust, dirt or any other undesirable materials like stains, spots, contents of an ashtray, etc.

*What happens if cleaning is not done on a regular basis*:

- Yes, your house will become the breeding ground of insects such as cockroaches, spiders, ants, flies and mosquitoes. It will look dirty and will be most uncomfortable.
- Living in such circumstances can also lead to diseases such as asthma, bronchitis, etc. Thus, cleaning is necessary for a general presentable appearance and also to ensure good hygienic conditions. What do you understand by dust and dirt?
- 'Dust' collectively refers to the loose particles, which are very easily moved by air and settle on any surface. It is easily removed with the help of a dry cloth.
- 'Dirt' refers to dust which sticks to any surface with the help of moisture or grease. It is more difficult to remove dirt as compared to dust. Dirt has to be removed either with a detergent or any other cleaning agent. Let us now read ahead of some general methods of cleaning.

## METHODS OF CLEANING

That dust and dirt can be removed by dusting, mopping etc.

*Based on these we can describe the cleaning methods as follows*:

- *Dusting*: You are already familiar with the term 'dust'. But how do you remove dust? When any surface is wiped with a piece of dry cloth, it carries the loose dust with it and the process is known as dusting. This should be done with a clean soft cloth.
- *Shaking and Beating*: What happens when you shake a cloth full of dust? Yes, the dust falls out. Similarly when you shake or beat any soft material, like a carpet/rug or a curtain, the dust falls out, making the object dust free to a large extent. This is mostly done in open air so that other things do not get dusty.
- *Sweeping*: When a broom or a brush is used to carry the dust laterally along the room, the process is known as sweeping. While sweeping any vertical surface as walls, you should remember to start from the top and sweep downwards. Similarly for lateral sweeping as for floors, start from one end of the room and move to another, preferably a door, and carry the dust all along or collect in a dust pan. All the movable objects kept on the floor should be lifted, swept under, and kept back in place.

- *Mopping*: You have read that wiping with a dry cloth is dusting, similarly, wiping a surface with a damp cloth is called 'mopping'. The piece of cloth used is known as a 'mop' and is generally coarser than a duster. In this process, both the dust, as well as easily removable dirt, is also removed. Mopping is mostly done on floors. Extra attention should be paid to nooks and corners otherwise it gets tougher to remove fixed grime later on.
- *Washing*: Sometimes mopping alone is not sufficient to remove dirt. Such surfaces are then scrubbed with the help of a yard broom along with plenty of water. Eventually the dirt loosens and is carried off by water. This process is known as 'washing'. In case of tougher stains or dirt, detergent may be added to the water.
- *Polishing*: When some reagent is rubbed on a surface to bring out the shine, the process is known as polishing and the reagent applied is known as the 'polish'. Similarly, many other objects/ decorative items made of brass, wood, marble etc, may be polished.

## CLEANING EQUIPMENTS AND MATERIALS

Let us now learn about the equipment and other materials, which assist us in the process of cleaning. Can you name a few? Let us try to make a list of such equipments.

### Equipments

*Following are some of the equipments which you will come across during the process of cleaning*:

- Brooms- brooms are either soft or hard. The soft ones are used to sweep the floors, whereas the hard ones are used to wash the floors.
- Brushes-are available in various sizes and shapes and are made of different materials. Different brushes are used for specific jobs. Brushes with nylon or plastic bristles are used for cleaning carpets or furniture, round feather brushes are used to remove cobwebs, metal brushes are used to clean wire mesh in the windows. You have special nylon brushes to clean the toilets.
- Buckets or basins- metal or plastic buckets/ basins of suitable sizes are used to carry water, detergents and chemicals so that there are no spills.
- Dust bins-these are available in plastic with a lid. These should be lined with paper so that the garbage does not stick to the surface. They should be emptied and washed daily.
- Dust pans- these are made of either plastic or metal and have flat surfaces, rounded at the sides. After sweeping, dirt and dust is

collected directly into these with the help of a broom and carried to a dustbin. Dustpans save sweeping the entire amount of dust from one room to another. Instead, dust can be collected from each room and disposed of simultaneously. Dust pans should be cleaned after use.

- Dusters - These are mostly made of soft cotton, flannel or artificial feathers mounted on a stick. These are used to clean loose dust and are also used for wiping various surfaces. You should use separate dusters for dusting and wiping surfaces such as dining table, mirrors, kitchen slabs, etc. They should be washed and dried after use.
- Mops- are mostly made of thick, loosely woven cotton cloth. These are used to wipe dust from the floors. These are dipped in clean water and squeezed before wiping the floors. You should change the water after mopping each room or when it gets dirty. You should thoroughly wash the mop and spread it for drying, after use.
- Polishing cloth- these are made of soft absorbent cloth such as flannel. Dry polishing cloth helps to clean and shine the polished surfaces by rubbing them vigorously.
- Vacuum cleaner- it works on electricity and has a fan. This sucks in the dirt and dust from the surfaces and stores it in a disposable bag inside. This bag should be emptied regularly.

**Materials**

There are many materials and reagents, which help in cleaning, scrubbing and polishing surfaces.

*Some of these are commercial preparations for cleaning and you may be already familiar with some of them*:

- Water- Water is the simplest cleaning reagent available to us. Some dirt may be loosened and dissolved in it. Although most of the time, some other cleaning agent is also used along with it.
- Detergents- Detergents are available in powder, solid and liquid form.These are used with water to clean various surfaces. The basic ingredients in a detergent are surface active agents, known as surfactants. A detergent may have more ingredients to make it more effective, like alkaline salts, bleaches, foam boosters, germicides and perfumes. The exact nature and use of a detergent will actually vary just as to its ingredients. However, there are a few points which should be kept in mind while choosing a detergent. It should –
  - Be readily soluble in water
  - Be effective in all types of water and produce no scum
  - Have good wetting powers so that the solution penetrates between the object and the dirt particles

- Have good suspending powers to suspend dislocated dirt and not allow it to settle back
- Be effective over a wide range of temperatures
- Be harmless to the object and the skin.
- Clean quickly
- Be easily rinsed away

- Abrasives- some of the common abrasives are sand, finely powdered brick, saw dust, wheat bran, emery paper, fine ash, filtered chalk etc. Besides these, steel wool, nylon mesh, coconut fibres are also used to scrub dirt. Their use depends on the surface to be cleaned and the type of dirt to be removed. The extent of cleaning will depend upon the nature of the abrasive used and on the scrubbing action.
- Acids- strong acids are used to clean toilets and are available in crystals or liquid form. Milder forms of acids are also used to clean very dirty tiles. Acids should be rinsed off as soon as possible after use and should be stored away from children. Vinegar and lemon are used to clean stains on metals like brass and copper.
- Alkalis- baking soda and ammonia are used as grease emulsifiers and stain removing agents.
- Bleaches- stains on fabrics are removed by bleaches such as sodium hypochlorite, sodium perborate, hydrogen peroxide, sodium hydrosulphite etc.
- Solvents – solvents such as methylated spirit, carbon tetrachloride, kerosene, petrol etc; are used to remove grease, wax and other stains from the surfaces. You should keep methylated spirit, kerosene, petrol, away from fire as they are inflammable. Carbon tetrachloride is harmful if inhaled.
- Polishes- polishes are used on surfaces such as floors, furniture, leather and even metals. When rubbed on a surface, they provide a protective covering to the surface and produce shine. The object also gets cleaned in the process.

## SCHEDULE OF CLEANING

Now the important question is how to do cleaning? You must have observed the cleaning process at your own house. Do you clean your rooms completely by removing all the furniture etc, every day? No, because that would require a lot of time and labour which can not be devoted everyday. Then how to do the cleaning? For this, it is important to follow a certain schedule of cleaning.

Everyday, a general cleaning of the open surfaces like floors, furniture and other such surfaces is required. Once in a while some more time is given to cleaning and you probably move heavy furniture and clean beneath it or beneath the carpets. Maybe once in six months or a year you empty the room completely and give it a complete wash, polish the floors, whitewash the walls, ceiling etc.

*Thus we can basically divide cleaning into three types of schedules*:

1. Daily clean
2. A weekly clean
3. A spring clean

A daily cleaning would be a general cleaning done every day; a weekly cleaning would be a more thorough cleaning done periodically, depending on the frequency of use. In a guest house, hotel, or a hospital, it may be done once a week or even earlier. Spring cleaning is usually done once a year or when particularly needed. It may be earlier in the case of a hospital.

**General Procedure for Daily Cleaning**

Let us now see how a room is cleaned daily.

*Similarly the kitchen can also be cleaned in the same way*:

- Collect all used utensils from the counters.
- Empty the dustbin, wash, wipe and line it with newspaper.
- Mop or wash the kitchen with a mild disinfectant.
- Sweep the floor.
- Wash all utensils. Drain and store.
- Wipe and clean the gas stove, electrical appliances and the counters.

*Can you suggest in what order the work should be carried on*:

- Brush or vacuum clean the carpet.
- Dust all surfaces including furniture and fixtures.
- In the end, adjust windows, do a general survey to see that everything is in order and to your satisfaction.
- Mop the whole area.
- Once you enter the room, open all windows in order to let the fresh air come in.
- Remove all unwanted objects like tea cups etc., and empty ash trays and dust bins.
- Replace linen wherever required, like in a bedroom, make the bed, in a restaurant cover the tables, in bathrooms, check for towels, soaps etc.
- Sweep the floor.

## General Procedure for Weekly Cleaning

You now know that special cleaning is more thorough than daily cleaning. *Let us now see in what order should one work for special cleaning of a room*:

- Check and clean thoroughly, all the drawers, furniture, fittings, all hangings or pictures, lights, etc.
- Remove all dirty linen.
- Remove all unwanted objects like trays, teacups, bottles etc. Empty the ash tray and dust bins.
- Remove stains from walls, doors, windows and furniture.
- Replace linen with clean linen
- Start in the same way as in a daily clean – that is, first open all the windows for fresh air.
- Survey the room for any discrepancy and adjust windows as desired.
- Sweep, dust and mop the surfaces.
- Vacuum clean the carpets and other upholstery. If vacuum cleaner is not available, use a brush.
- Wipe, dust or polish table lamps, accessories, telephone, if needed.

*In the case of kitchen*:

- Change the newspapers.
- Clean the jars and bins.
- Clean the sunmica on the cupboard door panels with a wet cloth.
- Clean the tiles.
- Rearrange the cupboards.
- You can empty out the shelves.

## General Procedure for Spring Cleaning

Spring cleaning is done after long intervals, the frequency being as less as once a year. Thus, it may also be called annual cleaning. It is the most thorough cleaning of a room.

*In the case of kitchen*:

- Clean exhaust fan and light switches.
- Clean the cobwebs.
- Clean tiles with detergent.
- Empty out the kitchen.
- Label and arrange all boxes back in place.
- Replace newspaper lining in cupboards.

- Spray insecticides in corners.
- Spread the pulses, spices, etc out in the sun.
- Tighten any loose screws.
- Wash kitchen counters with hot soapy solution and if needed, polish them.
- Wash the floor.
- Wipe stains on cupboard doors.

*Let us now see how a spring cleaning should be done*:

- Adjust windows, survey the room to satisfaction.
- Clean carpets thoroughly in the sun or send for dry cleaning. Re-lay it.
- Dust and mop.
- If any maintenance work is required, this is the right time to do it.
- If desired, rearrange the heavy furniture to give a new look.
- If necessary, remove all furniture and furnishings from the room. At least remove soft furnishings like carpets. Clean the cobwebs.
- Polish the furniture, decorative objects and floors.
- Remove all the movable objects including lamp shades, pictures, wall hangings etc., wipe and clean everything.
- Replace everything at the predetermined place, including all furniture and fixtures.
- Sweep the floors.
- Take off all linen, including curtains and remove them from the room.
- Ventilate the room.

# 7

# Dishwashers in Kitchen

## INTRODUCTION

A dishwasher is a mechanical device for cleaning dishes and eating-utensils. Dishwashers can be found in restaurants and private homes.

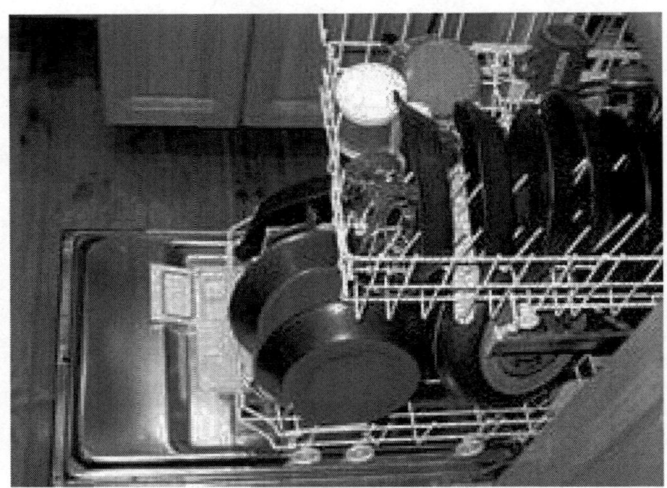

**Fig.** A dishwasher containing clean dishes

Unlike manual dishwashing, which relies largely on physical scrubbing to remove soiling, the mechanical dishwasher cleans by spraying hot water, typically between 55 and 75 °C (130 and 170 °F) at the dishes, with lower temperatures used for delicate items. A mix of water and detergent is circulated by a pump. Water is pumped to one or more rotating spray arms, which blast the dishes with the cleaning mixture. Once the wash is finished, the water is drained, more hot water is pumped in and a rinse cycle begins. After the rinse cycle finishes and the water is drained, a heating element in the bottom of the tub heats the air to dry the dishes. Sometimes a rinse aid is used to eliminate water spots for streak-free dishes.

**Fig.** An open dishwasher

## HISTORY

**Fig.** A hand-powered dishwasher and an early electric dishwasher both from about 1917.

The first reports of a mechanical dishwashing device are of an 1850 patent in the United States by Joel Houghton for a hand-powered good device. This device was made of wood and was cranked by hand while water sprayed onto the dishes. This device was both slow and unreliable. Another patent was granted to L.A. Alexander in 1865 that was similar to the first but featured a hand-cranked rack system. Neither device was practical or widely accepted.

The first reliable (hand-powered) dishwasher was invented in 1887 by Josephine Cochrane and unveiled at the 1893 Chicago World's Fair. Cochrane was quite wealthy and never washed dishes herself; she reportedly invented the dishwasher because her servants were chipping her fine china.

In England, William Howard Livens invented a small dishwasher suitable for domestic use in 1924. It was the first modern dishwasher, and incorporated most of the design elements that feature in the models of today; it included a front door for loading, a wire rack to hold the dirty crockery and a rotating sprayer.

Drying elements were even added to his design in 1940. It was the first machine suitable for domestic use, and it came at a time when permanent plumbing and running water in the house was becoming increasingly common.

Despite this, Liven's design did not become a commercial success, and dishwashers were only successfully sold as domestic utilities in the postwar boom of the 1950s, albeit only to the wealthy.

Initially dishwashers were sold as standalone or portable devices, but with the development of the wall-to-wall countertop and standardized height cabinets, dishwashers began to be marketed with standardized sizes and shapes, integrated underneath the kitchen countertop as a modular unit with other kitchen appliances.

By the 1970s dishwashers had become commonplace in domestic residences in North America andWestern Europe. By 2012, over 75 percent of homes in the US and Germany had dishwashers.

## CHARACTERIZATION

### Capacity

The international standard for the capacity of a dishwasher is expressed as standard place settings. Dishes or plates of irregular sizes may not fit properly in a dishwasher's cleaning compartment, so it is advisable to check for compatibility before buying a dishwasher.

Commercial dishwashers are rated as plates per hour. The rating is based on standard sized plates of the same size. The same can be said for commercial glass washers, as they are based on standard glasses, normally pint glasses.

## Size

**Fig.** North American counter-top dishwasher

Dishwashers that are installed into standard kitchen cabinets have a standard width and depth of 60 cm (Europe) or 24 inches (US), and most dishwashers must be installed into a hole a minimum of 86 cm (Europe) or 34 inches (US) tall. Portable dishwashers exist in 45 and 60 cm (Europe) 18 and 24 inch (US) widths, with casters and attached countertops. Dishwashers may come in standard or tall tub designs; standard tub dishwashers have a service kickplate beneath the dishwasher door that allows for simpler maintenance and installation, but tall tub dishwashers have approximately 20% more capacity and better sound dampening from having a continuous front door.

## Features

**Fig.** Clear model of a running dishwasher

Present-day machines feature a drop-down front panel door, allowing access to the interior, which usually contains two or sometimes three pull-out racks; racks can also be referred to as "baskets". In older U.S. models from the 1950s, the entire tub rolled out when the machine latch was opened, and loading/removing washable items was from the top, with the user reaching deep into the compartment for some items.

Today, "dish drawer" models mimic this style, while the half-depth design eliminates the inconvenience of the long reach that was necessary with older full-depth models. "Cutlery baskets" are also common. A drawer dishwasher, first introduced byFisher & Paykel in 1997, is a variant of the dishwasher in which the baskets slide out with the door in the same manner as a drawer filing cabinet, with each drawer in a double-drawer model being able to operate independently of each other.

The inside of a dishwasher in the North American market are either stainless steel or plastic. Stainless steel tubs resist hard water, provide better sound damping, and preserve heat to dry dishes faster. They also come at a premium price. Older models used a baked enamel on steel and are prone to chipping and erosion; chips in the baked enamel finish must be cleaned of all dirt and corrosion then patched with a special compound or even a good quality two-part epoxy. All European-made dishwashers feature a stainless steel interior as standard, even on low end models. The same is true for a built-in water softener.

The flutes (Or valve meters) of the dishwasher are prevalent in American models (With some appearing in European and Asian models influenced by US design)due to the higher pressure of the American water system. (Which averages at 90 torrs/min, as opposed to the 65 torrs/min pressure in other countries)The flutes help drain the excess water, preventing entropy within the system due to higher pressures at a lower volume. This is a removable fixture, as some areas require a higher or lower discharge based on their water system.

Mid-to-higher end North American dishwashers often come with hard food disposal units, which behave like miniature garbage (waste) disposal units that eliminate large pieces of food waste from the wash water. One manufacturer that is known for omitting hard food disposals is Bosch, a German brand; however, Bosch does so in order to reduce noise. If the larger items of food waste are removed before placing in the dishwasher, pre-rinsing is not necessary even without integrated waste disposal units.

Many new dishwashers feature microprocessor-controlled, sensor-assisted wash cycles that adjust the wash duration to the quantity of dirty dishes (sensed by changes in water temperature) or the amount of dirt in the rinse water (sensed chemically/optically). This can save water and energy if the user runs a partial load. In such dishwashers the electromechanical rotary switch often used to control the washing cycle is replaced by a microprocessor but most sensors and valves are still required to be present. However, pressure switches (some dishwashers use a pressure switch and flow meter) are not required in most microprocessor controlled dishwashers as they use the motor and sometimes a rotational position sensor to sense the resistance of water, when it senses there is no cavitation it knows it has the optimal amount of water. Abimetal switch or wax motor opens the detergent door during the wash cycle.

European dishwashers almost universally use two or three spray arms which are fed from the bottom and back wall of the dishwasher leaving both racks unimpeded and also such models tend to use inline water heaters, removing the need for exposed elements in the base of the machine that can melt plastic items near to them. Many North American dishwashers tend to use more basic,and old fashioned water distribution and exposed elements in the base of the dishwasher. Some North American machines use a large cone or similar structure in the bottom dish rack to prevent placement of dishes in the center of the rack.

he dishwasher directs water from the bottom of the dishwasher up through this structure to the upper wash arm to spray water on the top dish rack. Some dishwashers, including many models from Whirlpool and Kitchenaid, use a tube attached to the top rack that connects to a water source at the back of the dishwasher which allows full use of the bottom rack. Late-model Frigidairedishwashers shoot a jet of water from the top of the washer down into the upper wash arm, again allowing full use of the bottom rack (but requiring that a small funnel on the top rack be kept clear).

Some dishwashers include a child-lockout feature to prevent accidental starting or stopping of the wash cycle by children. A child lock can sometimes be included to prevent young children opening the door during a wash cycle. This prevents accidents with hot water and strong detergents used during the wash cycle.

A dishwasher should never be emptied before a complete process has been signified to be finished by the control system, as this will often leave the contents unwashed or still in a saturated state. It is a common misconception that to empty a dishwasher before the end of a cycle will save energy, as many of the contents may need to be re-run, hence almost doubling running costs.

**Plumbing**

Depending on the model, some dishwashers can be plumbed into either the hot or cold water supply, taking into account the maximum incoming water temperature recommended by the manufacturer where hot water is used. Plumbing a dishwasher into the hot or warm water supply can improve cleaning performance and reduce food debris in the interior of the dishwasher.

A few dishwashers may spend much less time on the wash phase if the incoming water is hot, which can compromise cleaning, so results will vary. Dishwashers may cost less to operate on a hot water supply if there are other forms of energy available that allow water to be heated more cost efficiently than an electrically powered heating element in a dishwasher.

### Sound Damping

Modern dishwashers are quieter than older models. Using blankets, panels, and sound-absorbing materials in various configurations, dishwashers can achieve sound damping levels down to 39 decibels or so. Undamped, low-end dishwashers generally output noise levels of anywhere from 65–70 decibels. Most manufacturers generally use their own nomenclature with trademark for sound damping.

## DETERGENT

**Fig.** A detergent tablet

Different kinds of dishwashing detergent contain different combinations of the items in the list below. Not all of the ingredients below are used in some detergent.

### Phosphates

Dissolves calcium and magnesium ions to prevent 'hard-water' type limescale deposits . They can cause ecological damage, so their use is starting to be phased out. Phosphate-free detergents are sold as eco-friendly detergents .

Oxygen-based bleaching agents (older-style powders and liquids contain chlorine-based bleaching agents)

Breaks up and bleaches organic deposits.

### Non-ionic Surfactants

Lowers the surface tension of the water, emulsifies oil, lipid and fat food deposits, prevents droplet spotting on drying .

### Alkaline Salts

These are a primary component, in older and original-style dishwasher detergent powders . Highly alkaline salts attack and dissolve grease, but are extremely corrosive (fatal) if swallowed. Salts used may include metasilicates, alkali metal hydroxides, Sodium carbonate etc.Alkali salts or basic salts are salts which are the product of the neutralization of a strong base and a weak acid.

Rather than being neutral (as some other salts) Alkali salts are bases as their name suggests. What makes these compounds basic is that the conjugate base from the weak acid hydrolyzes to form a basic solution. In sodium carbonate, for example, the carbonate from the carbonic acid hydrolyzes to form a basic solution. The chloride from the hydrochloric acid in sodium chloride does not hydrolyze, though, so sodium chloride is not basic.

The difference between a basic salt and an alkali is that an alkali is the soluble hydroxide compound of an alkali metal or an alkaline earth metal. A basic salt is any salt that hydrolyzes to form a basic solution. The hydroxide compounds are not salts.

Another definition of a basic salt would be a salt that contains amounts of both hydroxide and other anions. White lead is an example. It is basic lead carbonate, or lead carbonate hydroxide.

These salts are insoluble and are obtained through precipitation reactions.

**Enzymes**

Breaks up and dissolves protein-based food deposits, and possibly oil, lipid and fat deposits. Proteases do this by breaking down the proteins into smaller peptides that are more easily washed away .

**Anti-corrosion agent(s)**

Often sodium silicate, this prevents corrosion of dishwasher components .

Dishwashing detergent may also contain :

**Anti-foaming agents**

Foam interferes with the washing action.

Additives to slow down the removal of glaze & patterns from glazed ceramics

**Perfumes**

Anti-caking agents (in granular detergent)

Starches (in tablet based detergents)

Gelling agents (in liquid/gel based detergents)

Sand (inexpensive powdered detergents)

Dishwasher detergents are strongly alkaline (basic).

Inexpensive powders may contain sand, which can be verified by dissolving the powder in boiling water and then passing the solution through a coffee filter. Such detergents may harm the dishes and the dishwasher. Powdered detergents are more likely to cause fading on china patterns.

## BIODEGRADABLE DETERGENT

Besides older style detergents for dishwashers, biodegradable detergents also exist for dishwashers. These detergents may be more environmentally friendly than conventional detergents.

**Hand-washing Detergent**

Prior to the invention of the dishwasher in 1886, hand-washing primarily with simple detergents was common. The invention of the machine prompted the use of stronger detergents and rinse agents, thus saving time. Hand-washing dish detergent (washing up liquid) should not be used in a dishwasher, as it will create a large foam of bubbles which will leak from the dishwasher. If hand-washing detergent is accidentally used, the foam may be removed by spraying with salt, and the dishwasher should be forced into a drain cycle to remove the detergent and water.

## RINSE AID

Rinse aid (sometimes called rinse agent) contains surfactants that uses Marangoni stress to prevent droplet formation, so that water drains from the surfaces in thin sheets, rather than forming droplets.

The benefits of using it are that it prevents "spotting" on glassware (caused by droplets of water drying and leaving behind dissolved limescale minerals), and can also improve drying performance as there is less water remaining to be dried.

## DISHWASHER SALT

In some countries, especially those in Europe, dishwashers include a built-in water softener that removes calcium and magnesium ions from the water.Dishwasher salt, which is coarse-grained sodium chloride (table salt), is used to recharge the resin in the built-in ion-exchange system. The coarse grains prevent it from clogging the softener unit; unlike certain types of salt used for culinary purposes, it does not contain added insoluble anticaking agents or magnesium salts.

The presence of magnesium salts will defeat the purpose of removing magnesium from the water softener. Anticaking agents may lead to clogging or may contain magnesium. Table salt may contain added iodine in the form of sodium iodide or potassium iodide, but these compounds will not affect the ion-exchange system, but adding table salt to the dishwasher's water softening unit can damage it.

If a dishwasher has a built-in water softener there will be a special compartment inside the dishwasher where the salt is to be added when needed. This salt compartment is separate from the detergent compartment, and generally located at the bottom of the wash cabinet (this is below the bottom basket). On most dishwashers, an automatic sensing system will notify the user when more dishwasher salt is required.

Pouring detergent into the salt compartment will damage the water softening system, however this can be reversed if the user acts very quickly and the dishwasher is NOT used: with a suitable *wet and dry* vacuum cleaner, remove the foreign substance e.g. detergent, followed by adding water again and removing the water with the wet and dry vacuum and repeating the process several times.

Some newer dishwashers allow the use of "all in one" tablets/detergents (which include an amount of water softener along with detergent and a rinse agent) and are marketed as an alternative to using separate salt and rinse aid, but dishwasher salt must still be added to the salt compartment in very hard water areas. The use of such "all in one" detergents does not mean that separate salt and rinse aid is not required, as omitting separate salt and rinse aid will impair the cleaning and drying results and may cause limescale damage, also, incorrect use of "all in one" tablets/detergents may not be covered under the dishwasher's warranty..

Some dishwasher detergents are marketed for use in hard water areas for dishwashers which do not have a built-in water softener (and therefore do not use any dishwasher salt). These detergents use higher levels of phosphates to increase the solubility of hard water ions. In very hard water areas, the amount of phosphate may still be insufficient and the manual addition of dishwasher salt into the detergent compartment is recommended. Adding salt along with the detergent does not soften the water as does a dishwasher with an ion-exchange water softener, but the water will gain some additional ability to dissolve hard water ions. Note, however, that as water drops remaining on the dishware evaporate, deposits of the salt will likely remain. To combat this, the use of a rinsing agent which cause the water to "sheet" will help eliminate the spotting.

## HAZING OF GLASSWARE

Glassware washed by dishwashing machines can develop a white haze on the surface over time. This may be caused by any or all of the below processes, only one of which is reversible:

### Limescale Deposit

If the dishwasher has run out of the salt that recharges the ion exchange resin that softens the water, and the water supply is "hard", limescale deposits can appear on all items, but are especially visible on glassware. It can be removed by cleaning with vinegar or lemon juice, or a proprietary limescale removal agent. The dishwasher should either be recharged with salt, adjusted appropriately for the hardness of the supply water – or possibly this is a symptom of failure of the ion exchange resin in the water softener (which is one of the more expensive components). The resin may have stopped working because it has been poisoned by iron or manganese salts in the supply water.

### Silicate Filming/etching/Accelerated Crack Corrosion

This film starts as an iridescence or "oil-film" effect on glassware, and progresses into a "milky" or "cloudy" appearance (which is not a deposit) that cannot be polished off or removed like limescale. It is formed because the detergent is strongly alkaline (basic) and glass dissolves slowly in alkaline aqueous solution.

It becomes less soluble in the presence of silicates in the water (added as anti-metal-corrosion agents in the dishwasher detergent). Since the cloudy appearance is due to nonuniform glass dissolution, it is (somewhat paradoxically) *less* marked if dissolution is higher, i.e. if a silicate-free detergent is used; also, in certain cases, the etching will primarily be seen in areas that have microscopic surface cracks as a result of the items' manufacturing.

Limitation of this undesirable reaction is possible by controlling water hardness, detergent load and temperature. The type of glass is an important factor in determining if this effect is a problem. Some dishwashers can reduce this etching effect by automatically dispensing the correct amount of detergent throughout the wash cycle based on the level of water hardness programmed.

### Physical Abrasion

Glassware placed such that it is physically touching can abrade and produce a milky surface.

### Devitrification

Components found in dishwasher detergents can chemically scour the glass, causing tiny crystals, which can precipitate further crystal growth that can turn entire glasses cloudy

## COMMERCIAL DISHWASHERS

**Fig.** A commercial dishwasher

Large heavy-duty dishwashers are available for use in commercial establishments (e.g. hotels, restaurants) where a large number of dishes must be cleaned.

**Fig.** A Hobart commercial dishwasher

Unlike a residential dishwasher, a commercial dishwasher does not utilize a drying cycle (commercial drying is achieved by heated ware meeting open air once the wash/rinse/sanitation cycles have been completed) and thus are significantly faster than their residential counterparts.

Washing is conducted with 65-71 C / 150-160 F temperatures and sanitation is achieved by either the use of a booster heater that will provide the machine 82 C / 180 F "final rinse" temperature or through the use of a chemical sanitizer. This distinction labels the machines as either "high-temp" or "low-temp".

Some commercial dishwashers work similar to a commercial car wash, with a pulley system that pulls the rack through a small chamber (Known widely as a "rack conveyor" systems). Single-rack washers require an operator to push the rack into the washer, close the doors, start the cycle, and then open the doors to pull out the cleaned rack, possibly through a second opening into an unloading area.

In the UK, the British Standards Institution set standards for dishwashers. In the US, the NSF International (an independent not-for-profit organization) sets the standards for wash and rinse time along with minimum water temperature for chemical or hot water sanitizing methods. There are many types of commercial dishwashers including under counter, single tank, conveyor, flight type, and carousel machines.

Commercial dishwashers often have significantly different plumbing and operations than a home unit, in that there are often separate spray arms for washing and rinsing/sanitizing. The wash water is heated with an in-tank electric heat element and mixed with a cleaning solution, and is used repeatedly from one load to the next The wash tank usually has a large strainer basket to collect food debris, and the strainer may not be emptied until the end of the day's kitchen operations.

Water used for rinsing and sanitizing is generally delivered directly through building water supply, and is not reusable. The used rinse water falls into the wash tank reservoir, which dilutes some of the used wash water and causes a small amount to drain out through an overflow tube. The system may first rinse with pure water only, and then sanitize with an additive solution that is left on the dishes as they leave the washer to dry.

Additional soap is periodically added to the main wash water tank, from either large soap concentrate tanks or dissolved from a large solid soap block, to maintain wash water cleaning effectiveness.

## ENVIRONMENTAL IMPACT

The dishwasher has made cleaning and drying dishes much easier and more efficient. In the European Union, the energy consumption of a dishwasher for a standard usage is shown on a European Union energy label. In the United States, the energy consumption of a dishwasher is defined using the energy factor.

### Comparison with Washing by Hand

Comparing the efficiency of automatic dishwashers and hand-washing of dishes is difficult because hand-washing techniques vary drastically by individual. According to a peer-reviewed study in 2003, hand washing and drying of an amount of dishes equivalent to a fully loaded automatic dishwasher (nocookware or bakeware) could use between 20 and 300 liters of water and between 0.1 and 8 kWh of energy, while the numbers for energy-efficient automatic dishwashers were 15 to 22 liters and 1 to 2 kWh, respectively.

The study concluded that fully loaded dishwashers use less energy, water, and detergent than the average European hand-washer. For the automatic dishwasher results, the dishes were not rinsed before being loaded. The study does not address costs associated with the manufacture and disposal of dishwashers, the cost of possible accelerated wear of dishes from the chemical harshness of dishwasher detergent, the comparison for cleaning cookware, or the value of labour saved; hand washers needed between 65 and 106 minutes.

Several points of criticism on this study have been raised. For example, kilowatt hours of electricity were compared against energy used for heating hot water without taking into account possible inefficiencies. Also, inefficient human washers were compared against optimal usage of a fully loaded dishwasher without manual pre-rinsing that can take up to 100 liters of water.

### Detergents and Rinse Aids

Most dishwasher detergent contains complex phosphates, as they have several properties that aid in effective cleaning. However, the same chemicals have been removed from laundry detergents in many countries as a result of concerns raised about the increase in algal blooms in waterways caused by increasing phosphate levels. 17 US states have partial or full bans on the use of phosphates in dish detergent, and 2 US statesMaryland and New York ban phosphates in commercial dishwashing.

Detergent companies claimed it is not cost effective to make separate batches of detergent for the states with phosphate bans (although detergents are typically formulated for local markets), and so most have voluntarily removed phosphates from all dishwasher detergents.

In addition, rinse aids have contained nonylphenol and nonylphenol ethoxylates. These have been banned in the European Union by EU Directive 76/769/EEC.

## ALTERNATIVE USE AS A COOKING DEVICE

Many recipe websites have noted that a dishwasher can be used to cook certain foods, in particular salmon. It is very important that all foods be completely sealed to avoid contamination with soaps or rinse aids, and that the maximum temperature available in the washer is taken into account (as certain foods should not be prepared below a certain temperature, for food safety reasons).

# HOOD TYPE DISHWASHER

The Electrolux Dishwashing range is produced for customers with the highest conceivable demands for good efficiency, economy and ergonomics for dishwashing operation. The product range comprises glasswashers, undercounter dishwashers, hood type dishwashers, rack type dishwashers, flight type dishwashers and pot and pan washers.

The hood type dishwasher WT65E range consists of units with different voltages and has a capacity of 65 baskets per hour. The WT65E is available for cold or hot water connection, has insulated or uninsulated hood and manual hood opening.

### Easy To Install

- The WT65E requires 10.6 kW for hot water supply connection.
- Only one cable for electrical connection.
- External connecting board, protected by a waterproof plastic box.
- Simple service from the front and from the side panels.
- Pre-arrangements for drain pump available as an optional accessory that is possible to install on site.
- Pre-arrangements automatic detergent dispenser. For machines without detergent dispenser it is possible to add it on site.

- Pre-arrangement for connection to an energy management device.
- Corner or straight flow installation.
- Available on request model pre-arranged for HACCP implementation.
- Suitable to be connected to the tabling and roller conveyors (with appropriate kit) - included in Electrolux Handling System range - to create a functional and ergonomic lay-out.

**EASY TO CLEAN**

- Smooth surfaces and wash tank with rounded corners.
- Easily removable washing and rinsing arms, filters and rack support.
- Rack support guide pressed in the tank body.
- No pipes inside the washing chamber.
- Self cleaning cycle, easy to activate.
- Electronic control of the functions incorporating fault diagnosis system, number of cycles counter and number of drain cycles counter.
- Simple control panel with digital thermometres indicating both wash and rinse temperatures.
- Four dishwashing programmes: one for glass and lightly soiled items, one for normally soiled items, one for heavily soiled items and the fourth Programme is continuous.
- Height adjustable rounded feet.
- IP×5 water protection.

**EASY TO USE**

- Less hood friction thanks to a high sturdiness plastic guide.
- Double skin hood ceiling and completely closed and insulated back for less heat and noise dispersion.
- Pre-arrangement for connection to an Energy Management device.
- Available, on request, model pre-arranged for HACCP implementation.
- High efficiency non-return valve in water inlet circuit.

## STAINLESS STEEL FLAT WASHERS

Boker's is a leading metal stamping manufacturer of stainless steel flat washers. Stainless steel washers will not stain, corrode or rust as easily as ordinary steel. With outside diametres of 0.080" to 5.140" and a wide variety of inside diametres.

## CONVEYOR DISHWASHERS

It is abundantly clear that a commercial dishwasher is a vital piece of equipment for any catering business. Of course, the size of this dishwasher depends entirely on the size of your very own business - if you are running a small kitchen, you could well be fine with a dishwasher not much larger than your average domestic model, and at the same time, a larger dishwasher, the kind that can process thousands of plates an hour, may be much better suited to your restaurant or cafe.

Then again, what if even the larger machines will just not suffice? For example, a larger kitchen, with a much larger volume of dishes needing cleaned on a regular basis, such as in a canteen or a halls of residence, will not be able to invest in several of the larger dishwashers - not only will the cost be extremely prohibitive, but the sheer volume of work, of loading and unloading, and the time it would take to keep the system moving makes it clear that a larger unit is required, and that is where the Flight Conveyor Dishwasher, the largest model of commercial dishwasher, becomes a fantastic option to deal with an enormous amount of dishes.

The Flight Conveyor Dishwasher is an especially large model of commercial dishwasher which uses a conveyor belt system to clean a huge number of plates, cutlery and pans to ensure that your kitchen never runs out of supplies.

This works with three different types of conveyor, each specially designed for a different item of kitchenware - one for dishes, one for baskets and one for insulated food trays. These are all spaced to ensure that jets of water can hit each side equally, ensuring perfect cleaning, and each segment of conveyor has three rows, allowing you to quickly and efficiently unload the commercial dishwasher.

So how does the Flight Conveyor Dishwasher work? Well, unlike most commercial dishwashers, it has no exact size - it is built up of several pieces that you connect together, so it can be as big or small as you like, ultimately depending on the number of dishes you will be cleaning. Of course, two of the most important pieces you'd need for your machine will be the entry and exit modules - mainly because you'll need a way to unload and load your machine.

In between these key pieces you can fit in a lot more than just your washing unit; you can install a pre-wash segment, which will help ensure an even clean for all your dishes. Indeed, for baked-on food, it is even possible to add on a double rinsing module, which will ensure that your dishes are perfectly clean after every wash. So if your catering business requires a commercial dishwasher that surpasses the usual models in both size and efficiency, a Flight Conveyor Dishwasher may well be an excellent option - though strongly recommended only for larger kitchens, it has the dual benefit of being both an excellent way to keep your business working efficiently, as well as being totally customizable—you will be able to build exactly the commercial dishwasher you want and need.

## AUTOMATIC DISHWASHER

Automatic dishwashers represent a tremendous saving in time and effort; they minimize breakage through reduced handling of dishes; they help keep the kitchen neater and more clutter-free; and cleanup after entertaining is simplified. These are benefits that have much appeal to consumers.

In order to ensure that public health standards are maintained, hospitals and many other food service institutions are required by law to clean dishes by automatic dishwashing methods.

The benefits of an automatic dishwasher and the specially formulated detergents can only be realised if they are used correctly. It is, therefore, important for the user to understand how the dishwasher works, the purpose of its features and how to load and operate it properly. User's manuals and detergent packages contain this information.

### The Dishwasher

The function of the dishwasher is to provide the mechanical action necessary to distribute and direct the detergent solution and rinse waters over, under and around the dishes to loosen and remove soil. The dishwasher must also remove soil-laden waters from the machine after each phase of the cycle and provide for the drying of dishes after the cleaning process has been completed.

#### *Washing Systems*

Automatic dishwashers vary in the design of their washing systems. Some have a single water source, others may have several water sources. Water is distributed in dishwashers by spray arms or spray towers. The design of the spray arms or towers may differ in size, shape and placement in the dishwasher, or in the number, size and location of their water ports. All of the washing systems do a good job, but those with fewer water sources require greater care in loading the dishes to prevent blocking the washing action to various parts of the machine, especially the corners.

### The Water

The role of water is to dissolve and carry detergent, wet and loosen soil and effectively rinse the soil away. The velocity with which water is distributed in the dishwasher provides the scrubbing action to loosen and remove soil.

***Amount***

Cleaning in a dishwasher is accomplished with a relatively small volume of water. Contrary to what some people think, the dishwasher does not fill completely as does a clothes washer. The dishwasher, instead, employs several small fills during a cycle to accomplish the washing and rinsing operations. The total volume of water used in a complete cycle can vary from 6 - 10 gallons, depending on the number of washes and rinses included in that particular cycle.

Water pressure in a home may be noticeably reduced at some times because of numerous household water demands. As a result, insufficient water in the dishwasher could occur. This can be avoided by keeping bathing, laundering and other activities requiring quantities of water to a minimum while the machine is in use.

***Temperature***

The temperature of the water is an important factor in dissolving detergent, removing food soils and drying dishes properly. To do these things most effectively, the water temperature at the dishwasher should not be lower than 130 degrees F (54.4 degrees C). As temperature is reduced, the removal of greasy and oily soils becomes more difficult; spotting and filming on dishes may occur as well as improper drying.

***Hardness***

The amount of hardness minerals and other dissolved solids in water present obstacles to good automatic dishwashing results. Hardness minerals can cause spotting and filming on dishware. They must be effectively tied up or sequestered if the results are to be satisfactory. Hardness of water is determined by the amount of calcium and magnesium in the water. It varies from locality to locality and season to season. Water hardness is expressed in grains per gallon, parts per million or milligrams per litre (mg/L)

| | **Soft** | **Moderately Hard** | **Hard** | **Very Hard** |
|---|---|---|---|---|
| Grains per gallon | 0.0 to 3.5 | 3.6 to 7.0 | 7.1 to 10.5 | 10.6 - |
| Parts per million or milligrams per liter | 0.0 to 60 | 61 to 120 | 121 to 180 | More than 180 |

To find out the water hardness in your area, call the local water company, public utility consumer service department or the home economist at the Cooperative Extension Service office.

**The Detergent**

Automatic dishwashers require detergents with very special characteristics because of the conditions under which the detergent must work. One of its essential characteristics is that it must produce little or no suds or foam because too much foam can inhibit the washing action. Other important functions that a dishwasher detergent should perform are the following:

- Make water wetter to penetrate and loosen soil.
- Tie up water hardness minerals to permit the detergent to do its cleaning job.
- Emulsify greasy or oily soil.
- Suppress foam caused by protein soils such as egg and milk.
- Help water to sheet off surfaces of dishes, thus minimizing water spots.
- Protect china patterns and metals from the corrosive effects of heat and water alone.

### *Ingredients*

*To accomplish these functions, the following ingredients may be included depending on the formulation and product form*:

- *Surfactant*: Lowers the surface tension of water so that it will more quickly wet out the surfaces and the soils. Lowering the surface tension makes the water sheet off dishes and not dry in spots. The surfactant also helps remove and emulsify fatty soils like butter and cooking fat. Nonionic surfactants are used because they have the lowest sudsing characteristics.
- *Builder*: Combines with water hardness minerals and holds them in solution so that the minerals cannot combine with food soils and so that neither the minerals themselves nor the mineral/food soil combination will leave insoluble spots or film on dishes. A builder helps maintain a desirable level of alkalinity, necessary for good soil removal.
- *Corrosion inhibitor*: Helps protect machine parts, prevent the removal of china patterns and the corrosion of metals such as aluminum.
- *Chlorine compound*: Aids in sanitizing, helps make protein soils like egg and milk soluble, aids in removing such stains as coffee or tea and lessens spotting of glassware.
- Special additives (sodium aluminate, boric oxide, aluminum phosphate, etc.) may be used to inhibit overglaze and pattern removal from fine china.
- *Additional alkalis (sodium carbonate, trisodium phosphate)*: May be used to aid in handling greasy food soils.
- *Perfume*: Covers the chemical odor of the base product and stale food odors which might otherwise emanate from the dishwasher.

*Processing aids*: Generally inert materials that allow the active ingredients to be combined into a usable form.

### *A Specially Formulated Product*

There are no substitutes for an automatic dishwasher detergent. Only an automatic dishwasher detergent can be used in an automatic dishwasher. These products come in either powder or gel form. All other types of detergents or soaps produce too much suds and will smother the water action necessary for cleaning in the dishwasher. Furthermore, enough suds might be generated to cause a dishwasher to overflow. This could necessitate a service call and could be damaging to the dishwasher and the floor around it. No other type of cleaning product such as baking soda, borax, vinegar or hand dishwashing liquid can be substituted for an automatic dishwasher detergent. These other materials will not perform well and may be damaging to the items being washed or to the dishwasher itself.

### *Amount*

Enough dishwasher detergent must be used to soften the water effectively, suppress foam from food soils, provide the necessary cleaning and suspension of soil and protect materials being washed. Underuse will result in poor cleaning, redeposition of soil, spotting, filming and possibly damage to some items being washed. Both the dishwasher instruction booklet and the detergent package provide guidelines for proper usage. A good general rule is to fill the detergent dispenser cup or cups to the level recommended by the dishwasher manufacturer.

It should be remembered that water hardness in any area may vary from season to season and that more detergent may be needed at some times than is needed at other times.

### *Packaging*

Powder automatic dishwasher detergents readily take up and retain moisture and carbon dioxide gas from the atmosphere. Should this occur, the product may become lumpy. As long as it properly dissolves it can be used, but may be somewhat less effective. To help prevent this condition, the carton is specially designed to provide a moisture barrier. Consumers should open the package as directed, avoiding unnecessary tearing of the overwrap and closing the box after each use. Always select undamaged packages and purchase only one or two at a time to ensure maximum product effectiveness.

### *Storage*

Store these products in a cool, dry place. Storage under the sink is not advisable because this area is generally too warm and moist to keep the product in optimum condition.

**Rinse Agent**

Some dishwashers have automatic rinse agent dispensers which release a liquid wetting agent into the final rinse cycle. Rinse agents in solid form are also available for use in dishwashers without the dispenser.

The rinse agent allows the water to sheet off dishes rather than dry in droplets, thus helping to eliminate spotting. It is particularly helpful in hard water areas and when heat is eliminated in the dry cycle to conserve energy.

**Safety Tips**

- Store automatic dishwasher detergent out of the reach of children, especially toddlers who like to taste and touch everything within their reach.
- Never store automatic dishwasher detergent and other household cleaning products in low cabinets that are accessible to small children. An upper wall cabinet that is within easy reach for convenient use is safer.
- Store all household cleaning products away from food products.
- Keep automatic dishwasher detergent in original container.
- Another child safety measure is to add detergent just before turning on the dishwasher. Return the product to storage shelf immediately.
- On completion of the cycle, check to be sure that no detergent is left in the dispenser cups. Clean out if necessary.
- When discarding containers, be sure they are empty and placed in a covered receptacle.
- Hot water is essential to effective results in automatic dishwashing. To prevent possible burns and scalds, exercise caution, especially with young children, when hot tap water is being used in any area of the home.

**Energy Saving Tips**

- Load dishwasher correctly for best results.
- Use recommended amount of automatic dishwasher detergent.
- Operate dishwasher only when a full load is accumulated.
- Use shorter cycle if suitable for amount of soil on dishes.
- Eliminate heat during dry cycle if water spotting is not a problem.
- Run the appliance during off-peak hours.

## ULTRASONIC DISHWASHER

An improved dishwasher system utilizes ultrasonic signals to clean a wide range of kitchen and/or dining ware items. The system includes one or more ultrasonic signal generators submerged within a water bath and regulated by a controller to generate an ultrasonic signal, resulting in the production of a large quantity of cavitation bubbles which implode with a vigourous cleaning action against submerged kitchen ware items.

The controller rapidly varies the specific frequency of the generated ultrasonic signal, preferably in conjunction with a rapid on-off pulse cycling of the signal, to prevent damage to or breakage of fragile ware items.

## STAFF ORGANISATION IN RESTAURANTS

Staff organization is basically concerned with matters such as the decision of tasks within the restaurant, position of responsibility and authority and the relationship between them. It helps in introducing the conceps of span of control, level of management and delegation of power and responsibilities. However smaller organizations may combine a number of responsibilities according to the needs of the particular facility.

## DUTIES AND RESPONSIBILITIES OF RESTAURANT STAFF

All types of catering establishments require a variety of staff positions in order to operate effectively and efficiently. The food and beverage service department usually has the largest staff. Able leadership and supervision is required to effectively direct the department and guide the staff.

The personnel in the food and beverage service industry require practical knowledge of operations as even a small error can cause displeasure to the guest.

Coordination of activities of all outlets is essential to provide the guest with quality service at all times. Teamwork is the watchword in any food and beverage service department.

A dedicated and committed team, with able leadership, under ideal working conditions, helps in fulfilling the establishment's ultimate goal of guest satisfaction The important duties and responsibilities of the restaurant staffs.

### SERVICE STAFF

Dining Room Manager / Maitre D / Somelier, Responsibilities before service : Hire and train the Dining Room Staff, Supervises and coordinates activities of dining room staff, Checking the physical condition of the dining room before it opens, complete the "Mise en Place", Taking and Managing Reservations, Purchases and stores beverages (restaurant mgr) , Organise table and seat settings. If necessary re-arrange, Prepare the staff schedule and make sure enough service personnel will be on hand, Make sure the menus are in good condition, Turn on lights, heating or cooling units

Dining Room Manager / Maitre D / Somelier (p.31) Responsibilities during service : Welcome the guest, Seat the guest, Give the menu to the guest, Discuss menu specials, Take the F&B Order (Captain, Chef de Rang), Open and serve wine (somelier), Observe the job performances of service employees, Make sure the guest is satisfied and follow up guest complaints Detect dishonest servers and guests, Deal with unhappy or difficult guest in a discreet and appropriate manner, Provide special service (flambé), Check regularly the cleanness of the toilets, Maintain a pleasant atmosphere in the dining room, Prepare and present the guest bill / check(cashier), Take guest money / credit card (cashier, restaurant mgr)

Dining Room Manager / Maitre D / Somelier (p.31) Responsibilities after service : Turn off lights, heating or cooling units, Provide reports and statistics for management (sales per day, lunch, dinner, items, number of guests per day, lunch, dinner, average guest check)

Captain / Chef de Rang : The captain / Chef de Rang are responsible for a part of the restaurant. According to the type, size of the establishment, the restaurant's policy and the captain's ability, the captain may have some responsibilities that are usually reserved for the dining room manager / MaitreD, Control the "Mise en Place", Describe or suggest food with wine, Take the F&B Order, Open and serve wine (somelier), Bring the guest's Food Order to the Chef, Bring the guest's Beverage Order to the Bartender, Bring (and serve) Food & Beverages,

Food Servers (commis) : These employees serve food and beverage to guests, Clean the table and make the Mise en Place (busperson)

Buspersons : Clean the table, deserve, carry dirty dishes to the kitchen, Change the ashtray, Serve bred, Pour water, Buy stuff for the guest (cigarettes) Deliver Food, Make the Mise en Place (linen, tableware, candles), Clean the dining room (Vacuum, Polish, Take the dust)

## FOOD AND BEVERAGE MANAGER

The food and beverage manager is the head of the food and beverage service department, and is responsible for its administrative and operational work.

Food and Beverage Managers direct, plan and control all aspects of food and beverage services. Food and Beverage Managers require excellent sales and customer service skills, proven human resource management skills, and good communication and leadership skills.

Desired knowledge for this position includes knowledge of the products, services, sector, industry and local area, and knowledge of relevant legislation and regulations, as well. Hence it is said that food and beverage manager is a Jack-of-all-trades, as the job covers a wide variety of duties.

*In general, food and beverage manager is responsible for*:

- *Budgeting*: The food and beverage manager is responsible for preparing the budget for the department. He should ensure that each outlet in the department achieves the estimated profit margins.

- *Compiling New Menus and Wine Lists*: In consultation with the chef, and based on the availability of ingredients and prevailing trends, the food and beverage manager should update and if necessary, compile new menus. New and updated wine lists should also be introduced regularly.
- *Quality Control*: The food and beverage manager should ensure quality control in terms of efficiency in all service areas, by ascertaining that the staffs are adequately trained in keeping with the standards of the unit.
- *Manpower Development*: The food and beverage manager is responsible for recruitment, promotions, transfers and dismissals in the department. He should hold regular meetings with section heads, to ensure that both routine as well as projected activities of the department go on as planned. He must also give training, motivate and effectively control staff.

## ASSISTANT FOOD AND BEVERAGE MANAGER

The assistant food and beverage manager assists the food and beverage manager in running the department by being more involved in the actual day-to-day operations. This position exists only in large organisations.

*An assistant food and beverage manager's job includes*:

- Assisting section heads during busy periods.
- Taking charge of an outlet when an outlet manager is on leave.
- Setting duty schedules for all the outlet managers and monitoring their performance.
- Running the department independently in the absence of the food and beverage manager.

# 8

# Cooking Method

## INTRODUCTION

Cooking is the process of preparing food with heat. Cooks select and combine ingredients using a wide range of tools and methods. In the process, the flavor, texture, appearance, and chemical properties of the ingredients can change. Cooking techniques and ingredients vary widely across the world, reflecting unique environmental, economic, and cultural traditions. Cooks themselves also vary widely in skill and training. Preparing food with heat or fire is an activity unique to humans, and some scientists believe the advent of cooking played an important role in human evolution. Most anthropologists believe that cooking fires first developed around 250,000 years ago. The development of agriculture, commerce and transportation between civilizations in different regions offered cooks many new ingredients. New inventions and technologies, such as pottery for holding and boiling water, expanded cooking techniques. Some modern cooks apply advanced scientific techniques to food preparation.

## WHY DO YOU COOK FOOD?

### COOKING MAKES FOOD EASY TO DIGEST

When food is cooked it becomes soft so that it is easily chewed and swallowed. The juices that digest food are able to mix well with the softened food. Hence the food gets simplified for use by your body.

### COOKING IMPROVES THE APPEARANCE, TEXTURE, COLOUR, FLAVOUR, AND TASTE OF THE FOOD

Cooking improves the taste and flavour of food, changes its colour and appearance. When you cook meat or potatoes etc. you will find that the food has better taste. Cooking meat improves its taste, flavour and colour.

Addition of spices and condiments during cooking further improves the acceptability and palatability of foods. You must observe the changes that the foods undergo when you cook next.

## WHEN FOODS ARE COOKED YOU CAN MAKE A VARIETY OF DISHES

Cooked foods provide variety in your meals. You must have eaten potatoes cooked in different ways - such as pakora, potato chat, potato parantha, potato vegetables and potato chips etc. Can you list a few food items that can be made with atta? Yes, parantha, puree, chapati, bread, mathi, etc. So, you see that you can make variety of dishes with the same food.

## COOKING HELPS TO KEEP THE FOOD LONGER

Do you know why we boil milk? Yes, if you do not boil milk it will get spoiled soon. Boiling milk helps in killing of spoilage organism and makes it last longer. Atta dough gets spoilt after some time. You must have noticed that chapaties can be kept longer than the dough. Can you name a few more foods that will last longer after cooking?

## COOKING MAKES THE FOOD SAFE AND STERILE

Raw foods get spoilt because of the harmful micro-organism present in them. These micro-organism get destroyed, when you cook food. Killing germs by cooking makes the food sterile and safe for eating. Milk often contains bacteria that cause tuberculosis. Do you know what happens when you boil milk? Yes, the bacteria get killed and milk becomes safe for drinking.

## METHODS OF COOKING

You often say boil the rice, fry pakoras or bake a cake. What are boiling, frying and baking? These are the methods of cooking.

*Food can be cooked*:

- By moist heat
- By dry heat.
- By frying in ghee or oil.

## COOKING BY MOIST HEAT

In this method water is heated or boiled. The food is put into this boiling water or cooked in the steam which comes out from the boiling water. There are three ways by which you cook food by moist heat.

*These are*:

- Boiling
- Simmering or stewing
- Steaming

### Boiling

In this method food is covered with an adequate quantity of water and heated to a boiling. For example we boil potatoes, eggs, a number of vegetables, rice etc.

Usually green leafy vegetables such as cabbage, methi, and spinach are cooked with no water. Whereas vegetables such as green peas, green beans, are cooked with little water. Cereals such as rice and pulses such as dals, legumes, grams are boiled in large amounts of water. There are a few points which you should keep in mind while boiling foods.

- Before boiling, wash the food stuffs thoroughly.
- Cover the food with an adequate quantity of water.
- First boil the water and then put the food.
- Cook in a pan which has a well fitting lid. This way the steam from boiling water will not go out from the pan and the water will not dry up. Food gets boiled faster when the cooking pan has a lid on.
- Do not boil foods longer than needed. Once they are soft and tender, take them off the fire. If food is cooked for a very long time it looses its colour, shape and taste. Potatoes and other root vegetables should be boiled with their skins on.
- Water used for boiling should cover the food. Water soluble nutrients present in foods dissolve in water in which the food is being boiled. If you throw this water, nutrients will be lost. What can you do to save these nutrients? You can use this nutrient rich water to make gravy for another vegetable.

**Siimmering or Stewing**

Stewing is cooking for a long time in water, below the boiling point. In this method you cook food in a small quantity of water.

Once the boiling starts the flame is lowered and the food is allowed to cook slowly.

- *Suitability*: This method is suitable for cooking hard and tough foods like dals, meat and dried vegetables.
- *Advantages*: While cooking by this method we do not have to constantly keep an eye on food. And there are lesser chances of food getting burnt.

**Steaming**

Do you know what happens when the water boils? Yes, it gives off steam. When food is cooked in water vapour with or without pressure it is said to be steamed and this method of cooking is called steaming. Can you name some steamed foods that you have eaten? Yes, Idli and Dhokla. Steaming can be done for solid and semi-solid foods. Water is heated in a pan on fire. The pan is covered with a clean muslin cloth. Food is placed on the cloth.

The steam passes around the food and cooks the food placed above. When you are making idlis, the batter is put in the idli mould, which is then lowered into a container with water at the bottom. Once again it is the steam going around the moulds that cooks the idlis.

- *Suitability*: This method is suitable for making Dhokla, caramel custard etc.
- *Advantages*: Steaming shortens the duration of cooking and helps to conserve nutritive value, colour, flavour and palatability of food. Steamed food is light nutritious and easy to digest. Such foods are good for old people and little children.

**Pressure Cooking**

Pressure cookers are generally made of an Aluminium alloy which is very strong. Now a days stainless steel cookers are also available in the market. But these are quite expensive. Raw food is put in the container along with water and cooked under pressure. Under pressure the temperature of water is increased up to 1120C.

- *Advantages*: Pressure cooking kills all bacteria and hence the food is safe and hygienic for you to eat. Rice, dal, meat, potatoes, roots, beans, and peas and peas are cooked in the pressure cooker. The food gets cooked faster than boiling. *You can call pressure cooking high temperature short time cooking.*

## METHODS OF COOKING

There are very many methods of cooking, most of which have been known since antiquity. These include baking, roasting, frying, grilling, barbecuing, smoking, boiling, steaming and braising. A more recent innovation is microwaving.

Various methods use differing levels of heat and moisture and vary in cooking time. The method chosen greatly affects the end result. Some foods are more appropriate to some methods than others. Some major hot cooking techniques include:

***Boiling***

Boiling - Blanching - Braising - Coddling - Double steaming - Infusion - Poaching - Pressure cooking - Simmering - Steaming - Steeping - Stewing - Vacuum flask cooking

***Frying***

Frying - Deep frying - Hot salt frying - Hot sand frying - Pan frying - Pressure frying - Sautéing - Stir frying

### *Baking*

Baking - Baking Blind - Broiling - Flashbaking

### *Roasting*

Roasting - Barbecuing - Grilling - Rotisserie - Searing

### *Smoking*

Food smoking

## Food Safety

When heat is used in the preparation of food, it can kill or inactivate potentially harmful organisms including bacteria and viruses. The effect will depend on temperature, cooking time, and technique used. The temperature range from 41 °F to 135 °F (5 °C to 57 °C) is the "food danger zone." Between these temperatures bacteria can grow rapidly. Under optimal conditions, *E. coli,* for example, can double in number every twenty minutes.

The food may not appear any different or spoiled but can be harmful to anyone who eats it. Meat, poultry, dairy products, and other prepared food must be kept outside of the "food danger zone" to remain safe to eat. Refrigeration and freezing do not kill bacteria, but only slow their growth. When cooling hot food, it should not be left standing or in a blast chiller for more than 90 minutes.

Cutting boards are a potential breeding ground for bacteria, and can be quite hazardous unless safety precautions are taken. Plastic cutting boards are less porous than wood and have conventionally been assumed to be far less likely to harbor bacteria. This has been debated, and some research has shown wooden boards are far better.

Washing and sanitizing cutting boards is highly recommended, especially after use with raw meat, poultry, or seafood. Hot water and soap followed by a rinse with an antibacterial cleaner (dilute bleach is common in a mixture of 1 tablespoon per gallon of water, as at that dilution it is considered food safe, though some professionals choose not to use this method because they believe it could taint some foods), or a trip through a dishwasher with a "sanitize" cycle, are effective methods for reducing the risk of illness due to contaminated cooking implements.

### *Effects on Nutritional Content of Food*

Proponents of Raw foodism argue that cooking food increases the risk of some of the detrimental effects on food or health. They point out that the cooking of vegetables and fruit containing vitamin C both elutes the vitamin into the cooking water and degrades the vitamin through oxidation.

Peeling vegetables can also substantially reduce the vitamin C content, especially in the case of potatoes where most vitamin C is in the skin. However, research has also suggested that a greater proportion of nutrients present in food is absorbed from cooked foods than from uncooked foods.

Baking, grilling or broiling food, especially starchy foods, until a toasted crust is formed generates significant concentrations of acrylamide, a possible carcinogen. Cooking dairy products may reduce a protective effect against colon cancer. Researchers at the University of Toronto suggest that ingesting uncooked or unpasteurized dairy products may reduce the risk of colorectal cancer.

Mice and rats fed uncooked sucrose, casein, and beef tallow had one-third to one-fifth the incidence of microadenomas as the mice and rats fed the same ingredients cooked. This claim, however, is contentious. According to the Food and Drug Administration of the United States, health benefits claimed by raw milk advocates do not exist. "The small quantities of antibodies in milk are not absorbed in the human intestinal tract," says Barbara Ingham, Ph.D., associate professor and extension food scientist at the University of Wisconsin-Madison. "There is no scientific evidence that raw milk contains an anti-arthritis factor or that it enhances resistance to other diseases."

Several studies published since 1990 indicate that cooking muscle meat creates heterocyclic amines (HCAs), which are thought to increase cancer risk in humans. Researchers at the National Cancer Institute found that human subjects who ate beef rare or medium-rare had less than one third the risk of stomach cancer than those who ate beef medium-well or well-done. While eating muscle meat raw may be the only way to avoid HCAs fully, the National Cancer Institute states that cooking meat below 212 °F (100 °C) creates "negligible amounts" of HCAs.

Also, microwaving meat before cooking may reduce HCAs by 90%. Nitrosamines, present in processed and cooked foods, have also been noted as being carcinogenic, being linked to colon cancer.

Research has shown that grilling or barbecuing meat and fish increases levels of carcinogenic Polycyclic aromatic hydrocarbons (PAH). However, meat and fish only contribute a small proportion of dietary PAH intake - most intake comes from cereals, oils and fats. German research in 2003 showed significant benefits in reducing breast cancer risk when large amounts of raw vegetable matter are included in the diet. The authors attribute some of this effect to heat-labile phytonutrients. Heating sugars with proteins or fats can produce Advanced glycation end products ("glycotoxins"). These have been linked to ageing and health conditions such as diabetes.

## Science of Cooking

The application of scientific knowledge to cooking and gastronomy has become known as molecular gastronomy. This is a subdiscipline of food science. Important contributions have been made by scientists, chefs and authors such as Herve This (chemist), Nicholas Kurti (physicist), Peter Barham (physicist), Harold McGee (author), Shirley Corriher (biochemist, author), Heston Blumenthal (chef), Ferran Adria (chef), Robert Wolke (chemist, author) and Pierre Gagnaire (chef). Chemical processes central to cooking include the Maillard reaction - a form of non-enzymatic browning involving an amino acid, a reducing sugar and heat.

**Home-cooking vs. Factory Cooking**

Although cooking has traditionally been a process carried out informally at home or around a communal fire, cooking is often, and increasingly, carried out outside the home. Bakeries were an early form of cooking outside the home, and bakeries in the past often offered the cooking of foods provided by their customers as an additional service. In the present day, factory food preparation is rapidly becoming the norm, with many "ready-to-eat" foods being prepared and cooked in factories.

"Home-cooking" may be associated with comfort food, and some commercially produced foods are presented as having been "home-cooked", regardless of their actual origin.

## HISTORY OF COOKING

There is no clear evidence as to when cooking was invented. Primatologist Richard Wrangham stated that cooking was invented as far back as 1.8 million to 2.3 million years ago. Other researchers believe that cooking was invented as late as 40,000 or 10,000 years ago. Evidence of fire is inconclusive as wildfires started by lightning-strikes are still common in East Africa and other wild areas, and it is difficult to determine when fire was first used for cooking, as opposed to just being used for warmth or for keeping predators away.

Most anthropologists contend that cooking fires began in earnest barely 250,000 years ago, when ancient hearths, earth ovens, burnt animal bones, and flint appear across Europe and the middle East. The only evidence of human use of fire more than two million years ago is burnt earth with human remains, which most anthropologists consider coincidence rather than evidence of intentional.

However, some Fire-cracked rock, such as that in Central Texas (United States) are burned rock middens, or enormous piles fire-damaged rock dated to c. 3,500 years ago. These may represent the remains of earth ovens used in cooking since they contain evidence of *Dasylirion wheeleri* bulbs and other plants. In Great Britain similar Neolithic, Bronze Age and Iron Age features exist, but are commonly called 'burnt mounds'.

## COOKING BY DRY HEAT

What do we normally eat for breakfast? Some times we eat chapaties, paranthas, purees and some times bread. We also eat rusks and buns.

Do you know how these are cooked? Yes, they are cooked by dry heat.

Cooking food by dry heat means using hot air to cook the food. There are three methods of cooking food by dry heat using hot air.

- Baking
- Roasting
- Grilling
- *Baking*: Baking is the method in which food is placed inside a closed box called an oven. The air inside the oven is made hot by fire or electricity. The food gets cooked by hot air. Have you seen a bakery in your village or neighbouhood? You must have also seen the big ovens heated by fire in which biscuits, breads and pastries are made in these bakeries.

  These ovens are also known as 'bhattis'. It is in these ovens that the food is cooked. In the very big bakeries, the air is heated by electricity.You can easily make an oven at home to bake foods. Take an empty oil pin. Put a layer of sand in it and fit it with a lid. Heat this over coal, kerosence or a gas stove. Once it becomes hot, put the food inside and close the lid. Place the tin on a low fire. Bake food till it is light brown in colour. Do not open the lid very often because the hot air from inside will go out and make the food dry and hard.
- *Roasting*: Another method of cooking food by dry heat is called roasting. Roasting is cooking on a glowing fire. While roasting, the food is put directly on the hot tava, hot stand or hot fire and cooked. For eg. channas, brinjals, potatoes, maize, ground nuts, cashew nuts, papad, meat etc. are cooked by this method. You must, have had chicken or paneer tikkas cooked in this way.
- *Grilling*: Grilling is cooking over a glowing fire. The food is supported on a iron grid over the fire, or between electrically heated grill bars. The grill bars are brushed with oil to prevent food sticking and can be heated by charcoal, coke, gas or electricity. The food is cooked on both sides to give the distinctive flavour of grilling. Potato, sweet potato.

## FRYING

Frying is the process of cooking food in hot fat or oil.

*Food can be fried in two ways*:

- Shallow frying
- Deep frying

*Advantages of frying are*:

- Fried food is very appetizing

- Quick method of cooking
- The keeping quality of food is increased.

*Some precautions while frying food*:

- Food should be cut in suitable size and shape.
- Do not put in too many pieces of food at the same time. It will lower the temperature.
- Food should be fried to golden brown colour on both sides by turning over the food if necessary.
  - *Shallow frying*: When you make paranthas or an omellette, you need very little oil for frying. You can fry them on a tava or a frying pan. The food is turned over so that both sides may be browned and cooked. This method is called shallow frying.
  - *Deep frying*: Do you know how to fry foods? Yes, ghee/oil in a karahi is heated to the smoke point. Carefully put the food to be fired in the hot ghee/ oil. The food should fully dip in ghee/ oil. Put only a few pieces of food to be fried at a time. Avoid using large quantity of oil/ ghee or overheating. If some ghee is left over after frying, drain and store in a closed container to be used again. Frying is a quick method of cooking as compared to boiling or stewing.

**ACTIVITY**

Observe dal, rice, potato curry and brinjal bhartha before and after they have been cooked. Record your observations in the table given below.

| **Food** | **Colour Before Cooking** | **Textrure Flavour After Cooking** |
|---|---|---|
| Dal | | |
| Palak Pakora | | |
| Potato curry | | |
| Brinjal Bharta | | |

## Nutrients Lost During Cooking

So far we have only read about the importance of cooking. Do you know that some nutrients are lost during cooking? Even when we cut and wash the foods, some nutrients are destroyed. Let us understand how some of the nutrients are lost during cooking.

- *Vitamin A*: Vitamin A is found in foods like spinach, methi, carrots etc.When we cook these vegetables not much of vitamin A is lost, but when we fry these foods, like when we make palak pakoras, vitamin A gets destroyed. Can you tell why? If you remember, vitamin A dissolves easily in fats and oils. So, when you fry such foods in oil, vitamin A comes out from the food and goes into oil.

- *Vitamin B*: How is rice cooked? First of all you clean rice and then wash it. Vitamin B being water soluble, goes out of the rice and washes away with the water. If you wash rice by rubbing you are letting more vitamin B wash away. After washing rice, it is soaked in water. Some more vitamin B goes out from the rice into the water during this process. Next, rice is boiled in water. If you use a lot of water to cook rice and throw away the extra water some dissolved vitamin B also goes out with this water. Sometimes, you add cooking soda to soften foods like rajmah and channas. Cooking soda also destroys vitamin B.
- *Vitamin C*: Vitamin C is an important nutrient which is easily destroyed by cooking. When you cut vegetables and fruits rich in vitamin C, some of it is lost. Vitamin C is also lost when you wash vegetables and fruits after cutting and exposing cut vegetables to air for long periods before cooking. When the foods are cooked for a long time or when you throw away water in which you cook them, you loose Vitamin C. You also loose vitamin C when you add cooking soda to the foods. Therefore, cooking procedures that minimize the loss of vitamin C result in conserving all other nutrients.
- *Proteins*: All proteins present in the foods coagulated by heat. Cooking results in softening of proteins in foods such as egg, fish, and meat, becomes water is bound in the process of coagulation. If the coagulated protein is further heated, it loses moisture and becomes dry and rubbery. They also become difficult to digest.
- *Oils and Fats*: When food containing fat are heated, the fat has the tendency to separate from the food. You must have seen that heating milk results in the fat layer floating on top. Oils and fats are used as a cooking medium. Some fat is absorbed during frying. Therefore fried foods such as pakoras, etc. gives us more energy than the boiled foods. When fats, ghee and oil, are heated for long periods of time over and over again, to fry pakoras or purees etc. its quality becomes poor.
- *Minerals*: Minerals like sodium, potassium, etc. dissolve in water. Minerals get lost when food is first cut, then washed and the extra water in which they are boiled, is thrown away.

**Conservation of Nutrients**

Now you all know that some nutrients are lost when foods are cooked. Nutrients like vitamin B and C are lost when foods are boiled or soaked in water and the water is thrown away. Nutrients like vitamin A are lost when fats are used for cooking foods. If all these nutrients will be destroyed, how will our body get energy to do work, repair body tissues and fight disease germs?

Therefore, you must think of ways of saving these nutrients. Saving nutrients during the process of cooking is called conservation.

- Wash vegetables before cutting them so that minerals and vitamins are not destroyed. Do not wash the foods more than necessary.
- Peel vegetables thinly as vitamins and minerals are found just under the skin.
- Cut vegetables into large pieces just before cooking. Small pieces mean greater loss of nutrients.
- If vegetables are to be cooked in water, put them into boiling water.
- Scrape the peels very thin. Use dry tori or jute to remove peels from potatoes, etc.
- Use just enough water for cooking. Do not throw away the extra water. Use this extra water to cook some other food.
- Do not use cooking soda. Use of tamarind or lemon juice helps to conserve the vitamins.
- Cook rice in just enough water which gets absorbed during cooking? Do you know how much water should be used for one katori rice? Yes, two katori water.
- Cook in a pan which has a well fitting lid. When you cook in an uncovered pan most nutrients are lost.
- Do not overcook the food as many nutrients will be destroyed.

## Enchancing Nutrients Content of Food

You are already familiar with the different ways that help you to conserve nutrients during cooking. It would be so nice if we could increase the nutritive value of foods without increasing the cost. Can you suggest some ways of doing so? Let us find out how to do it.

### *Definition of Enrichment*

The process of improving the nutrients in foods by special methods is called Enrichment.

*Importance of enhancing nutritive value of food*:

- To meet the nutritional requirements of the body.
- To make proper selection and preparation of foods.
- To consume food in a balanced manner.
- To improve the flavour and texture of the food.

- To get variety in food.
- To assist in planning the daily menu, keeping in view the nutrient content of the food.
- To prevent deficiency diseases in the body.
- To develop good food habits.

***Methods of Enrichment of Nutrients***

There are three methods by which you can enhance or increase the nutrients present in your food.

(a) Combination
(b) Fermentation
(c) Germination

## Combination

We all eat combination of variety of foods. For example, you eat a dal or channas etc. with vegetables, salad, curd and chapati or rice.

Chapaties or rice will give you carbohydrates, dal and curd will give you proteins, vegetables and salad will give you vitamins and minerals. Combining of foods from different food groups is the easiest way of eating all nutrients.

You can also mix a number of foods in one dish and get all the nutrients from it. Such a combination of foods improves the quality of nutrients.

When you eat rice and dal together you get better nutrients. Do you know why? Cereals lack certain amino acids. And these are present in dals. On the other hand dals lack some other amino acids that are present in cereals. Do you know when you eat dal and rice together, the quality of proteins becomes as good as that of milk.

Do you remember the food group to which the carrots belong to? What are carrots rich in? Vitamin A. What will happen to your khichri if you add carrots to it? And what will happen if you eat this khichri with curd?

The khichri will also become rich in vitamin A, calcium and proteins (curd). Can you name some other foods that can be added to your dal rice preparations? Yes, methi, peas, beans, ghee, etc.

Can you name some other rice and dal dishes that your family eats? Yes, Paushtik roti, Kachauri, Idli, Dosa, Sambhar, mixed dal, etc. The combination of a variety of foods ensures better availability of nutrients. Combination is the process of combining cheaper and commonly available foods from different food groups to improve the quality of nutrients.

*Combination helps you to*:

- Eat a diet that has good quality nutrients.
- Use cheaper and easily available foods that enhance the nutrient content of food considerably.
- Provide balanced diet to your family.

**Fermentation**

Have you ever made bhuturas? These are made by mixing a little curd in maida which is kneaded into a dough and kept covered for few hours. In these few hours the dough rises. Do you know why? When you add curd to maida you introduce micro-organisms which begin to grow at a very fast rate. They start a process called fermentation.

Fermentation makes the dough rise and become almost double in quantity. During fermentation the micro-organisms use up some of the nutrients present in the atta and change them into other better quality nutrients. They also make some new nutrients.

*Definition of Fermentation*: Fermentation is a process in which some micro-organisms are added to the food. They change nutrients already present in the foods into simpler and better forms and also make other new nutrients. Can you name some fermented foods? Curd, bread, khaman-dhokla, idli, etc. are all examples of fermented foods.

*Advantages of Fermentation:*

- Fermentation improves the digestibility of foods. The micro-organisms which cause fermentation break the proteins and carbohydrates into smaller parts, which are easier to digest.
- During fermentation of cereals and foods like peas, beans etc. the minerals, calcium, phosphorus, and iron are changed into better quality ones. These are then easily absorbed by the body.
- Fermented foods become spongy and soft and are liked by children and adults.

***Germination***

Take some whole 'moong' or 'channa' and soak them overnight in a small quantity of water. What do you see the next day? Yes, they become big in size and soft to touch. Now if you tie the soaked dal in a wet cloth and keep for another 12 to 24 hours, you will notice that small, white shoots have started growing from these dals. This process is called germination or sprouting.

**Definition of Germination**

Germination is a process in which small shoots come out of the dal or cereal when these are kept with small amount of water. The grains and pulses to be sprouted need to be soaked in just enough water so that all of it is absorbed. If the extra water in which they are soaked is thrown away, you will be loosing a lot of nutrients.

Grains like wheat, bajra, jawar, etc. can also be sprouted. These grains can then be dried in shade and roasted lightly on a tava. They can be ground and used in many dishes. Pulses like moong, peas, kala chana etc. are also sprouted first and then steamed and eaten after adding salt, chilli powder, lemon juice etc. The time and water which each grain or pulse needs for soaking and sprouting is different. Normally 8-16 hours are needed for soaking and 12-24 hours for sprouting. The cloth in which the soaked dal is tied should be kept moist all the time. In the winter months sprouting can be done faster by using warm water.

If you sprout wheat you can grind it into a fine powder after sprouting. This can then be fermented and bathuras made from the dough. Such a dough will be rich in vitamins. Here the food is first sprouted then fermented.

*Germination helps you to*:

- Increase the digestibility of foods. Do you know why?
  - Some carbohydrates and proteins are broken down into smaller and easily digestible forms.
  - Grains and pulses become soft after sprouting, so they take less time for cooking and are easy for you to digest.
- Increase the nutritive value of food with no additional cost. Some vitamins and minerals become more when foods are germinated Vitamin B becomes almost double in quantity while vitamin C increases almost 10 times.

When you soak pulses like rajmah, soyabeans etc. in water for a few hours before cooking, it helps to increase their vitamins content.

## INDIAN COOKING

Like any art form, the foundation of Indian cooking is based on technique. There is a body of knowledge about the food itself-the vegetables, the spices, the herbs, the sauces-but this information is meaningless unless applied with sensitivity. I use the words sensitivity and knowledge in all of their nuances: knowing when a vegetable like the bitter melon, Karela, is perfectly in season; understanding how to remove the bitterness; and, finally being aware of its healing properties.

There's a perfect moment to eat karela, just as there's an appropriate time for an Indian raga to be played. There are monsoon ragas, morning ragas, and ragas that are played when the lover has gone. Music and food are always respected for their ability to cleanse the soul, and heal.

Indian cooking has always found a willing companion in art and music. They always seem to go together. Any musical gathering first begins with prayers to the gods and offering of food to them. Just as emotions are a part of music so are they a part of cooking. Thus in India one finds that to evolve ones palate one also studies the appreciation of music and art. In the Indian kitchen one entertains spices or masalas. The seeds, stalks and powders are all found. There are masalas that can set ones palate to receive taste sensations in the most profound ways.

There are those that can alter feelings. Grains are an integral part of cooking throughout India. A vegetarian cuisine that would otherwise be nutritionally weak is complete by the mixing of lentils, beans, rice and vegetables. Rice has been know in India for over 5 thousand years... maize, barley, semolina, millet, countless types of lentils and beans and many peas form a crucial part of the Indian pantry. Over many ages and several dynastic rules later, cooking in India has been honed into a fine art in itself. One of the older civilizations known to man, this country also proudly boasts a culinary repertoire that is eclectic at the least.

Over the length and breadth of India, in the different homes in India, of the rich and the poor, one comes across a wide range of flavours, styles and tastes. Many styles of cooking seen in different parts of the world can also be found in one or the other part of India. In India one can find Indian-Chinese cooking, Parsee cooking, Baghdadi cooking and within that the Jewish cooking of that area, Portuguese influenced, French influenced, British inspired and then the well known Mughal cooking.

One sees these styles emerge from the invasion of India by many of these foreign powers and then in the case of the Parsee community, one sees the creation of a cuisine by a people that came as refugees. The Parsees are Zoroastrians who came to India to flee religious persecution in the middle east. Today they seem as much a part of India as any other segment of the population. They speak Gujerati, their food is loved by one and all and they are welcome members of the community. There is a very small Jewish population scattered across India.

It may be small in number, but has been able to maintain its clean status and has kept its cultural independence. Their foods and their customs are still a part of that heritage that makes India so diverse. In Cochin, in Calcutta and in Bombay one sees how these small pockets of a minority community has managed to influence a larger community and also taken from the other community. It is this secular fabric of India that has kept a vibrancy in an otherwise very old culture. In India one sees society, culture, language, food and people change dramatically as one goes from North to South or East to West.

A country that has a couple of dozens of languages and several hundred dialects, also boasts of many different art form and food styles. It is this change from region to region that gives India a very mixed blessing. It adds greatly to the cultural wealth of this country and is a great teacher for a hungry traveller. But it also brings with it a mixed socioeconomic bag. Each region, each state and each community in India, is steeped in local traditions.

Many of these traditions are based upon the history of that region, the religious fabric of its people and the agricultural diversity. In India all the culinary styles are based upon the local produce found in that area. Thus to study Indian food as a whole one studies the regional influences that shape its many styles. Spices which today signal the advent of cooking are found in abundance in India.

Most come from that region and many have been studied not just for the culinary uses but also for the healing powers. Spices and fresh herbs are used in good measure and are a very intricately woven part of Indian life. Food, prayer and medical uses are some of many roles played by these inanimate ingredients.

Turmeric is revered as an antiseptic, asafoetida to fight flatulence, carom to counter nausea and ginger as an aphrodisiac. Fenugreek and cumin seeds are given to nursing mothers to aid secretion. How a spice is used and when it is added to a meal can easily tell you where the food is from and who it has been cooked for.

Every kitchen has a masaal-daan, a spice box. In this box are found seeds, stalks, barks, stems and leaves that exalt Indian cooking. What combination one sees is typical of that chefs repertoire or of the region. In the north one would see whole garam masala, cumin seeds, coriander seeds, turmeric, red chili powder, fennel seeds and some other spice blends. In the south one would find mustard seeds, fenugreek seeds, curry leaves, whole red chilies, urad daal and chana daal, and other spice blends.

In each of the region one will also find spices that are used in the other. This shows how deep the fusion of the styles is already. Each day, after the vegetable vendor has made his trip, the cook then plans a menu and will prepare the spices accordingly. Spices are ground daily to ensure freshness. A mortar and pestle is used most often as this gives the cook control over how fine to grind them. There are dishes for which one needs very finely ground spices and then there are those that require coarsely ground powders.

Every region of India has its own staple cooking medium, or fat. There is mustard oil in the north and the east, peanut oil in the south and the west. There are also other oils used from region to region. The one common fat used across India is clarified butter or ghee. Often recipes call for mixing the two.

Ghee adds a very distinct flavour to dishes and makes them seem very organic. Every home makes its own ghee. Ghee is made with butter from cows milk. The preparation of ghee is almost a religious chore as ghee is also used to burn the oil lamps in the home temple. It is also the medium with which most navaidyum is prepared. Navaidyum is the food that is first offered to the Gods and then eaten by families. This is the case in most traditional homes. One sees less and less of this in big cities today.

Milk and yogurt are found across the country. In home cooking one often sees wide usage of yogurt. Yogurt is used as an end to a meal with just some sugar. Yogurt is mixed into curries to reduce use of fat. Yogurt is mixed with flour to make sauces that replace those made with any vegetables. Yogurt can be the sauce by itself with bean dumplings. Yogurt is used in dressing Indian style salads like chaat papri. This shows the affinity Indians have for dairy. Yogurt is believed to aid digestion. Yogurt also gives protein to an otherwise vegetarian diet. Cows are holy in India. This has been a part of Indian tradition for as long as India has been there. In old India cows milk was fed to babies that had lost their mother at birth. It was because of this that cows were treated as another form of the mother goddess. Cow milk is used in making all the many desserts that are offered to the gods and then help sate the Indian sweet tooth.

It is said that during the days of the rule of the Kauravas and the Pandavas, the Mahabharat setting, Indians lived decadently. The cuisine was very rich and very complex. India which is predominantly vegetarian today seemed to have enjoyed eating many different meats. Curries were made from cow, deer, wild boar, goat, sheep, poultry and other animals. Meats were grilled and roasted and broiled.

They were cooked on spent flames, on spits and under a hot flame inside the ground. Often larger animals were stuffed with smaller and so on until there could be no more stuffing. These were then cooked under the ground below a flame that was kept alive overnight. Meats and rice were cooked together. In the north fruits and vegetables were mixed with these rice and meat preparations. The old texts mention the use of milk instead of water to cook some rich savory casseroles of meat and rice. Spices were used generously and dried fruit and nuts were added during and after cooking to add to the lavishness of a meal.

It was only after this excessive era that one finds a change in the eating habits. What was mostly a meat enriched diet now became vegetarian. Decadence was replaced by humble simplicity. Vegetarianism found new appeal. Brahmans the stalwarts of Hinduism became ardent supporters of this austere vegetarian diet. As Buddhism and Jainism came along, they furthered the rise of vegetarianism.

Within these religions one saw other factors develop that changed the cuisine. Hindus encouraged not eating onions and garlic as they had aphrodisiacal properties. It was believed that these ground vegetables would arouse people. Widows and certain other classes of society were forbidden their use. The Jains believed that eating root vegetables would harm the organisms that lived alongside them. But then there were contradictions to the rule. In Bengal the Brahmins ate fish, calling it the gourd of the ocean. In the south certain Brahman communities also ate seafood with the same reasoning.

In Kashmir the Brahmins eat all meat other than beef and pork. There have been socio-historical reasons for that occurrence. But for the most part India was now a vegetarian society and thus began the exploration of how to make an austere practice seem lavish. With their desire to eat meals with meat and yet a ardent faith that said otherwise, cooks took it upon them to come up with recipes that would make a meatless diet seem just as tasty. It was with regards to their food that the Brahmins take most excessive precautions. They are never allowed to touch meat and this includes not only anything that has had life, fish included, but also anything that has contained even any form of life, such as an egg.

Vegetables were cooked by themselves, whole, stuffed, steamed, sauteed, fried and cooked as mince. Dumplings were made with grains, lentils and beans. Rice and beans were cooked together. Lentils and beans were prepared as soups and into stews with mixed vegetables. Patties were made with vegetables and grains. Fritters were prepared. Yogurt was added to the curries and chutneys and preserved were prepared. The murrabas (preserves) and the aachaars (pickles) were used as condiments and also for their medicinal use. These pickles and preserves also enabled one to have the flavour of certain vegetables and fruits all year long. It is thus no surprise that mango chutney has remained ever popular today just as it was then.

Meat made a come back in the realm on Indian cooking. With the arrival of the Afghans, Turks and other Central Asians there was another introduction of meat to India. The non-vegetarian cuisine of India is very different from the Muslim cooking of other Central Asian nations. The common roots exist but the changes are stark and clean. One can see how local ingredients and the influences of the societal structure have played a huge role in the development of this cuisine.

Onions, garlic, ginger found a robust re-entry. Rice which had been found here for ages was made into Pilafs seasoned with the many spices found in India. Layered with different meats and vegetables, teased with dried fruits and nuts and tempered with saffron and screwpine essence and served as biryanis.

The Muslim invaders also brought with them communal eating. They reintroduced pomp and extravagance into Indian society. Multi course meals were made in homes. Week long festivities were planned on special occasions. Music, dance and drinks accompanied good food. Eating became a revered ritual and good cooks were guarded carefully. Each family had its own secrets and these were passed on only by word of mouth through members of the family alone, lest anyone else find out.

Fruits play a very important role in the Indian diet. The Muslim invaders realized that the barren northern plains did not bare some of their loved fruits. This led to the import of melons, cantaloupes and grapes into India. India has a natural abundance of Mangoes, some of the most flavourful and varied ones found in the world.

Oranges of many varieties, guavas, figs, plantains, berries of many different kinds, mulberries that are delectable, shareefas (custard apples) that exude an aroma that can change any persons mood for the better, and pineapple. Pomegranates were introduced into India and quickly became a favourite and also became an ingredient to cook savory dishes with.

The entry of Europeans into India, many exotic ingredients entered the Indian kitchen. Potatoes, chilies, tomatoes and cheeses came into India and were used generously.

Tomatoes were not a favourite of many old fashioned Indians as the vegetable seemed very fleshy and the colour blood like. Indians have traditionally rejected any vegetable whose roots or stems grow in the shape of a head.

Thus onions, garlic and mushrooms have had trouble finding there place. In this era, all of these vegetables were given a gallant re-entry and more and more dishes were made using them. Jams, jellies, yeast risen breads, pastries and casseroles were prepared with hints of Indian spices. Chilies, potatoes and tomatoes found much love in India and have become staples of the Indian kitchen. Most Indians would not even realize that these were until very recently unknown ingredients.

After the partition of India in 1947 into Pakistan and India, the northern states had an influx of refugees from Central Asia. Tandoori foods that were found mostly in stately homes were now made a part of the local cuisine. Frontier cooking took over the regional cooking in popularity. Vendors who would have traditionally sold chaats and fritters and vegetable patties now started selling kebabs, tikkas, kormas, pasindas and other meat laden curries.

## METHODS OF MIXING FOOD

### STIRRING

Food is stirred by a rotary motion of the arm. The purpose of stirring is to mix thoroughly all ingredients.

### BEATING

Food is beaten when the motion in mixing brings the contents at the bottom of the bowl to the top and there is a continual turning over and over of a considerable part of the contents of the bowl. The purpose of beating is to enclose a large amount of air.

### FOLDING IN

Two foods are blended by putting the spoon or egg-whip vertically down through the foods, turning it under the mass, and bringing it vertically up. This process is repeated until the mixing is complete. The purpose of folding in is to prevent the escape of air or gases that have already been introduced into the mixture.

### CUTTING IN

A process used to blend fat with flour. It consists of cutting the fat into the flour with a knife or two knives until it is distributed in as small particles as desired.

## CREAMING

A rubbing together of fat and sugar, or a pressing and beating of fat to soften it.

## KNEADING

A stretching motion applied to dough when more flour is to be added than can be either stirred or beaten into the mixture; or used to make a dough smooth and even in consistency.

## *LARDING*

A process of inserting match-like strips of salt pork about one-fourth inch in thickness into a dry meat or fish. These strips are called lardons, and are inserted either by making an incision in the surface and laying the lardon in the slashing or by the use of a larding-needle. The pork is clamped into one end of the needle and is threaded into the meat, as in any sewing process.

# FRYING METHOD IN COOKING

Frying is the cooking of food in oil or another fat, a technique that originated in ancient Egypt around 2500 BC. Chemically, oils and fats are the same, differing only in melting point, but the distinction is only made when needed.

Foods can be fried in a variety of fats, including lard, vegetable oil, rapeseed oil and olive oil. To fry in olive or vegetable oil is sometimes seen as healthier than doing so in lard, because the chief fat in olive oil is Monounsaturated fat, not saturated fat. In commerce, many fats are called oils by custom, *e.g.* palm oil and coconut oil, which are solid atroom temperature. A variety of foods may be fried, including the Potato chip, bread, eggs and foods made from eggs, such as omelettes or pancakes.

## History

Frying is thought to have originated in ancient Egypt around 2500 BCE.

## Details

Fats can reach much higher temperatures than water at normal atmospheric pressure. Through frying, one can sear or even carbonize the surface of foods while caramelizing sugars. The food is cooked much more quickly and has a characteristic crispness and texture. Depending on the food, the fat will penetrate it to varying degrees, contributing richness, lubricity, and its own flavor, as well as calories.

Frying techniques vary in the amount of fat required, the cooking time, the type of cooking vessel required, and the manipulation of the food.Sautéing, stir frying, pan frying, shallow frying, and deep frying are all standard frying techniques.

Sautéing and stir-frying involve cooking foods in a thin layer of fat on a hot surface, such as a frying pan, griddle, wok, or sauteuse. Stir frying involves frying quickly at very high temperatures, requiring that the food be stirred continuously to prevent it from adhering to the cooking surface and burning. Shallow frying is a type of pan frying using only enough fat to immerse approximately one-third to one-half of each piece of food; fat used in this technique is typically only used once. Deep-frying, on the other hand, involves totally immersing the food in hot oil, which is normally topped up and used several times before being disposed. Deep-frying is typically a much more involved process, and may require specialized oils for optimal results.

Deep frying is now the basis of a very large and expanding worldwide industry. Fried products have consumer appeal in all age groups and in virtually all cultures, and the process is quick, can easily be made continuous for mass production, and the food emerges sterile and dry, with a relatively long shelf life. The end products can then be easily packaged for storage and distribution. Examples are potato chips, french fries, nuts, doughnuts, instant noodles, etc.

## MENU PLANNING

*Menu planning doesn't have be complicated. A small investment of time can reap great rewards*:

- *A menu plan saves money*: Reducing trips to the supermarket, a menu plan reduces impulse spending. Using leftovers efficiently cuts food waste, while planned buying in bulk makes it easy to stockpile freezer meals at reduced prices.
- *A menu plan saves time*: No dash to the neighbours for a missing ingredient, no frantic searches through the freezer for something, anything to thaw for dinner.
- *A menu plan improves nutrition*: Without the daily dash to the supermarket, there's time to prepare side dishes and salads to complement the main dish, increasing the family's consumption of fruits and vegetables.

### DARE TO DO IT

For too many of us, making a menu plan is something we intend to do . . . when we get around to it. Instead of seeing menu planning as an activity that adds to our quality of life, we dread sitting down to decide next Thursday's dinner. "I'll do that next week, when I'm more organized."

Wrong! Menu planning is the first line of Defence in the fight to an organized kitchen, not the cherry on the icing on the cake.

*Take the vow*: "I, [state your name], hereby promise not to visit the supermarket again until I've made a menu plan!"

## START SMALL AND SIMPLE

Still muttering, "But I don't wanna ..."? Break into menu planning easily by starting small and simple.

Think, "next week." Seven little dinners, one trip to the supermarket. Sure, it's fun to think about indexing your recipe collection, entering the data in a relational database and crunching menus till the year 2010, but resist the urge. Slow and steady builds menu planning skills and shows you the benefits of the exercise. Elaborate hoo-rah becomes just another failed exercise in home management overkill.

Where to start? The food flyers from your local newspaper. Try to make your menu plan and shopping list the day the food ads appear.

You'll use the ads to get a feel for the week's sales and bargains. Use that feeling to guide your menu plan.

This week in Eastern Washington, for instance, two local chain supermarkets are offering whole fryers for the low, low price of 59 cents a pound. Clearly, this is the week for Ginger Chicken and Fajitas, not a time to dream about Beef Stew and Grilled Pork Tenderloins.

## MENU PLANNING BASICS

Okay, it's food ad day. Ready? Time to rough out a simple menu plan. The goal is two-fold: shop efficiently to obtain food required for seven dinner meals, while minimizing expenditure, cooking, shopping and cleaning time.

*Here's the overview of the process*:

- Scan the food ads for specials and sales. Rough out a draft menu plan: seven dinner entrees that can be made from weekly specials, side dishes and salads.
- Wander to pantry and refrigerator to check for any of last week's purchases that are languishing beneath wilting lettuce or hardening tortillas. Check for draft recipe ingredients. Review your shopping list and note needed items.
- Ready, set, shop—but shop with an open mind. That 59-cent fryer won't look like such a bargain next to a marked-down mega-pack of boneless chicken breasts at 89 cents a pound. Be ready to substitute if you find a great deal.
- Return from shopping. As you put away groceries, flesh out the menu plan. Match it up with the family's calendar, saving the oven roast for a lazy Sunday afternoon, the quick-fix pizza for soccer night.
- Post the menu plan on the refrigerator door. Refer to it during the coming week as you prepare meals.

That's it! The bare bones of menu planning. You've made a draft plan, shopped from a list, retained flexibility in the marketplace, firmed up your plan and held yourself accountable.

## COAST IN THE CALM OF A ROUTINE

Yes, there are some well-organized souls among us who don't make formal meal plans. Look close, and you'll discover that household meal service dances to a routine.

Sunday's a big dinner, and Tuesday gets the leftovers. Monday is burger night, and Wednesday sees spaghetti, year in and year out. Thursday's the day for a casserole, and Dad grills on Friday. Saturday night, it's take-out or pizza.

Create a routine around your menu planning. Sure, you can try new recipes—just don't let your enthusiasm for the glossy pages of the cookbook con you into doing so more than twice a month. Cooking tried-and-true speeds dinner preparation and streamlines menu planning.

To do it, look for cues in the family schedule. At-home days with more free time can handle a fancy meal—or can signal soup, sandwiches and Cook's Night Off. Running the evening kid carpool is a great time to plan for pick-up sandwiches. Make the routine yours, and it will serve you well.

## STAY FLEXIBLE

Menu plans aren't written in stone. So you're dodging cramps on the "big" cooking day? Swap it out with Pizza Night and go to bed early with a cup of herb tea.

A posted menu plan promotes accountability, but family members will forgive you, as long as they get their postponed Favourite a day or two later. Build flexibility into your plan and serve the aims of thrift with Cook's Choice Night.

Traditionally held the night before grocery shopping, you can slide a neglected dinner into Cook's Choice, or chop up the contents of the refrigerator for a clean-out stir-fry. Either way, you'll feel smug at your frugality and good planning.

## MAKE IT A HABIT

Simple or not, a menu plan won't help you if you don't make one. Weekly menu planning is a good candidate for the Habit Patrol. Get into the habit of planning before you shop, and you'll get hooked—one addiction of great value.

## RECYCLE MENU PLANS

After you've made menu plans for a few weeks, the beauty of the activity shines through: recycle them! Your family won't mind, and you'll save even more time and energy.

Instead of an ambitious plan for 30-day menus, tuck completed menu plans in a file folder or envelope. Next time fryers are 59 cents a pound at the market, pull out the plan you made this week. Done!

## BENEFITS

- You can extract a grocery list from your menu choices.
- Because you buy only what you need, less food is wasted.
- You know with plenty of notice what's for dinner – no more frantic 5 p.m. crazyness.
- Cooking is more enjoyable, because odds are you'll be more prepared.
- You'll have more variety, because you've planned it.
- It's healthier, because it cuts down on drive-thru runs.
- It's cheaper, too, because you're eating out less, you can menu plan around your coupons, and you can intentionally cook with seasonal ingredients.

## MENU PLANNING TIPS

*Use the menu planner and grocery list shown below as you follow these steps*:

- Get out your cookbooks and plan several main meals. Make a list of these menu ideas on a menu planner. Plan some quick meals for busy nights. You also can double some recipes that freeze well, and save half for other busy nights when you don't have time to cook.
- Check your pantry for all the ingredients called for in recipes. Write down all the ingredients you need to purchase. If you notice you are running low on certain basic items, put these on your grocery list as well.
- Now fill in foods that you use to make breakfast, lunches, and snacks, such as eggs, cereals, breads, tuna, milk, and juice. List plenty of fruits and vegetables.
- Post this list on the refrigerator and add to it as you run out of foods or think of other things you need.
- Take the list to the store and stick to it. You save money by not making impulse buys. However, you don't need to be so rigid that you pass up a good sale item.
- When you get home, cut out and post the menu planner in your kitchen. You may want to write down page numbers from recipe books for quick reference. This way, whoever gets home first can start dinner.

The first few times you do this, it will seem like a fair amount of work. But the rewards are worth it, and you will become faster at the planning process. You can even save some of the menus and grocery lists and use them again in a few weeks.

## BOILING METHOD IN COOKING

In cooking, *boiling* is the method of cooking food in boiling water, or other water-based liquid such as stock or milk. Simmering is gentle boiling, while inpoaching the cooking liquid moves but scarcely bubbles. Boiling is a very harsh technique of cooking. Delicate foods such as fish cannot be cooked in this fashion because the bubbles can damage the food. Foods such as red meat, chicken, and root vegetables can be cooked with this technique because of their tough texture.

The boiling point of water is typically considered to be 100 °C or 212 °F. Pressure and a change in composition of the liquid may alter the boiling point of the liquid. For this reason, high elevation cooking generally takes longer since boiling point is a function of atmospheric pressure. In Denver, Colorado, USA, which is at an elevation of about one mile, water boils at approximately 95 °C or 203 °F.

Depending on the type of food and the elevation, the boiling water may not be hot enough to cook the food properly. Similarly, increasing the pressure as in a pressure cooker raises the temperature of the contents above the open air boiling point. Adding a water soluble substance, such as salt or sugar also increases the boiling point.

This is called boiling-point elevation. At palatable concentrations of salt, the effect is very small, and the boiling point elevation is difficult to notice. However, while making thick sugar syrup, such as forGulab Jamun, one will notice boiling point elevation. Due to variations in composition and pressure, the boiling point of water is almost never exactly 100 °C, but rather close enough for cooking.

Bringing water to a boil is generally done by applying maximal heat, then shutting off when the water has come to a boil, which is known as bang–bang control. Keeping water at or below a boil requires more careful control of temperature, particularly by using feedback. In places where the available water supply is contaminated with disease-causing bacteria, boiling water and allowing it to cool before drinking it is practiced as a valuable health measure. Boiling is the most certain way of killing all microorganisms in emergency situations.

Foods suitable for boiling include vegetables, starchy foods such as rice, noodles and potatoes, eggs, meats, sauces, stocks and soups. Boiling has several advantages. It is safe and simple, and it is appropriate for large-scale cookery. Older, tougher, cheaper cuts of meat and poultry can be made digestible. Nutritious, well flavoured stock is produced. Also, maximum colour and nutritive value is retained when cooking green vegetables, provided boiling time is kept to the minimum. On the other hand, there are several disadvantages.

There is a loss of soluble vitamins from foods to the water (if the water is discarded), and some boiled foods can look unattractive. Boiling can also be a slow method of cooking food. Boiling can be done in several ways: The food can be placed into already rapidly boiling water and left to cook, the heat can be turned down and the food can be simmered; or the food can also be placed into the pot, and cold water may be added to the pot. This may then be boiled until the food is satisfactory.

Water on the outside of a pot, *i.e.* a wet pot, increases the time it takes the pot of water to boil. The pot will heat at a normal rate once all excess water on the outside of the pot evaporates. Boiling is also often used to remove salt from certain foodstuffs, such as bacon, if a less saline product is required.

## FOOD COOKING METHOD OF BAKING

Baking is a food cooking method using prolonged dry heat acting by convection, rather than by thermal radiation, normally in an oven, but also in hot ashes, or on hot stones. The most common baked item is bread but many other types of foods are baked. Heat is gradually transferred "from the surface of cakes, cookies and breads to their centre. As heat travels through it transforms batters and doughs into baked goods with a firm dry crust and a softer centre".

Baking can be combined with grilling to produce a hybrid barbecue variant, by using both methods simultaneously or one before the other, cooking twice. Baking is related to barbecuing because the concept of the masonry oven is similar to that of a smoke pit.

Baking has been traditionally done at home by women for domestic consumption, by men in bakeries and restaurants for local consumption and when production was industrialised, by machines in large factories. The art and skill of baking remains a fundamental one and important for nutrition, as baked goods, especially breads, are a common food, economically and culturally important. A person who prepares baked goods as a profession is called abaker.

### Foods and techniques

All types of food can be baked but some require special care and protection from direct heat. Various techniques have been developed to provide this protection.

As well as bread, baking is used to prepare cakes, pastries, pies, tarts, quiches, cookies, scones, crackers and pretzels. These popular items are known collectively as "baked goods," and are sold at a bakery.

Meat, including cured meats, such as ham can also be baked, but baking is usually reserved for meatloaf, smaller cuts of whole meats, and whole meats that contain stuffing or coating such as bread crumbs or buttermilk batter. Some foods are surrounded with moisture during baking by placing a small amount of liquid (such as water or broth) in the bottom of a closed pan, and letting it steam up around the food, a method commonly known asbraising or slow baking. Larger cuts prepared without stuffing or coating are more often roasted, which is a similar process, using higher temperatures and shorter cooking times.

Roasting, however, is only suitable for the finer cuts of meat, so other methods have been developed to make the tougher meat cuts palatable after baking. One of these is the method known as *en croûte* (French for "in a crust"), which protects the food from direct heat and seals the natural juices inside.

Meat, poultry, game, fish or vegetables can be prepared by baking *en croûte*. Well-known examples include Beef Wellington, where the beef is encased in pastry before baking; pâté en croûte, where the terrine is encased in pastry before baking; and the Vietnamese variant, a meat-filled pastry called pâté chaud.

The *en croûte* method also allows meat to be baked by burying it in the embers of a fire - a favourite method of cooking venison. In this case, the protective case (or crust) is made from a paste of flour and water and is discarded before eating.

Salt can also be used to make a protective crust that is not eaten. Another method of protecting food from the heat while it is baking, is to cook it *en papillote*(French for "in parchment"). In this method, the food is covered by baking paper (or aluminium foil) to protect it while it is being baked. The cooked parcel of food can be served unopened, with an element of surprise, allowing diners to discover the contents for themselves.

Eggs can be baked to produce savoury or sweet dishes. In combination with dairy products and/or cheese, they are often prepared to serve as adessert. Although a baked custard, for example, can be made using starch (in the form of flour, cornflour, arrowroot or potato flour), the flavour of the dish is much more delicate if eggs are used as the thickening agent. Baked custards, such as crème caramel, are among the items that need protection from an oven's direct heat, and the *bain-marie* method serves this purpose.

The cooking container is half submerged in water in another, larger one, so that the heat in the oven is more gently applied during the baking process. Baking a successful soufflé requires that the baking process be carefully controlled - the oven temperature must be absolutely even and the oven space not shared with another dish.

These factors, along with the theatrical effect of an air-filled dessert, have given this baked food a reputation for being a culinary achievement. Similarly, a good baking technique (and a good oven) are also needed to create a baked Alaska because of the difficulty of baking hot meringue and cold ice cream at the same time.

Baking can also be used to prepare various other foods, such as for example, baked potatoes, baked apples, baked beans, some casseroles and pastadishes such as lasagne.

**History**

The first evidence of baking occurred when humans took wild grass grains, soaked them in water, and mixed everything together, mashing it into a kind of broth-like paste. The paste was cooked by pouring it onto a flat, hot rock, resulting in a bread-like substance. Later, this paste was roasted on hot embers, which made bread-making easier, as it could now be made any time fire was created.

The Ancient Egyptians baked bread using yeast, which they had previously been using to brew beer. Bread baking began in Ancient Greecearound 600 BC, leading to the invention of enclosed ovens. "Ovens and worktables have been discovered in archaeological digs from Turkey (Hacilar) to Israel (Jericho) and these date from about 5600 BCE."

Baking flourished in the Roman Empire. In about 300 BC, the pastry cook became an occupation for Romans (known as the pastillarium). This became a respected profession because pastries were considered decadent, and Romans loved festivity and celebration.

Thus, pastries were often cooked especially for large banquets, and any pastry cook who could invent new types of tasty treats was highly prized. Around 1 AD, there were more than three hundred pastry chefs in Rome, and Cato wrote about how they created all sorts of diverse foods, and flourished because of those foods.

Cato speaks of an enormous amount of breads; included amongst these are the libum (sacrificial cakes made with flour), placenta (groats and cress), spira (our modern day flour pretzels), scibilata (tortes), savaillum (sweet cake), and globus apherica (fritters).

A great selection of these, with many different variations, different ingredients, and varied patterns, were often found at banquets and dining halls. The Romans baked bread in an oven with its own chimney, and had mills to grind grain into flour. A bakers' guild was established in 168 BC in Rome.

Eventually, the Roman art of baking became known throughout Europe, and eventually spread to the eastern parts of Asia. From the 19th century, alternative leavening agents became more common, such as baking soda. Bakers often baked goods at home and then sold them in the streets. This scene was so common that Rembrandt, among others, painted a pastry chef selling pancakes in the streets of Germany, with children clamoring for a sample.

In London, pastry chefs sold their goods from handcarts. This developed into a system of delivery of baked goods to households, and demand increased greatly as a result. In Paris, the first open-air café of baked goods was developed, and baking became an established art throughout the entire world.

**Commercial baking**

Baking developed into an industry using machinery that enabled more goods to be produced and which then had to be distributed more widely. In the United States the baking industry "was built on marketing methods used during feudal times and production techniques developed by the Romans."Some makers of snacks such as potato chips or crisps have produced baked versions of their snack items as an alternative to the usual cooking method of deep-frying in an attempt to reduce the calorie or fat content of their snack products. Baking has opened up doors to businesses such as cake making factories and private cake shops where the baking process is done with larger amounts in bigger and open furnaces.

The aroma and texture of baked goods as they come out of the oven is strongly appealing but it is a quality that is quickly lost. Since the flavour and appeal largely depend on this freshness, commercial producers have had to compensate by using food additives as well as imaginative labelling. As baked goods are more and more purchased from commercial suppliers, producers try to capture that original appeal by adding the label "home-baked". Such a usage seeks to make an emotional link to the remembered freshness of baked goods and seeks also to attach any positive associations the purchaser has with the idea of "home" to the bought product. Freshness is such an important quality that restaurants, although they are commercial (and not domestic) preparers of food, bake their own products for their customers. For example, scones at The Ritz London Hotel "are not baked until early afternoon on the day they are to be served, to make sure they are as fresh as possible."

**Equipment**

Baking needs an enclosed space for heating - an oven. The fuel can be supplied by wood or coal; gas or electricity. Adding and removing items from an oven may be done by a long handled tool called a peel.

Many commercial ovens are provided with two heating elements: one for baking, using convection and thermal conduction to heat the food, and one for broiling or grilling, heating mainly by radiation. Another piece of equipment still used in the 21st century for baking is the Dutch oven. "Also called a bake kettle, bastable, bread oven, fire pan, bake oven kail pot, tin kitchen, roasting kitchen, *doufeu* (French: "gentle fire") or *feu de compagne* (French: "country oven") [it] originally replaced the cooking jack as the latest fireside cooking technology," combining "the convenience of pot-oven and hangover oven."

## FOOD SAFETY

Food safety is a scientific discipline describing handling, preparation, and storage of food in ways that prevent foodborne illness. This includes a number of routines that should be followed to avoid potentially severe health hazards. Food can transmit disease from person to person as well as serve as a growth medium for bacteria that can cause food poisoning.

Debates on genetic food safety include such issues as impact of genetically modified food on health of further generations and genetic pollution of environment, which can destroy natural biological diversity. In developed countries there are intricate standards for food preparation, whereas in lesser developed countries the main issue is simply the availability of adequate safe water, which is usually a critical item.

## REGULATORY AGENCIES

### European Union

The parliament of the European Union (EU) makes legislation in the form of directives and regulations, many of which are mandatory for member states and which therefore must be incorporated into individual countries' national legislation. As a very large organisation that exists to remove barriers to trade between member states, and into which individual member states have only a proportional influence, the outcome is often seen as an excessively bureaucratic 'one size fits all' approach. However, in relation to food safety the tendency to err on the side of maximum protection for the consumer may be seen as a positive benefit. The EU parliament is informed on food safety matters by the European Food Safety Authority.

Individual member states may also have other legislation and controls in respect of food safety, provided that they do not prevent trade with other states, and can differ considerably in their internal structures and approaches to the regulatory control of food safety.

### United States

#### *Federal Level Regulation*

The Food and Drug Administration publishes the Food Code, a model set of guidelines and procedures that assists food control jurisdictions by providing a scientifically sound technical and legal basis for regulating the retail and food service industries, including restaurants, grocery stores and institutional foodservice providers such as nursing homes. Regulatory agencies at all levels of government in the United States use the FDA Food Code to develop or update food safety rules in their jurisdictions that are consistent with national food regulatory policy. The FDA, 48 of 56 states and territories, representing 79% of the U.S. population, have adopted food codes patterned after one of the five versions of the Food Code, beginning with the 1993 edition.

In the United States, federal regulations governing food safety are fragmented and complicated, just as to a February 2007 report from the

Government Accountability Office. There are 15 agencies sharing oversight responsibilities in the food safety system, although the two primary agencies are the U.S. Department of Agriculture (USDA) Food Safety and Inspection Service (FSIS), which is responsible for the safety of meat, poultry, and processed egg products, and the Food and Drug Administration (FDA), which is responsible for virtually all other foods.

The Food Safety and Inspection Service has approximately 7,800 inspection Programme personnel working in nearly 6,200 federally inspected meat, poultry and processed egg establishments. FSIS is charged with administering and enforcing the Federal Meat Inspection Act, the Poultry Products Inspection Act, the Egg Products Inspection Act, portions of the Agricultural Marketing Act, the Humane Slaughter Act, and the regulations that implement these laws. FSIS inspection Programme personnel inspect every animal before slaughter, and each carcass after slaughter to ensure public health requirements are met. In fiscal year (FY) 2008, this included about 50 billion pounds of livestock carcasses, about 59 billion pounds of poultry carcasses, and about 4.3 billion pounds of processed egg products. At U.S. borders, they also inspected 3.3 billion pounds of imported meat and poultry products.

***State and Local Regulation***

A number of U.S. states have their own meat inspection programmes that substitute for USDA inspection for meats that are sold only in-state. Certain state programmes have been criticized for undue leniency to bad practices.

However, other state food safety programmes supplement, rather than replace, Federal inspections, generally with the goal of increasing consumer confidence in the state's produce. For example, state health departments have a role in investigating outbreaks of food-borne disease bacteria, as in the case of the 2006 outbreak of *Escherichia coli* O157:H7 from processed spinach. Health departments also promote better food processing practices to eliminate these threats.

In addition to the US Food and Drug Administration, several states that are major producers of fresh fruits and vegetables have their own state programmes to test produce for pesticide residues.

Restaurants and other retail food establishments fall under state law and are regulated by state or local health departments.

Typically these regulations require official inspections of specific design features, best food-handling practices, and certification of food handlers. In some places a letter grade or numerical score must be prominently posted following each inspection. In some localities inspection deficiencies and remedial action are posted on the Internet.

**China**

Food safety is a growing concern in Chinese agriculture. The Chinese government oversees agricultural production as well as the manufacture of food packaging, containers, chemical additives, drug production, and business regulation. In recent years, the Chinese government attempted to consolidate food regulation with the creation of the State Food and Drug Administration of China in 2003, and officials have also been under increasing public and international pressure to solve food safety problems.

However, it appears that regulations are not well known by the trade. Labels used for "green" food, "organic" food and "pollution-free" food are not well recognized by traders and many are unclear about their meaning. A survey by the World Bank found that supermarket managers had difficulty in obtaining produce that met safety requirements and found that a high percentage of produce did not comply with established standards.

Traditional marketing systems, whether in China or the rest of Asia, presently provide little motivation or incentive for individual farmers to make improvements to either quality or safety as their produce tends to get grouped together with standard products as it progresses through the marketing channel.

Direct linkages between farmer groups and traders or ultimate buyers, such as supermarkets, can help avoid this problem. Governments need to improve the condition of many markets through upgrading management and reinvesting market fees in physical infrastructure. Wholesale markets need to investigate the feasibility of developing separate sections to handle fruits and vegetables that meet defined safety and quality standards.

**Australia**

Australian Food Authority is working toward ensuring that all food businesses implement food safety systems to ensure food is safe to consume in a bid to halt the increasing incidence of food poisoning, this includes basic food safety training for at least one person in each business. Smart business operators know that basic food safety training improves the bottom line, staff take more pride in their work; there is less waste; and customers can have more confidence in the food they consume.

Food Safety training in units of competence from a relevant training package, must be delivered by a Registered Training Organization (RTO) to enable staff to be issued with a nationally-recognised unit of competency code on their certificate. Generally this training can be completed in less than one day. Training options are available to suit the needs of everyone. Training may be carried out in-house for a group, in a public class, via correspondence or online.

*Basic Food Safety Training includes*:

- Understanding the hazards associated with the main types of food and the conditions to prevent the growth of bacteria which can cause food poisoning

- The problems associated with product packaging such as leaks in vacuum packs, damage to packaging or pest infestation, as well as problems and diseases spread by pests.
- Safe Food handling. This includes safe procedures for each process such as receiving, re-packing, food storage, preparation and cooking, cooling and re-heating, displaying products, handling products when serving customers, packaging, cleaning and sanitizing, pest control, transport and delivery. Also the causes of cross contamination.
- Catering for customers who are particularly at risk of food-borne illness, including allergies and intolerance.
- Correct cleaning and sanitizing procedures, cleaning products and their correct use, and the storage of cleaning items such as brushes, mops and cloths.
- Personal hygiene, hand washing, illness, and protective clothing.

People responsible for serving unsafe food can be liable for heavy fines under this new leglislation, consumers are pleased that industry will be forced to take food safety seriously.

9

# Kitchen Utensil

## INTRODUCTION

A kitchen utensil is a hand-held, typically small tool or utensil that is used in the kitchen, for food-related functions. A cooking utensil is a utensil used in the kitchen for cooking. Other names for the same thing, or subsets thereof, derive from the word "ware", and describe kitchen utensils from a merchandising (and functional) point of view: kitchenware, wares for the kitchen; ovenware andbakeware, kitchen utensils that are for use inside ovens and for baking; cookware, merchandise used for cooking; and so forth.

**Fig.** An exhibit of a batterie de cuisine, from the beginning of the 20th century, at the Musée Cernuschi in Paris.

**Fig.** Biodegradable plastic utensils made frombioplastic

A partially overlapping category of tools is that of eating utensils, which are tools used for eating (c.f. the more general category of tableware). Some utensils are both kitchen utensils and eating utensils.Cutlery (i.e. knives and other cutting implements) can be used for both food preparation in a kitchen and as eating utensils when dining. Other cutlery such as forks and spoons are both kitchen and eating utensils.

Other names used for various types of kitchen utensils, although not strictly denoting a utensil that is specific to the kitchen, are according to the materials they are made of, again using the "-ware" suffix, rather than their functions: earthenware, utensils made of clay; silverware, utensils (both kitchen and dining) made of silver; glassware, utensils (both kitchen and dining) made of glass; and so forth. These latter categorizations include utensils — made of glass, silver, clay, and so forth — that are not necessarily kitchen utensils.

## MATERIALS SCIENCE

Benjamin Thompson noted at the start of the 18th century that kitchen utensils were commonly made of copper, with various efforts made to prevent the copper from reacting with food (particularly its acidic contents) at the temperatures used for cooking, including tinning, enamelling, and varnishing. He observed that iron had been used as a substitute, and that some utensils were made of earthenware. By the turn of the 20th century, Maria Parloa noted that kitchen utensils were made of (tinned or enamelled) iron and steel, copper, nickel, silver, tin, clay, earthenware, and aluminium. The latter, aluminium, became a popular material for kitchen utensils in the 20th century.

### Copper

Copper has good thermal conductivity and copper utensils are both durable and attractive in appearance. However, they are also comparatively heavier than utensils made of other materials, require scrupulous cleaning to remove poisonous tarnish compounds, and are not suitable for acidic foods.

### Iron

Iron is more prone to rusting than (tinned) copper. Cast iron kitchen utensils, in particular, are however less prone to rust if, instead of being scoured to a shine after use, they are simply washed with detergent and water and wiped clean with a cloth, allowing the utensil to form a coat of (already corroded iron and other) material that then acts to prevent further corrosion (a process known as seasoning).

Furthermore, if an iron utensil is solely used for frying or cooking with fat or oil, corrosion can be reduced by never heating water with it, never using it to cook with water, and when washing it with water to dry it immediately afterwards, removing all water. Since oil and water are immiscible, since oils and fats are more covalent compounds, and since it is ionic compounds such as water that promote corrosion, eliminating as much contact with water reduces corrosion.

For some iron kitchen utensils, water is a particular problem, since it is very difficult to dry them fully. In particular, iron egg-beaters or ice cream freezers are tricky to dry, and the consequent rust if left wet will roughen them and possibly clog them completely. When storing iron utensils for long periods, van Rensselaer recommended coating them in non-salted (since salt is also an ionic compound) fat or paraffin.

Iron utensils have little problem with high cooking temperatures, are simple to clean as they become smooth with long use, are durable and comparatively strong (i.e. not as prone to breaking as, say, earthenware), and hold heat well. However, as noted, they rust comparatively easily.

**Earthenware and Enamelware**

Earthenware utensils suffer from brittleness when subjected to rapid large changes in temperature, as commonly occur in cooking, and the glazing of earthenware often contains lead, which is poisonous. Thompson noted that as a consequence of this the use of such glazed earthenware was prohibited by law in some countries from use in cooking, or even from use for storing acidic foods. Van Rensselaer proposed in 1919 that one test for lead content in earthenware was to let a beaten egg stand in the utensil for a few minutes and watch to see whether it became discoloured, which is a sign that lead might be present.

In addition to their problems with thermal shock, enamelware utensils require careful handling, as careful as for glassware, because they are prone to chipping. But enamel utensils are not affected by acidic foods, are durable, and are easily cleaned. However, they cannot be used with strong alkalis.

Earthenware, porcelain, and pottery utensils can be used for both cooking and serving food, and so thereby save on washing-up of two separate sets of utensils. They are durable, and (van Rensselaer notes) "excellent for slow, even cooking in even heat, such as slow baking". However, they are comparatively *un*suitable for cooking using a direct heat, such as a cooking over a flame.

**Aluminium**

James Frank Breazeale in 1918 opined that aluminium "is without doubt the best material for kitchen utensils", noting that it is "as far superior to enamelled ware as enamelled ware is to the old-time iron or tin". He qualified his recommendation for replacing worn out tin or enamelled utensils with aluminium ones by noting that "old-fashioned black iron frying pans and muffin rings, polished on the inside or worn smooth by long usage, are, however, superior to aluminium ones".

Aluminium's advantages over other materials for kitchen utensils is its good thermal conductivity (which is approximately an order of magnitude greater than that of steel), the fact that it is largely non-reactive with foodstuffs at low and high temperatures, its low toxicity, and the fact that its corrosion products are white and so (unlike the dark corrosion products of, say, iron) do not discolour food that they happen to be mixed into during cooking. However, its disadvantages are that it is easily discoloured, can be dissolved by acidic foods (to a comparatively small extent), and reacts to alkaline soaps if they are used for cleaning a utensil.

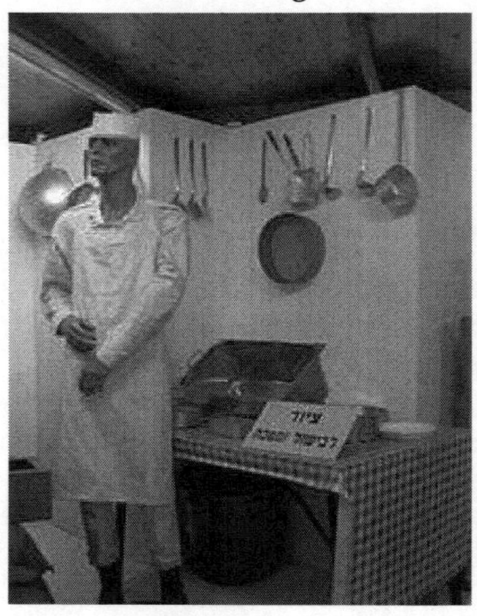

**Fig.** An exhibit of Israeli Defence Forceskitchen utensils at the Batey ha-Osef Museum in Tel Aviv.

In the European Union, the construction of kitchen utensils made of aluminium is determined by two European standards: EN 601 (*Aluminium and aluminium alloys — Castings — Chemical composition of castings for use in contact with foodstuffs*) and EN 602 (*Aluminium and aluminium alloys — Wrought products — Chemical composition of semi-finished products used for the fabrication of articles for use in contact with foodstuffs*). These define maxima for the percentages (by mass) of impurities or added elements present, other than aluminium, in such products, as follows:

Unalloyed aluminium

- Iron and silicon: less than 1%
- Chromium, manganese, nickel, zinc, titanium, tin: less than 0.1% each
- Copper: less than 0.1% (or less than 0.2% if the proportions of chromium and manganese both do not exceed 0.05%)
- Other elements: less than 0.05%

Alloyed aluminium

- Silicon: less than 13.5%

- Iron: less than 2%
- Copper: less than 0.6%
- Manganese: less than 4%
- Magnesium: less than 11% (less than 5% in pressure cooking utensils)
- Chromium:less than 0.35%
- Nickel: less than 3%
- Zinc: less than 0.25%
- Antimony: less than 0.2%
- Tin: less than 0.1%
- Strontium: less than 0.3%
- Zirconium: less than 0.3%
- Titanium: less than 0.3%
- Other elements: less than 0.05% each, and less than 0.15% in total

## DIVERSITY AND UTILITY

**Fig.** Various kitchen utensils. At top: a spice rack with jars of mint, caraway, thyme, andsage. Lower: hanging from hooks; a small pan, a meat fork, an icing spatula, a whole spoon, a slotted spoon, and a perforated spatula.

### Before the 19th Century

"Of the culinary utensils of the ancients", wrote Mrs Beeton, "our knowledge is very limited; but as the art of living, in every civilized country, is pretty much the same, the instruments for cooking must, in a great degree, bear a striking resemblance to one another".

Archaeologists and historians have studied the kitchen utensils used in centuries past. For example: In the Middle Eastern villages and towns of the middle first millennium AD, historical and archaeological sources record that Jewish households generally had stone measuring cups, a *mey%am* (an wide-necked vessel for heating water), a *kederah* (an unlidded pot-bellied cooking pot), a *ilpas* (a lidded stewpot/casserole pot type of vessel used for stewing and steaming), *yorah* and *kumkum* (pots for heating water), two types of *teganon*(frying pan) for deep and shallow frying, an *iskutla* (a glass serving platter), a *tam%ui* (ceramic serving bowl), a *keara* (a bowl for bread), a *kiton* (a canteen of cold water used to dilute wine), and a *lagin* (a wine decanter).

Ownership and types of kitchen utensils varied from household to household. Records survive of inventories of kitchen utensils from London in the 14th century, in particular the records of possessions given in the coroner's rolls.

Very few such people owned any kitchen utensils at all. In fact only seven convicted felons are recorded as having any. One such, a murderer from 1339, is recorded as possessing only the one kitchen utensil: a brass pot (one of the commonest such kitchen utensils listed in the records) valued at three shillings.

Similarly, in Minnesota in the second half of the 19th century, John North is recorded as having himself made "a real nice rolling pin, and a pudding stick" for his wife; one soldier is recorded as having a Civil War bayonet refashioned, by a blacksmith, into a bread knife; whereas an immigrant Swedish family is recorded as having brought with them "solid silver knives, forks, and spoons [...] Quantities of copper and brass utensils burnished until they were like mirrors hung in rows".

## 19th Century Growth

The 19th century, particularly in the United States, saw an explosion in the number of kitchen utensils available on the market, with many labour-saving devices being invented and patented throughout the century. Maria Parloa's *Cook Book and Marketing Guide* listed a *minimum* of 139 kitchen utensils without which a contemporary kitchen would not be considered properly furnished. Parloa wrote that "the homemaker will find [that] there is continually something new to be bought".

A growth in the range of kitchen utensils available can be traced through the growth in the range of utensils recommended to the aspiring householder in cookbooks as the century progressed. Earlier in the century, in 1828, Frances Byerley Parkes (Parkes 1828) had recommended a smaller array of utensils. By 1858, Elizabeth H. Putnam, in *Mrs Putnam's Receipt Book and Young Housekeeper's Assistant*, wrote with the assumption that her readers would have the "usual quantity of utensils", to which she added a list of necessary items:

| | | | | | |
|---|---|---|---|---|---|
| 1 Tea-kettle | 6s. 6d. | 1 Colander | 1s. 6d. | 1 Flour-box | 1s. 0d. |
| 1 Toasting-fork | 1s. 0d. | 3 Block-tin saucepans | | 3 Flat-irons | 3s. 6d. |
| 1 Bread-grater | 1s. 0d. | | 5s. 9d. | 2 Frying-pans | 4s. 0d. |
| 1 Pair of Brass | | 5 Iron Saucepans | 12s. 0d. | 1 Gridiron | 2s. 0d. |
| Candlesticks | 3s. 6d. | 1 Ditto and Steamer | | 1 Mustard-pot | 1s. 0d. |
| 1 Teapot and Tray | 6s. 6d. | | 6s. 6d. | 1 Salt-cellar | 8d. |
| 1 Bottle-jack | 9s. 9d. | 1 Large Boiling-pot | | 1 Pepper-box | 6d. |
| 6 Spoons | 1s. 6d. | | 10s. 0d. | 1 Pair of Bellows | 2s. 0d. |
| 2 Candlesticks | 2s. 6d. | 4 Iron Stewpans | 8s. 9d. | 3 Jelly-moulds | 8s. 0d. |
| 1 Candle-box | 1s. 4d. | 1 Dripping-pan and | | 1 Plate-basket | 5s. 6d. |
| 6 Knives & Forks | 5s. 3d. | Stand | 6s. 6d. | 1 Cheese-toaster | 1s. 10d. |
| 2 Sets of Skewers | 1s. 0s. | 1 Dustpan | 1s. 0d. | 1 Coal-shovel | 2s. 6d. |
| 1 Meat-chopper | 1s. 9d. | 1 Fish and Egg-slice | | 1 Wood Meat-screen | |
| 1 Cinder-sifter | 1s. 3d. | | 1s. 9d. | | 30s. 0d. |
| 1 Coffee-pot | 2s. 3d. | 2 Fish-kettles | 10s. 0d. | | |
| | | | | The Set | £8 11s. 1d. |

Copper saucepans, well lined, with covers, from three to six different sizes; a flat-bottomed soup-pot; an upright gridiron; sheet-iron breadpans instead of tin; a griddle; a tin kitchen; Hector's double boiler; a tin coffee-pot for boiling coffee, or a filter — either being equally good; a tin canister to keep roasted and ground coffee in; a canister for tea; a covered tin box for bread; one likewise for cake, or a drawer in your store-closet, lined with zinc or tin; a bread-knife; a board to cut bread upon; a covered jar for pieces of bread, and one for fine crumbs; a knife-tray; a spoon-tray; — the yellow ware is much the stringest, or tin pans of different sizes are economical; — a stout tin pan for mixing bread; a large earthen bowl for beating cake; a stone jug for yeast; a stone jar for soup stock; a meat-saw; a cleaver; iron and wooden spoons; a wire sieve for sifting flour and meal; a small hair sieve; a bread-board; a meat-board; a lignum vitae mortar, androlling-pin, &c. — Putnam 1858, p. 318

Mrs Beeton, in her *Book of Household Management*, wrote:

The following list, supplied by Messrs Richard & John Slack, 336, Strand, will show the articles required for the kitchen of a family in the middle class of life, although it does not contain all the things that may be deemed necessary for some families, and may contain more than are required for others.

As Messrs Slack themselves, however, publish a useful illustrated catalogue, which may be had at their establishment gratis, and which it will be found advantageous to consult by those about to furnish, it supersedes the necessity of our enlarging that which we give:

*— Isabella Mary Beeton, The Book of Household Management*

Parloa, in her 1880 cookbook, took two pages to list all of the essential kitchen utensils for a well-furnished kitchen, a list running to 93 distinct sorts of item.

The 1882 edition ran to 20 pages illustrating and describing the various utensils for a well-furnished kitchen. Sarah Tyson Rorer's 1886*Philadelphia Cook Book* (Rorer 1886) listed more than 200 kitchen utensils that a well-furnished kitchen should have.

### "Labour-saving" Utensils Generating More Labour

However, many of these utensils were expensive and not affordable by the majority of householders. Some people considered them unnecessary, too. James Frank Breazeale decried the explosion in patented "labour-saving" devices for the modern kitchen—promoted in exhibitions and advertised in "Household Guides" at the start of the 20th century—, saying that "the best way for the housewife to peel a potato, for example, is in the old-fashioned way, with a knife, and not with a patented potato peeler".

Breazeale advocated simplicity over dishwashing machines "that would have done credit to a moderate sized hotel", and noted that the most useful kitchen utensils were "the simple little inexpensive conveniences that work themselves into every day use", giving examples, of utensils that were simple and cheap but indispensable once obtained and used, of a stiff brush for cleaning saucepans, a sink strainer to prevent drains from clogging, and an ordinary wooden spoon.

The "labour-saving" devices didn't necessarily save labour, either. While the advent of mass-produced standardized measuring instruments permitted even householders with little to no cooking skills to follow recipes and end up with the desired result and the advent of many utensils enabled "modern" cooking, on a stove or range rather than at floor level with a hearth, they *also* operated to raise expectations of what families would eat. So while food was easier to prepare and to cook, ordinary householders at the same time were expected to prepare and to cook more complex and harder-to-prepare meals on a regular basis. The labour-saving effect of the tools was cancelled out by the increased labour required for what came to be expected as the culinary norm in the average household.

# Index